Trading STIR Futures

An introduction to short-term interest rate futures

By Stephen Aikin

HARRIMAN HOUSE LTD

43 Chapel Street
Petersfield
Hampshire
GU32 3DY
GREAT BRITAIN

Tel: +44 (0)1730 233870
Fax: +44 (0)1730 233880
email: enquiries@harriman-house.com
website: www.harriman-house.com

First published in Great Britain in 2006

Copyright Harriman House Ltd

The right of Stephen Aikin to be identified as author has been asserted
in accordance with the Copyright, Design and Patents Act 1988.

ISBN 1-897597-81-9
978-1-897597-81-1

British Library Cataloguing in Publication Data
A CIP catalogue record for this book can be obtained from the British Library.

Printed and bound by Biddles Ltd, Kings Lynn, Norfolk.
Index by Indexing Specialists (UK) Ltd

Contents

Index of tables

Chapter 1

Chapter 2

Chapter 3

Appendices

Index of charts

Chapter 1

Chapter 2

Chapter 3

Chapter 3

Index of figures

Chapter 1

Chapter 2

Biography

Stephen Aikin has been trading STIR futures for almost 20 years, after working for several banks, primarily in the equity options markets. He became a member of the London International Financial Futures Exchange (LIFFE) in 1987, where he started trading in the open outcry markets, joining loud young men in even louder coloured trading jackets shouting and jostling in the trading pit of the fledging Euromark contract, a STIR future on German interest rates. He has traded STIR futures ever since, including a busman's holiday in Sydney during 1990, trading Australian STIR futures. Stephen specialises in spread trading, both intra and inter contract and has only ever traded STIR futures for his own account. With the advent of computerised trading in the late 1990s, Stephen continues to trade STIR futures in south west London and is grateful to be able to trade sitting down without shouting.

Preface

Who the book is for

This book is written for the aspiring trader but will also appeal to the experienced trader looking for a new market or trading strategy.

Although the book is introductory in title, the learning curve is steep and constant. Even those traders already experienced in trading STIR futures might find new inspiration and trading ideas from the sophisticated trading strategies presented in the trading section.

Hopefully, all the information and concepts needed by the aspiring trader are simply presented and easily understood but some prior knowledge of buying and selling securities might be helpful. The web sites of the futures exchanges listed in the Appendix are useful sources of introductory information.

What the book covers

This book does not pretend to be a guide to making a trading fortune, and neither is it selling a trading system. Instead, it is a comprehensive guide to the STIR futures markets, showing how professional traders can profit from its unique risk reward profile, particularly by using spreads and similar trading strategies. It contains all the necessary tools and methodologies for the sophisticated trading strategies, appealing to the experienced STIR futures trader, whilst also providing guidance and contacts for the aspiring trader to make an informed judgement on trading as a career.

Any book on financial markets has to contain some amount of quantitative methodology but this book deliberately avoids over succinct notation and expands all equations and workings into easily followed market examples. The majority of trading examples used in the book can be calculated by the use of pre-built functions that are standard within Microsoft Excel, rather than assuming that everyone has access to expensive subscription based-quantitative software.

Furthermore, all the examples presented in this book are drawn from real market data and situations, taken from trading applications in use during the course of writing this book, which covered the period of late 2005 into early 2006. Consequently, most of these examples are based upon European STIR futures but the methods are completely transferable to any other STIR futures, whether they are denominated in Yen, Dollars or Swiss Francs.

How the book is structured

The book consists of five main parts.

1. **The Basics of STIR futures**

   Part one is the basics of STIR futures and describes what they are, where they are traded and how they are priced. This is followed by a comprehensive review of the drivers of STIR futures, which describes the underlying fundamental influences that create the price movement and how this should be interpreted by traders.

2. **The Mechanics of STIR futures**

   Part two is concerned with the mechanics of the market, including the clearing and settlement procedures, how the markets are accessed, the software options and the influences on the choice of which STIR futures contracts to trade.

3. **Trading STIR futures**

   Part three is the trading section, with the majority comprising a thorough analysis of the spread relationships that exist both within STIR futures and against other interest rate products. STIR futures are often described as the 'building blocks of finance' which makes them perfect for spread trading, providing many more trading permutations with lower risk profiles than traditional directional trading instruments.

4. **Trading considerations of STIR futures.**

   The fourth part is trading considerations and comprises an insight into the market place and its population, characteristics and the trading decision making process.

5. **Endgame**

   The book concludes with two pieces: a fictional day in the life of a trader and an interview with an established trader , both of which serve to bring everything from the book together and hopefully give the reader a glimpse into a possible trading future.

The appendices provide a range of information, referenced from the text that will supply details and contact information to those interested in taking matters further.

Supporting web site

A web site supporting this book can be found at: www.stirfutures.co.uk

Introduction

Most people are only aware of interest rate changes when they make the newspaper or television headlines, but interest rates are moving all the time. They are driven by the supply and demand of money being borrowed and lent in the interbank money markets and STIR futures are one of the key financial instruments in this market.

STIR futures first appeared in the 1970s as the Eurodollar contract, based on US interest rate deposits traded on the Chicago Mercantile Exchange (CME). Its success encouraged European emulation resulting in the formation of the London International Financial Futures Exchange (LIFFE – now Euronext.liffe) in the early eighties and the creation of the Short Sterling (UK rates), Euromark (German rates), Euroswiss (Swiss rates) and Eurolira (Italian rates) STIR futures.

All Futures were then traded by a method called *open outcry* which physically involved the shouting out of order flow into a circular pit, populated by traders wearing the colourful jackets of their company's livery. Nowadays, almost all trading is computerised, creating a global virtual trading pit with no restriction on the number of participants it can hold. Consequently, STIR futures volumes have exploded in recent years and they are now arguably the largest financial market in the world. It is not unusual for the leading STIR futures contracts, the Eurodollar and Euribor, to each trade over one trillion dollars or euros worth of interest rate transactions every day. Compare that with the $75 billion traded on a good day at the New York Stock Exchange, or even with the entire foreign exchange markets, which trade approximately $1.5 trillion of all currencies per day in its entirety, and it gives a clear idea of just how large the STIR futures markets are.

However, STIR futures are unique amongst financial markets in that individual traders can compete and trade on equal terms as the other participants such as the banks and large funds. It's a completely level playing field, unlike other markets which are dominated by middlemen and market makers. Today's fully computerised STIR futures markets support a global network of professional individual traders who benefit from the unique characteristics of these markets. Traders are not restricted to using a broker's service or trading platform but can directly buy and sell into the central marketplace with the same technology and market information as the largest players.

Futures are generally perceived as risky investments, not helped by their portrayal in the media as highly volatile instruments. Films such as *Trading Places* and *Rogue Trader* depicted easy routes to bankruptcy. Admittedly, orange juice futures and stock index futures can be extremely risky instruments, but futures are a broad asset class, making it unfair to categorise all futures as having the same risk profile. STIR futures are lower risk than most other types of futures contract and they can provide a lower trading risk than shares, currencies or spread betting alternatives by providing consistent returns from a diverse range of low risk strategies not available in any other financial market.

Recent years have seen a growing number of individuals trading STIR futures for their own account, attracted by the professional market access and level competition terms. Some traders have been very successful and many more are content with an attractive and flexible lifestyle. Of course, some aspiring traders realise that a life in the markets is not for them, but the vast majority of time it is a personal decision and not dictated by the massive losses popularised by Hollywood. Hopefully, this book will provide the knowledge to trade STIR futures intelligently, allowing the reader to make their own informed decisions about this unique market.

STIR Futures – Quick Summary

1. STIR futures are one of the largest financial markets in the world. The two largest contracts, the Eurodollar and Euribor, regularly trade in excess of one trillion dollars and euros each day.

2. The STIR futures markets are fully computerised.

3. Professional STIR future traders need a minimum capital of £25,000 to start trading their own account, or nothing to join a trading arcade's proprietary trading scheme.

4. STIR futures are one of the lowest risk financial futures contracts and trading spreads or similar strategies provides an even lower risk profile. Trading STIR futures can provide more frequent and consistent returns with lower risk than most other kinds of financial market.

5. STIR futures are essentially financial building blocks, which make them very suitable for trading against each other or other interest rate contracts. The sheer number of trading permutations offered by their range of contracts and spreads allow traders to find their own professional niche.

1

Basics of STIR Futures

Introduction to STIR Futures

What are STIR futures?

STIR futures are financial futures. The 'STIR' in STIR futures stands for Short Term Interest Rate and futures can be defined as:

Legally binding agreements of a standardised product at an agreed price for either physical or cash delivery at a pre-determined date in the future.

This means that contracts on a particular commodity, whether it is something tangible like gold, or intangible in the case of short-term interest rates, can be negotiated between buyers and sellers for a known amount at a known price for delivery at a known future date.

Similarities with other futures contracts

STIR futures are similar to other futures contracts in that they are:

- Traded on regulated futures exchanges that provide the legal framework, contract specifications and the trading mechanism.

- Settled via a central counterparty to remove credit risk between market participants.

- Are characterised by a unit of trading, tick size and settlement procedures.

Differences with other futures contracts

STIR futures differ from other futures in that they:

- Have multiple delivery cycles, sequential to several years, covering a broad spectrum of the near dated yield curve. This means that STIR futures have many different expiries trading simultaneously within the same contract which allows a unique trading perspective.

- Have highly similar risk characteristics between delivery cycles.

- Include spread trading and other trading strategies, allowing many different trade permutations and ideas, with different risk profiles.

- Are arguably the most liquid class of futures by nominal value.

Derived from interest rates

Futures are broadly classed as derivatives since they are derived from another product; and are called futures since they are not for immediate purchase or sale but at a future date.

STIR futures are derived from interest rates covering a deposit period of three months, extending forward from three months up to ten years. These interest rates refer to near term money market interest rates which are comprised of the unsecured inter-bank deposits markets (also known as the depo market) and the secured paper market covering instruments such as treasury bills, floating rate notes and certificates of deposits.

From these money markets come the daily fixing of London Inter-Bank Offered Rate (LIBOR), or its European equivalent: European Inter-Bank Offered Rate (EURIBOR). This is the reference rate that is used to settle STIR futures on expiry.

Movement of interest rates

Chart 1.1 opposite shows how these LIBOR rates for Switzerland (CHF), UK (GBP), USA (USD) and EURIBOR rates for the Eurozone (EUR) have moved over time and how they have been influenced by major events.

It can be seen that interest rates are rarely static for long. They are influenced by the state of their economies and market expectations for interest rate levels in the future. Sharper movements are often caused by economic or political events. UK interest rates fell sharply in 1992 when sterling withdrew from the European Exchange Rate Mechanism (ERM) and global rates were cut sharply after the stock market boom of the late 1990s as well as in the aftermath of 9/11.

Chart 1.1: 3-month LIBOR rates for GBP, USD, CHF and 3-month Euribor for EUR

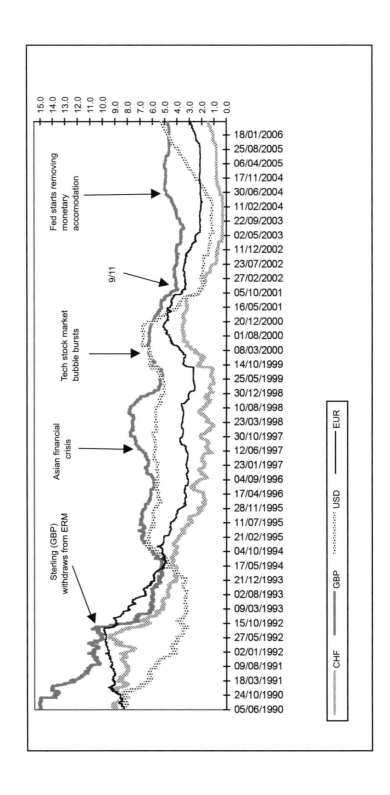

Traded on exchanges

STIR futures are traded on regulated futures exchanges, such as Euronext.liffe in London or the Chicago Mercantile Exchange (CME). Nowadays virtually all contracts are transacted electronically via computerised trading. These exchanges provide the mechanism and legal framework for access to their particular markets.

Different exchanges have different STIR products, usually determined by their geographical origins. Euribor futures (based on European interest rates) are traded on Euronext.liffe and the Eurodollar futures (based on US interest rates) are mainly traded by the CME. Although sometimes the same contract can be quoted on several exchanges, in the spirit of competition.

Buyers and sellers of STIR futures connect to these exchanges, either directly as members of the exchange or indirectly using a member as an agent. These buyers and sellers can be banks, corporate treasurers or speculative traders such as hedge funds, proprietary groups or individuals, formerly called locals but now known as Independent Liquidity Providers (ILP). These speculative traders attempt to make money from price action whereas banks and treasurers tend to use the markets as hedging tools to risk manage other interest rate exposures.

As with most exchange-traded futures, credit risk between the counterparties to a trade is removed by the intermediation of a highly capitalised Clearing House, which effectively guarantees each side of the deal, meaning that a buyer of a futures contract need not worry about the credit worthiness of the seller.

Where and how are they traded

Futures on short-term interest rates are traded by exchanges all over the world including Europe, the United States, South America, Australia, Asia and Japan. A list of these futures is included in the appendix.

The list contains futures on short-term interest rates, and not just STIR futures which are based on three-month forward deposits. The list is not exhaustive and does not include different contracts on the same instruments – for example Eurodollar forward rate agreement futures when the Eurodollar STIR future is already listed. Furthermore, some economic areas such as China and Russia have no interest rate futures currently but this will certainly change in time.

Focus on just the four main contracts

Not all contracts are of equal trading stature. Some are a lot larger and more liquid than others and some, although being large and liquid, are not readily accessible or are of different contract design. Examples of the former include Euroyen, and the latter Australian 90 day bank bills. Consequently, this book will focus on four contracts, based upon liquidity and ease of access to the broadest range of users. These contracts tend to be the major western economic powers such as US, Europe, UK, and Switzerland and include the Eurodollar, Euribor, Short Sterling and Euroswiss respectively. The Eurodollar is traded on the American CME, whilst the other three are traded on UK-based Euronext.liffe and they are largely similar to each other.

As can be seen in the contracts table in the appendix, some like Eurodollar and Euribor are traded on two or even three exchanges. Most exchanges will try to capture business from other exchanges where they think they may have a competitive advantage, such as time zone or cross-margin incentives. However, even though the computerisation of futures trading has become a global phenomenon, the main pool of liquidity usually remains with the domestic exchange. The UK-based Euronext.liffe, hosting the European Euribor contract, is not really an exception given London's status as the capital of Europe's financial markets.

Trading is now computerised

STIR futures used to be traded by open outcry, mainly by loud young men in even louder coloured jackets on crowded trading floors. With the advent of computerisation, the vast majority of STIR futures are now traded electronically. The exceptions tend to be where some degree of negotiation is required during a transitional phase from floor to screen – examples being back month trading or complex strategies.

Most exchanges' computer systems have an Application Program Interface (API) architecture that allows third parties to build software to run on it. This has led to a market of Independent Software Vendors (ISV) plying a variety of commercial packages, offering the trader functionality and connectivity to the majority of exchanges from most major locations. However, unless the trader is a full Clearing Member of an exchange, they will need to appoint a Clearing Agent to process and guarantee their trades. This agent is usually a larger financial entity and will assume the trader's risk based on a capital deposit in return for transaction based commissions. [Directories of Clearing Members/Agents and ISVs can be found in the appendix.]

Contract structure and general specifications

The selling and buying of STIR futures represent a notional borrowing or lending from the money markets. They confer the borrowing or lending at a rate determined by the price at which the future was transacted, for a period of three months after the expiry and settlement of the contract, effectively a forward interest rate.

They are notional in the sense that they are cash settled and so a holding of STIR futures is not used to physically place or remove money from the markets. Instead, this notional value or unit of trading, usually a denomination of one million, is used as a proxy. The futures will mirror movements in the underlying market and provide a representative profit and loss.

Expiry cycle

Each STIR future has a finite life and trades on a quarterly expiration cycle: **March, June, September** and **December** (usually denoted by the symbols H, M, U and Z respectively). The year is usually added to these symbols so that the cycle in 2006 would be H6, M6, U6 and Z6 going into 2007 as H7, M7 and so on. Serial months in between do exist but are mainly aimed at specific users such as option traders.

Unit of trading

The unit of trading is the *notional value* attached to each STIR future, normally in denominations of one million or £500,000, as in the case of Euronext.liffe Short Sterling. This unit of trading is the notional amount that would be nominally deposited or borrowed for three months at the contracts expiry. But since STIR futures are cash settled, these amounts never actually change hands. These units of trading are never at risk and are integral to the contract design only in that they permit a minimum movement increment to be derived.

A Euribor future has a notional value of €1,000,000 and this number is used to calculate its minimum movement, usually one or one half of a basis point*. The figure of €1,000,000 is multiplied by the minimum permitted increment as designated by the exchange, in this case 0.005 (half a basis point), and then by the quarterly expiry cycle to give:

```
€1,000,000 x 0.005/100 x ¼ = €12.50
```

* A *basis point* is one hundredth of one percent (one percent being the difference between, for example, 4% interest rates and 5% interest rates).

Quotation and minimum increments/tick sizes

Method of quotation

STIR futures trade as a quote of 100 minus the interest rate. For example, if interest rates were 4.50 %, the futures would be quoted as 95.50. This methodology provides price synchronicity to other interest rate products such as bonds, which fall as interest rates rise and rise as interest rates fall. If interest rates were suddenly cut by ¼ point, or 25 basis points to 4.25%, the STIR future would rise to 95.75. Usually though, they move intra-day by much smaller amounts, in increments of 0.01 or even 0.005 basis point.

Tick size

The smallest permitted increment is known as the *minimum price movement* and is expressed in basis points. Derived from this figure and the notional value of the contract is the *tick value* which is the monetary value of the minimum price movement.

In the case of the Short Sterling contract, the minimum movement is 1 basis point with a value of £12.50. This can be expressed as:

```
500,000 (unit of trading) x 0.01/100 (minimum price movement) x ¼
(quarterly expiry cycle) = £12.50
```

Tick values are known figures and do not need to be calculated by the trader. They are used to determine profit and loss. If a trader were to buy one Short Sterling STIR future at 95.50 and sell it at 95.51, they would have a profit of 1 x £12.50. If they had bought and sold 2 contracts at the same prices, the profit would be £25.

[Contract specifications for the four main STIR futures can found in the appendix.]

Hopefully by now, the structure of a STIR future should be becoming apparent. A STIR future is a contract with a notional value or unit of trading, a quarterly delivery cycle going out over several years, known minimum price movements and tick values and defined trading days and settlement procedures.

Price quotations

A quick look in the financial pages or exchange website might show the following quotes.

Table 1.1: Euronext.liffe Short Sterling historic quote

Month	Symbol	Price	High	Low
Mar	H	95.50	95.48	95.53
Jun	M	95.45	95.43	95.48
Sep	U	95.41	95.39	95.44
Dec	Z	95.38	95.35	95.41

Each quarterly month has a price, which is the settlement price or closing price for that day's business. Note that all four quarterly expiries trade concurrently and in relation to each other. The high and low values show the day's range or the minimum and maximum prices traded during that session. However, this display is of historical prices from a previous trading session and if current price data were to be used, then the prices would appear something like this.

Table 1.2: Euronext.liffe Short Sterling current quote

Month	Symbol	Bid	Offer	Last	Volume	Change
Mar	H	95.50	95.51	95.51	40555	+0.01
Jun	M	95.46	95.47	95.47	30667	+0.02
Sep	U	95.41	95.42	95.42	28909	+0.02
Dec	Z	95.39	95.40	95.40	18909	+0.02

Some notes on the quote:

- **Bid/offer spread**
  The notable difference with the historic quote is the bid/offer spread. These are the selling/buying prices. The trader could sell March at 95.50 or buy it at 95.51, similar to the way shares are traded. The difference between the bid price and offer price usually reduces to the minimum price movement, in this example 0.01; but in Eurodollar or Euribor would be 0.005, such as 95.505 bid 95.510 offered.

- **Last price**

  The last price shows where business is currently being transacted. In this case it appears to be buying at the offer price and this is supported by the change column depicting the positive difference between the last traded price and the previous settlement price.

- **Volume**

  The volume shows the liquidity in the market. In this example, the combined four months have traded a total of 119,040 contracts, being just over 119 billion of notional interest rate trade.

The examples above have only used the first four months for the sake of expediency. In reality, the prices extend out for several years on the same quarterly cycle to the extent dictated by their individual contract specifications.

The quarterly cycle is also colour coded, the first four quarters being called the whites, the next four being the reds, the next four being the greens, the next four being the blues and the next four being the gold's – contract specifications permitting. Sequences of STIR futures are generically called *strips* and so the first four quarterly expiries can be called the white strip, followed by the red and green strips. However, strips can comprise any number of futures and not just be determined by colour.

Table 1.3: Example of coloured yearly sequences

Code	Expiry year	Colour
Z5	First quarterly expiry	WHITE
H6		WHITE
M6		WHITE
U6		WHITE
Z6	Year 2 quarterly expiry	RED
H7		RED
M7		RED
U7		RED
Z7	Year 3 quarterly expiry	GREEN
H8		GREEN
M8		GREEN
U8		GREEN

As time progresses, and the front contract expires, the contracts will move forward one place so that, for example, on the expiry of the Z5, the H6, M6, U6 and Z6 will be the new white strip.

Buying and selling STIR futures and spreads

The principles of buying and selling STIR futures and spreads are similar to those of stocks, bonds or commodities. Buying low and selling high will return a profit, and selling high and buying low will do the same.

If one STIR future is purchased at 95.50 and sold at 95.51, a profit of one tick is made. If this were a Euronext.liffe Short Sterling future, where one tick is equivalent to £12.50, then this would be the profit on the trade. If it were a CME Eurodollar, where the value of one tick is $25, then that would be the profit.

The profit or loss on any STIR future or spread trade can be simply calculated by:

```
number of contracts x difference between opening price and closing
price x tick value
```

For example, if 100 Euribor are sold to open at 96.62 and bought back to close the position at 96.605, the profit would be:

```
100 x 0.015 x €25 = €3750
```

If 50 Short Sterling H6M6 spreads are bought at 0.05 and sold at 0.04, the loss would be:

```
50 x 0.01 x £12.50 = £625
```

Note how the results need to be multiplied by 100 to compensate for the basis point convention.

Futures are transacted to *open* or *close*. This is market terminology for entering and exiting trades. A purchase or sale to open is entering a new trade or position. A purchase or sale to close is exiting an existing trade or position. Remember that in futures markets, it is as easy to sell to open, as it is to buy to open.

Brief introduction to spreads and strategies

STIR futures are unique amongst financial markets in that they have many different months or expiries trading simultaneously as part of the same contract. For example, a STIR future such as the CME Eurodollar can have as many as forty different quarterly expiries trading at the same time. All of these expiries are based on the same STIR future, and will have the same specifications, but will differ slightly in that they all have different expiries and so their prices will change at slightly differing rates according to underlying drivers such as the movement of interest rates over time.

These small differences in the price action between expiries gives rise to the spread markets and similar trading strategies.

Spreads

A *spread* is simply the differential between two expiries, created by buying one month and selling another. For example, a H6 future can be purchased and a M6 future sold in equal quantity, which will result in a H6M6 spread. If H6 was purchased at 95.51 and M6 sold at 95.46, the spread would be bought at a difference of 0.05 (95.51-95.46). This spread is called a 3-month spread since there is 3-months difference between expiries. Spreads can have many different permutations such as 6-month, 9-month and 12-months but are subject to some common rules.

The nearest dated expiry is always quoted first in the calculation of the spread price so that its formula will appear as:

$$Future_{nearestdated} - Future_{furthestdated}$$

Spreads are quoted with a bid and offer price just like the outright futures contracts, but are quoted as a differential. They can be positive or negative and are quoted as separate instruments so that, for example, the H6 and M6 expiries will have individual quotations and so will the H6M6 spread. Trading the spread as an independently quoted contract involves the simultaneous transaction in both underlying months but with no execution risk.

The table shows some prices for the outright futures in the top box and some strategies in the lower box.

Table 1.4: Quotes for standard STIR futures

Futures	Symbol	Bid	Offer
March	H6	95.50	95.51
June	M6	95.46	95.47
Sept	U6	95.41	95.42
Dec	Z6	95.39	95.40

Table 1.5: Quotes for standard STIR spreads

Strategies	Symbol	Bid	Offer
3 month spread	H6M6	0.03	0.05
3 month spread	M6U6	0.04	0.06
6 month spread	H6U6	0.08	0.10
Butterfly	H6M6U6	-0.03	0.01

The 3-month and 6-month spreads are the differentials between the outright futures. Note how the bid/offer spreads in the two component outright futures of a spread will create a wider spread bid/offer, totalling the combined bid/offer spreads of the two futures. In reality, market participants would tighten these quotes

Butterfly

The last entry in the lower table is a *butterfly*, which is a variation on a spread. Whereas a spread is the differential between two futures contracts, a butterfly is the differential between two spreads. It can be quoted in two ways, firstly as the difference between two spreads so that in the example above, it would be created by:

H6M6 – M6U6

Since the individual spreads are quoted as 0.03/0.05 and 0.04/0.06 respectively, the butterfly quote will be buying the first spread at 0.05 and selling the second spread at 0.04 to give an offer price of 0.01 (0.05-0.04) and a bid price of 0.03-0.06, equalling -0.03.

The second method of quoting the butterfly is by using the outright futures in the following formula:

$$(Future_{nearestdated} + Future_{furthestdated}) - (2 \times Futures_{middledated})$$

So that the butterfly offer price would be:

```
(buying H6 at 95.51 + buying U6 at 95.42) - (2 x selling M6 at
95.46) = 0.01
```

And the butterfly bid price would be:

```
(selling H6 95.50 + selling U6 at 95.41) - (2 x buying M6 at
95.47) = -0.03
```

Spreads and other trading strategies will be examined in much more detail later in the book, but hopefully this introduction will have highlighted the many trading permutations that spreads and strategies offer, as opposed to purely directional outright trading.

> Spreads and butterflies carry lower risk than outright futures and can move in more predictable fashions, making them ideal instruments for the professional trader.

A typical traders screen

Although there are many different software packages offering access to the STIR futures markets, they are usually of a typical layout, and will be considered in greater depth later.

Figure 1.1: Typical STIR trading screen

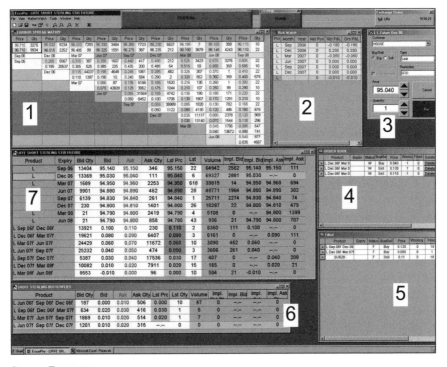

Source: Eccoware

The screenshot above shows a Windows-based display with the principal trading windows as follows:

1. Spread matrix displaying a large range of Euribor calendar spreads

2. Risk watch window displaying real time position and profit and loss

3. Order tickets, in this case to buy 1 December 2006 Short Sterling future at 95.04

4. Order book which shows current, working orders.

5. Filled window displaying completed orders

6. Short Sterling price display showing Butterfly strategies

16

7. Main price window showing Short Sterling futures from Sept 06 to June 08 and the 3-month sequential calendar spreads. Customisable columns show market bid and offer price and quantities as well as information such as last price traded, volume and implied price functionality.

The advantages of trading STIR futures compared to other financial products

Be a price maker, not a taker

The modern trader is faced with the choice of many products to trade. There are stocks and shares, contracts for differences, foreign exchange and options to name a few. However, there always seems to be a middleman getting in between the trader and the market, be it someone obvious like a stockbroker or something less tangible like a wide bid/offer spread on a currency quote. Most markets will only offer the non-institutional trader agency access, meaning that the trader will usually be required to trade off someone else's price quotes, which creates an instant disadvantage. If a security is bought with a quoted selling buying price of 50 – 52 at 52, there is an immediate loss since the selling price to exit the position is now 50. The trader might not want to sell immediately but there's no denying that paper loss on a mark to market basis. Furthermore, the market needs to rise two points before a breakeven point is reached. Add in a commission, if applicable, and it's easy to understand why many traders fail. A trader would need to be right seven or eight trades out of ten to get ahead.

Futures offer a different approach to trading. Traders can still be price takers like in the example above, but they can also be a price maker. This means that the trader can be the guy quoting 50 – 52, hoping that someone sells to them at 50 or buys from them at 52. It's immediately apparent that this can be a much more advantageous way to trade, particularly when in reality, the huge liquidity of STIR futures markets create a tight bid/offer spread which gives guidance as to where the market is and, most importantly, has other buyers and sellers bidding and offering the same prices in case the trader wishes to close out the position. Traders also have the benefit of being able to sell short just as easily as buying long. There are no additional costs involved.

Deep liquidity

STIR futures are amongst the most liquid financial markets in the world. It is virtually unheard of not to have a liquid market in all conditions, even in times of economic or political turmoil. Indeed, events that might cause problems in other financial markets, such as 9/11 which closed the NYSE, led to huge trading volumes in global STIR futures.

The liquidity of STIR futures is based on the cumulative order flow of thousands of traders and institutions, and not just quotes provided by a few market makers. This means that large orders, for example trades of between 1000 and 10,000 lots (1 to 10 billion) can trade at any one time, particularly in the larger Euribor or Eurodollar contracts and are usually easily absorbed by the markets.

A mathematical dependency

STIR future prices have a very clear reference to their underlying interest rates and market expectations for future interest rate levels, which provides traders with a good idea of their value, either absolutely or relative to each other, as in the case of spread trading.

Low costs

Trading costs are low to trade relatively large amounts of interest rate futures. To buy and sell one lot of Euribor (which is €1m of interest rate futures) would cost approximately €1.50 but would yield a potential profit (or loss) of €12.50 on a minimum movement. Trading rebate schemes can reduce these fees substantially.

Lower volatility

STIR futures have much lower volatilities than most other financial markets, meaning that they move around a lot less. Chart 1.2 shows the volatilities for the Dow Jones index, German bonds, the £/$ rate and Euribor futures. It is quite apparent that the Euribor futures are consistently and substantially less volatile than the other asset classes, making them a more predictable product to trade.

Chart 1.2: Volatilities (close-to-close with 10-day observations) for DJIA, Bund, £/$ and Euribor futures (Jan 2004 to Jun 2006)

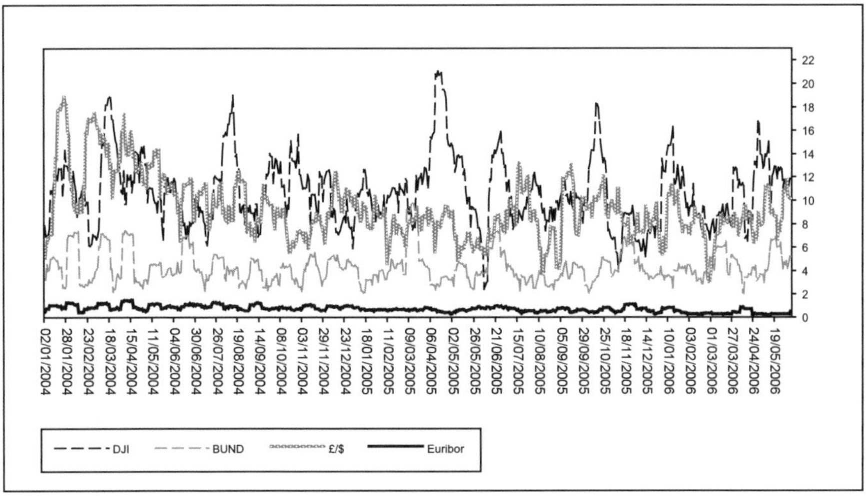

Source: Reuters

Many trading permutations

All these advantages can apply to most financial futures, but STIR futures offer further trading advantages. Because they have multiple expiries listed on the same contract, this offers the trader more choices. They could sell H5 or M6, or buy red September or buy green December. Indeed, many traders specialise in trading certain maturity cycles such as the reds or greens, rarely trading the front whites. Traders can also trade one maturity or expiry against another. For example, you might purchase H7 and sell M7 against it to trade the spread between the two contracts. You might buy H7, sell M7, sell M7 and buy U7 and trade the differential between the two spreads. It doesn't stop there either. There are many trading permutations within STIR futures, which allow the traders to find a niche for themselves. However, make no mistakes, there's little easy money in STIR futures but undoubtedly many choices. Subsequent chapters will be looking at the trading of STIR futures in much greater detail but first it's important to appreciate how STIR futures are priced relative to the underlying interest rates.

STIR Futures Pricing

Spot and forward rates

STIR futures are derived from the underlying interest rate, and those interest rates are short-term rates from the money markets. Money markets comprise both cash deposits rates (also known as depos or spot rates) and money market instruments. It is the former with which this section is primarily concerned.

Deposit rates

Most readers will be familiar with the concept of deposit rates. A bank will offer the depositor a choice of term and interest rate for the money. Usually, but not always, the longer the money is left, the higher the interest rate that is received. This depends on the outlook for interest rates but, generally, depositors will be rewarded with higher rates for the longer they leave their money. This shape of the deposit rate structure (or *yield curve*) where longer-term rates are higher than short-term rates, is often termed *positively sloping*. The deposit rate will be fixed for the term of the deposit. Table 1.6 shows the deposit rates for pounds sterling available on 8 November 2005.

Table 1.6: Deposit rates as at 8 November 2005

Term	Rate %
1 month	4.45
2 months	4.52
3 months	4.54
6 months	4.58
9 months	4.62
12 months	4.66

Let's say an author agreed a £200 advance for a book. Half is receivable in November 2005, and the other half in nine months time when the manuscript is delivered. The first £100 could be deposited at a fixed rate and be assured that the rate quoted at inception would be the rate for the term of the deposit, whether it be one month or three. (There is a little credit risk associated with deposits: banks *can* fail, but it can be regarded as a minor risk.)

Continuing this analogy, £100 is duly deposited on 8 November at the rate of 4.54% for three months. The author is happy, although a bit concerned about newspaper reports suggesting lower UK interest rates in the future. He is increasingly concerned that in 9 months time, deposit rates may not be as high as they are today. Since he will not receive the other £100 for 9 months, the deposits market is not applicable and he really wants to lock in an interest rate for, say, 3 months that starts, not today as in the case of deposits, but in 9 months time which introduces the forwards market.

Forward markets

The forwards markets is concerned with forward interest rates. They are rates that commence for a fixed term at a certain date in the future. They can also be known as forward-forward rates.

The author is then faced with the problem of determining the 3-month interest rate starting in 9-months time. The diagram below shows that the nine-month rate is 4.62% and the 12-month rate is 4.66 % and so it's just a question of working out the value of the missing 3-month period between 9 and 12 months. This can be viewed diagrammatically as:

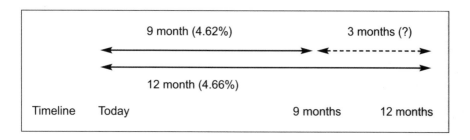

It's possible to mathematically solve for the 'missing' 3-month period between 12 months and 9 months by working through the cash flows.

Since the 12-month rate is known to be 4.66%, funds could be deposited for that period at that rate. A similar sum could also be deposited for nine months starting from now until 9 months hence at the rate of 4.62%. What needs to be done now is solve for the rate at which the 9-month deposit could be reinvested for a further 3 months so that the total of interest received from both 9 month and 3 month deposits is the same as that the single 12-month deposit. This rate will be the 9- month implied forward rate.

Working this through gives the following cash flows.

Depositing £100 for 12 months at 4.66% would provide £4.66 interest at maturity.

Alternatively, depositing £100 for 9 months at 4.62% will give £3.465 (£4.62 x 270/360). From this, an additional £1.195 (£4.66 – £3.465) needs to be earned by reinvesting the 9-month deposit for a further 3 months so that this method equals the amount that could have been made by just investing in the 12-month deposit.

However, the original £100 is now worth £103.465 after 9 months and so this is reinvested for a further 3 months. This concept of earning interest on the interest is called compound interest. The rate at which it is reinvested for the £103.465 to generate £1.195 in interest is then calculated by:

£1.195 / (£103.465 x 90/360) = 4.62 % and this is the implied forward rate for 3 months, starting in 9 months time.

There needs to be no advantage in depositing in either a single 12-month deposit or by investing in a 9 month deposit rate and a 9 month forward for 3 months These rates need to be in equilibrium with each other or arbitrage opportunities will exist.

This concept can be expressed mathematically by the formula for implied forward rates. This allows for the easy calculation of implied forwards by use of a spreadsheet omitting the need to work out cashflows each time.

$$\left(\left(\frac{1+ \text{(long period rate x long period /Year)}}{1+ \text{(Short period rate x short period/Year)}}\right)-1\right) \times \frac{\text{Year}}{\text{Actual}} = 4.62\%$$

Substituting the values gives:

$$\left(\left(\frac{1+ (0.0466 * 360 / 360)}{1+ (0.0462 * 270 / 360)}\right)-1\right) \times \frac{360}{90} = 4.62\%$$

Note: This example is using a 360-day year to equate the periods, so that 3 months equals 90 days, which in turn equals a quarter of a year.

This gives the same answer as the manual example using the cashflows. 4.62% is the implied forward rate that could be expected based upon the given deposit rates and this is the rate, fixed today, at which the author could expect to place £100, receivable in nine months time, on deposit for three months.

Implied forward rates are very dependant on the shape of the yield curve. If the yield curve is positively sloped, implied forward rates are higher than spot rates. Conversely, in a negatively sloped curve, implied forward rates are lower. This is an effect of compound interest, and this and the other variables of day count and deposit rates used can influence the final values.

The STIR Future Theoretical Price

Basic pricing concepts

It was mentioned earlier that STIR futures-

confer the borrowing or lending at a rate determined by the price at which the future was transacted, for a period of three months after the expiry and settlement of the contract.

This is the same concept as the implied forward rate. Both determine interest rates for a borrowing and lending for a specified period that will occur at a date in the future. Indeed, it is from the implied forward rate that the theoretical value of a futures contract can be calculated. The value of the equivalent STIR future can be expressed as:

```
STIR theoretical value = 100 - implied forward rate
```

or, in the case of the example above:

```
100 - 4.62% = 95.38
```

At the time of writing, on 8 November 2005, the nearest future expiring in 9 months time would be the U6 (September 2006) contract, which is currently trading at 95.32. However, the U6 future has 316 days to expiry whereas the implied forward rate uses 270 days that results in a wider difference between the STIR theoretical value and the actual market price.

Day counts

It is very important when comparing the two that all conventions are identical. The day count in particular needs special attention since the above example has used a 360-day year whereas the UK money markets, and so Short Sterling STIR futures, use a 365-day year. Also, the 3-month periods assumed a convenient 90 days per quarter, but 3-months can be anything from 89 days to 93 days depending on the time of year. Furthermore, the start and end date need to be on business days and so day counts need to be adjusted for weekends and Bank holidays.

If the periods were equated between the U6 future and the period at which a forward rate were to be established (so that the period would be 316 days, not 270 and a 365 day count), the implied forward rate would be 4.67% (using deposit rates for 316 days and 406 days) Transforming this number into the theoretical futures price would give 95.33.

The basis

This difference between the STIR future theoretical price and the STIR future market price is called the *value basis* and is expressed as:

STIR future market price - STIR future theoretical price

The basis is a measure of how under or over valued the futures contract is relative to its fair value. A positive basis will indicate futures being overpriced relative to the theoretical price and conversely, a negative basis would show futures to be cheap when compared to the theoretical value. In the case of above example, the value basis would be -1 basis points (95.32-95.33 = -0.01), indicating that the futures are cheap to theoretical.

There is another basis figure in use in the markets called the *simple basis* and is the difference between the 3 month LIBOR or EURIBOR rate, expressed as an equivalent futures price and the front STIR future. It is mainly used to value the front contract when close to expiry.

Valuing the short sterling STIR futures

The above methodology can be applied using the deposit rate curve to value the short sterling STIR futures trading in the market. Firstly, it is necessary to calculate the day counts for the futures contracts for their expiry and subsequent 3-month forward period and to align this with the deposits yield curve.

The Short Sterling contract specification states that the Z5 contract will expire on the third Wednesday of the month, which is 21 December, or 43 days from the start date of 8 November 2005. Adding a forward period of 3-months to this Z5 expiry date will give another date point of 133 days from which the implied forward rate for the Z5 contract can be calculated. The H6 future will expire on 15 March 2006, or in 127 days time and adding 3-months to this gives a date point of 217 days, allowing the calculation of the its implied forward rate and so the H6 theoretical value. This can be carried on throughout the range of futures to be valued but note that this is a simplified process to demonstrate the principal. The day counts do not exclude bank holidays or include settlement periods and three months are deemed to be a constant 90 days, all of which will have an effect on the rates generated. It should also be noted that Short Sterling is unique among most STIR futures in that it uses the British day count convention of 365 days per year, compared to 360 days for most other contracts.

Interpolation

So far, date points have been calculated for the Z5 futures of 43 days to expiry with the three-month forward period of 90-days continuing this to 133 days. The H6 expiry is 127 days from the start date of 8 November and the three-month forward period of 90-days continues this to 217 days. However, the cash deposit rates in table 1.6 are for 30 days, 60 days, 90 days, 180 days and 270 days that do not match those of the futures. Consequently, these date gaps need to be to filled by interpolating the rates between these dates to match the futures. Interpolation is the process of estimating new values between existing discrete values, and linear interpolation is most widely used for money market instruments. It is a weighted mean, assuming two known data points and that the rate of change between them is constant. Linear interpolation can be used to fill in the deposit date gaps in the example to provide a smooth range of deposit rates for the required periods.

Table 1.7 shows the results of this interpolation. The date points are shown on the left hand side and are the number of days forward from the start date of 8 November. Next to them are the Short Sterling futures contract codes and prices followed by the market prices. The deposit rate column shows the given deposit rates in normal font and the interpolated rates in bold. Note how the bold interpolated rates now match the date points for the futures. Once those rates are determined, it's then just a case of putting those numbers into the implied forward rate calculation to calculate the theoretical futures price. To value the Z5 future, the 43-day date point and corresponding rate of 4.45% and the 133-day point and rate of 4.57% would be used.

Table 1.7: Implied forward rates from UK deposit rates

Number of days from 8th Nov 2005	Futures contract (Short Sterling)	Futures price	Depo rates (%)	LIBOR (%)	2 Yr Swap rate (%)	Implied forward rate (%)	Theoretical Futures price	Value basis
30			4.45					
43	Z5	95.39	4.45			4.60	95.40 (95.38)	-0.01
60			4.52					
90			4.54	4.62				
127	H6	95.40	4.56			4.58	95.42	-0.02
133 Z5			4.57					
180			4.58					
217 H6			4.60					
225	M6	95.39	4.61			4.58	95.42	-0.03
270			4.62					
315 M6			4.64					
316	U6	95.32	4.64			4.67	95.33	-0.01
365			4.66					
406 U6			4.69					
407	Z6	95.27	4.69			4.66	95.34	-0.07
497 Z6			4.73					
498	H7	95.23	4.73			4.62	95.38	-0.15
588 H7			4.76					
730					4.78			

Substituting them into the implied forward calculation would give:

$$\left(\left(\frac{1+ (0.0457 \times 133/365)}{1+ (0.0445 \times 43/365)}\right) -1\right) \times \frac{365}{90} = 4.60\%$$

From this implied forward rate, the Z5 theoretical value can be calculated as:

```
100 - 4.60 = 95.40
```

The actual Z5 futures price is shown in the table as 95.39 giving a value basis of – 0.01 indicating that the market price of the future is marginally cheap compared to its theoretical value. Since Z5 is the front or nearest dated contract, the 3-month LIBOR rate can be used to establish the simple basis. In this case 100 – 4.62% = 95.38, which when compared to the market price gives a basis of 0.01.

Finding interest rates beyond 1 year

This procedure can be continued all along the sequence of futures until there is a theoretical futures price for the first four contracts or white strip. It can be seen that they are priced quite closely to the actual futures prices since the process of interpolating the deposit rates and calculating the implied forward rates is fairly straightforward. However, the red strip including Z6 and H7 is not as accurate and this is where things become a bit more difficult. Deposit rates really only go out to 12 months. (Some brokers will quote deposit rates beyond 1-year but they are not quite the same instrument since they have an interim interest payment after 12 months and then every 6-months hence. Furthermore, the rates will be susceptible to a given brokers' quotes). But the futures continue forward for several years. One pricing solution is to use another adapted form of interest rate security, which provides a representative interest rate beyond one year.

A popular choice is the interest rate swap. These instruments notionally swap a fixed rate of interest for a floating one, are conveniently quoted in a rate format and are popular instruments representing the yield curve between 2 years and 50 years. Table 1.7 shows the 2-year Swap rate as being 4.78 % at 730 days. However, this causes an increasingly inaccurate value basis for the Z6 and H7 contracts and so a more advanced pricing methodology is needed to value STIR futures beyond 1 year.

Advanced pricing concepts

It has been seen how it is fairly straightforward to value near-dated STIR futures using deposit rates to calculate the implied forward rates, but how it becomes more difficult moving beyond the barrier of 1-year due to the necessity of having to choose another instrument to give a representative longer dated rate value. The usual choice is swaps but although they are interest rate products they are dissimilar to deposits in terms of cash flows and sometimes day conventions.

Zero yield curve

Deposits are sometimes called spot rates since they are the rates quoted today for what you will receive in x periods. For example, a £100 deposited in a 12-month deposit at 5 % will return £100 principal plus £5 interest in a year's time. However, swaps are based upon notional cashflows (interest payments) which can be made every 6-months or so. The effects of compounding make themselves clear when a £100 investment in a 1-year swap at 5% returns £105.60 a year later, making the assumption that the interest received after 6 months could be reinvested at the same rate. This assumption is apparent in the quoted price/rate of the swap. Consequently, these instruments need to be re-formatted so that they have the same characteristics as the deposits, that is being spot products paying interest at maturity but expressed as a discounted security. These products are also known as zeros or zero coupons and a curve made up of these instruments is known as a zero yield curve.

A zero yield curve is a term structure of interest rates, usually comprising deposits rates, futures rates and swap rates. Each instrument needs to be equated in terms of cash flow periods and compounding and date conventions.

Deposit rates are effectively already zero rates and they only need to be converted to a uniform compounding and day count convention, usually a continuously compounded rate. Swap rates are usually compounded semi-annually because of their cashflow exchange every 6 months and normally quoted as par rates (the par rate is the fixed rate at which the swap has a zero present value). The zero rates are derived from the swap par rates by a method called bootstrapping. This is a complicated process that starts from the shortest term cashflow and steps through each subsequent one, effectively valuing the next cashflow from the preceding one. This will produce continually compounded zero rates from which the forward rates can be calculated and used to value the STIR futures.

This is a complex procedure, fortunately made easier by software packages, which can calculate results with real time data. It is possible for the mathematically able to construct a zero curve in a spreadsheet but there is plenty of scope for error and the whole procedure is rendered rather academic by the need for real time swap rate data, which is usually only available from the same data vendors as those containing pre-built zero curves. Furthermore, zero curves do not lend themselves well to the use of end of day data since the different component instruments have differing settlement times of up to several hours apart.

It should also be noted that STIR futures should not be used in zero curves to be used for pricing STIR futures since it effectively becomes a circular reference. They should ideally be replaced with deposits to nine months and swap rates thereafter. However, even using this construction in a real time environment yields mixed results since most swaps are quoted on a 2 or 3 basis point bid and offer, which when converted to zero rates and then combined in a forward rate calculation, introduce a measure of variance which makes interpretation difficult.

Table 1.8 shows the same data used before to value the Short Sterling STIR futures but valued more accurately by using forward rates from zero rates in a zero yield curve derived from the deposit rates and 2-year swap rate. It can be seen from the table that this approach provided more accurate results for the basis figures after 1 year's duration.

Table 1.8: Implied forward rates calculated from a zero curve

Future	Market price	Implied forward rate (%) (linear int)	Theoretical futures price (100-implied rate)	Value basis (market price – theoretical price)
Z5	95.39	4.59	95.41	-0.02
H6	95.40	4.61	95.39	0.01
M6	95.39	4.63	95.37	0.02
U6	95.32	4.65	95.35	-0.03
Z6	95.27	4.71	95.29	-0.02
H7	95.23	4.75	95.25	-0.02
M7	95.21	4.77	95.23	-0.02
U7	95.20	4.79	95.21	-0.01

Source: Reuter 3000xtra

Note: The zero curve will have higher yields than the standard yield curve when the curve is positively sloping This is because the discount rate attached to each cash flow must increase as maturity increases along the curve in order to maintain an arbitrage free equilibrium of zero coupon rates. Accordingly, the implied forward curve is higher in the table above than the one in the earlier table resulting in more accurate pricing of the longer dated futures.

There will always be discrepancies between fair value and price

It would be unrealistic to expect that any level of sophistication used to calculate STIR futures fair values will result in values that are identical to that of the underlying future. Factors such as the choice and source of which deposit and swap rates to use, whether to use the bid, offer or mean price, which day count and settlement period, which interpolation method and the inherent characteristics of compounding all affect the final values. It is unlikely that any STIR future theoretical value will be an absolutely fair value when the variables are so subjective and market sentiment toward the incidence of future interest rate moves plays a role.

Basis values can reflect market expectations of higher or lower interest rates and so futures can trade cheap or dear to the theoretical levels. Consequently, traders should use discretion towards the valuation of STIR futures and not necessarily assume that one particular future is absolutely cheap or expensive relative to it's theoretical value but use it more as an indicative tool that can reflect the market outlook.

Convexity adjustments

There is a further consideration to be taken into account when valuing STIR futures and that is convexity.

There is a difference between forward rates and those rates implied by STIR futures caused by the different settlement procedures. Futures are settled daily and their profit or loss added or subtracted to or from their margin account whereas the forward rates settle only at maturity. There is an inherent benefit or bias to being short STIR futures against forward rates. If interest rates increase, the futures will fall, returning a margin credit that can be reinvested at higher rates. If interest rates fall, the margin deficit can be financed at lower rates. The difference in reinvestment opportunity of the cash flows between the futures and forward rates causes the forward rate to be less than the futures rate and this difference is termed the *convexity bias*. Convexity only becomes a meaningful issue in pricing STIR futures for longer dated futures (in excess of two years) and is greatly affected by interest rate volatility.

There are several methods of calculating the convexity adjustment, most of which are a function of volatility but they can be intricate in their construction. Consequently, those readers with further interest are directed to the recommended reading below[1] but for the purpose of example it suffices to say that convexity adjustment for Short Sterling 2-year futures would be approximately 2.0 basis points.

This convexity adjustment of approximately 0.02 for the 2-year Short Sterling contract needs to be added to the forward rate (4.79%) of the nearest future to two years, which table 1.8 gives as being the U7 future (95.20). This changes the forward rate to 4.81% (4.79 + 0.02) and returns a convexity adjusted theoretical futures price of 95.19 (95.21 – 0.02).

Arbitrage considerations

It has been shown that deposit and forward rates must exist in equilibrium with each other. There has to be no difference between an investor depositing in a 12-month spot rate or in a combination of a 9-month deposit and 3-month forward starting in 9 months time. The sum of the parts should equal the whole otherwise the potential

[1] 1. 'Options Futures & Other Derivatives', JC Hull, Prentice Hall

2 'The Eurodollar Futures And Options Handbook', Burghardt G, McGraw Hill

3 'Convexity Conundrums', George Kirikos and David Novak, RISK, March 1997 (see www.powerfinance.com/convexity).

to make money from simply borrowing and lending exists. This is called arbitrage and can be simply described as a free lunch or, more formally, as a strategy involving the simultaneous purchase and sale of near identical securities that exploits a price differential for a risk-free profit.

It has also been shown that differences between the theoretical futures and market futures price do exist, shown by a basis other than zero. Basis calculations can be complicated by the type of security selected to calculate forward rates, date conventions need to match and market sentiment can cause distortions since investors will often tend to go to the quickest source of liquidity, which tends to be the futures markets.

Defining an arbitrage channel

However, it should be possible to define an arbitrage channel around the futures contract by careful use of all the variables. This would make the assumption that transaction expenses do not apply but that the bid/offer spread on deposit rates does. Now, a 4-basis point bid/offer spread will be incorporated, reflecting the actual money market dealing rates whereas, before, only the mid point of the deposit rates was used.

Given the following data:

Date:	8 November
U6:	95.32
316 day bid/offer rate:	4.62/4.66
406 day bid/offer rate:	4.67/4.71

Changing the implied forward equation to incorporate the bid/offer spread would give:

Implied forward bid rate:	4.52%
Implied forward offer rate:	4.83%

Which converted into STIR futures theoretical prices would give a bid price of 95.17 and an offer of 95.48 against a mean price of 95.33, making an arbitrage channel of 31 ticks wide. This means that assuming that the above bid/offer rates were the only dealing rates available at that time, the U6 STIR future could either fall to 95.17 or rise to 95.48 without attracting the attention of arbitrageurs.

Every arbitrageur has their own arbitrage channel

In reality, an arbitrageur might have the advantage of better rates to deal at than those quoted above and so improve upon this arbitrage channel considerably, but this exercise shows that a change of 1 basis point in the deposit rate bid/offer spread can have an effect of approximately 5 ticks to the value of the underlying STIR futures theoretical value. Tighter dealing rates might reduce the arbitrage channel from say, 31 ticks to perhaps 15 ticks – approximately 7 ticks either side of the theoretical mean price, but the arbitrageur still then needs to find a mis-pricing in excess of this.

Arbitrage example

If an arbitrageur defined his arbitrage channel as being 15 ticks for the U6 future given his dealing rates, he might find a mis-pricing as follows:

Date:	21 December 2005
U6:	95.30
3 month rate:	4.54%
9 month rate:	4.62%
12 month rate:	4.66%

It's the 21st December and the markets are quiet. A bank trader notices that the Short Sterling U6 future has traded down to 95.30 on thin business. Deposit rates have remained unchanged. The trader calculates the theoretical future price to be 95.38 based upon an implied forward rate calculation using his dealing rates at which he can borrow or lend money and sees an opportunity:

- He decides to buy 200 U6 futures at 95.30, which at £500,000 per contract, confers a lending of £100,000,000, whilst simultaneously depositing £100,000,000 for 9-months at 4.62% and borrowing £100,000,000 for 12-months at 4.66%.

- On 20 September 2006, rates are unchanged and his futures expire at 95.46 (100-3-month rate of 4.54%) making him £40,000 (200*£12.50*16). His £100,000,000 9-month deposit matures returning £103,465,000 and he reinvests this at 4.54% for another 3-months.

- Three months later, on 20 December 2006, the trader's deposit matures returning £104,639,328. His 12- month borrowing also matures, having cost him £4,660,000 in interest losing a total of £20,672. However, given the £40,000 profit in hand and additional £454 interest that that money has earned in the last 3-months makes a net profit of £19,782. This profit is approximately equal to the trader buying the futures at 95.30 and selling them at the theoretical value of 95.38.

Of course, this is a very simplistic version but it illustrates some important points:

1. The amount of capital is large and the time period long compared to the relatively small profit being made. The deposits market is deemed to be on-balance sheet meaning that the initiating bank would need to make reserves against it's capital to finance this arbitrage. These reserves would reduce the amount of capital being available for other, perhaps more profitable ventures.

2. The dates in this example are conveniently synchronised so that the deposit dates match the futures dates. Dealing on days away from this date harmony would involve a different, more complex approach to the arbitrage. The usual approach is to ratio different futures maturities in order to try to cover the mismatched (broken) dates but it is difficult to be exact.

It can be seen how arbitrage can define an acceptable range in which the futures should trade. However, the above has shown how arbitrage might not be the pure equaliser as proposed in theory. Practical and commercial considerations probably extend the arbitrage boundaries beyond these theoretical limits as each transgression has to be also evaluated in terms of opportunity and resources cost. However, that's not to say that prices can or will get wildly out of line. The existence of other interest rate products on that segment of the yield curve including forward rate agreements, swaps and treasury bills and notes will combine to eliminate the easy arbitrage since traders will trade these instruments relative to each other.

The Drivers Of STIR Futures Prices

The drivers of STIR futures are what influences and changes the prices of the futures contracts and how those prices can change relative to each other. There are two broad categories of drivers: the yield and price sensitive effects. Each of these will be looked at in turn. First, the yield curve.

Changing shape of the yield curve

Yield curves are the term structure of interest rates over time, which in its simplest form is a graphical display of interest rates plotted against time. These interest rates are compiled from representative instruments of certain maturity such as deposits, STIR futures and swap rates. This kind of yield curve is called a *spot curve* or *cash curve*. The spot curve is based on rates starting from the inception date until maturity.

But there is also another type of yield curve called the *forward curve*, which is a term structure of forward starting rates over time. These are rates that do not start until a specified date and it is upon these that STIR futures are priced.

Incidence of interest rate expectations

The previous section on pricing explained how STIR futures are based on forward rates and how forward rates are effectively what the market expects interest rates to be in the future, but by nature of their calculation, there is usually a positive bias. STIR futures will most closely map a yield curve of forward rates, but it can be interesting to observe differences in interest rate expectations by comparing the futures rates to the cash or spot yield curve.

The yield curve is constantly changing

Although it has been said earlier that the yield curves tend to be positively sloping, that is, longer dated rates tend to be higher than nearer dated rates, the yield curve can take many shapes, all dependent on interest rate outlook. In times of falling interest rates, all or part of the curve might be negatively sloping, where the longer dated rates are lower than the near dated ones. Yields can move sharply from one shape to another as illustrated by Chart 1.3 that shows two snapshots of UK data.

The first is taken on 8 July 2005 when expectations were for interest rates to move lower. Surveys had 90% of polled economists expecting a 25 bps (basis points) rate cut in August based on slowing economic growth, weakening retail sales and falling employment.

This is reflected in the negatively sloping yield curve between 3-months and 2-years and the futures strip were aggressively pricing in further cuts. The base rate was duly cut to 4.5% in August and forecasters started predicting rates even lower by year-end.

Chart 1.3: GBP cash and futures curves 8 July 2005 and 8 November 2005

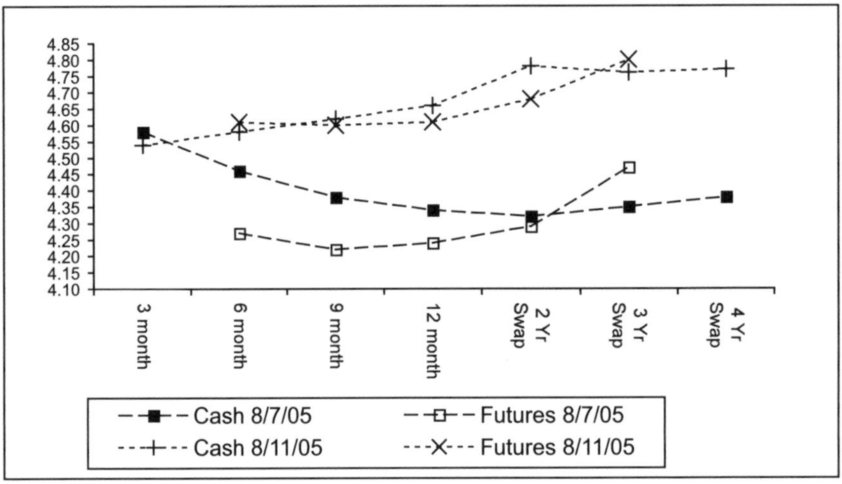

This enthusiasm towards lower rates continued into October until a series of central banker's comments to the media reversed the outlook. An increased inflationary outlook and a dawning realisation amongst economists that August's rate cut might have been a one-off had them revising their expectations.

By 8 November, short sterling futures had dropped approximately 40 ticks and some forecasts started emerging for the possibility of a rate increase in early 2006. Chart 1.3 shows this change of sentiment with the second snapshot taken on 8 November 2005. The curve has clearly shifted upwards in yield, steepened and is fully positive. The futures curve is sitting close to the curve indicating some indecision as to the future direction of rates. It's neither aggressively predicting lower rates as it was in July, nor indicating substantially higher rates than those already in the market. Time will tell!

Interest rate expectations are rarely static for long. New data and forecasts, right or wrong, constantly influence the outlook for rates and hence the STIR futures price curve. The yield curve will always be a melting pot of opinion and expectations, ensuring that STIR futures will be active products to trade!

Quantifying interest rate expectations

Interest rate expectations can be quantified by assigning a probability to the chance of an expected move. Market strategists usually calculate this by subtracting the 3-month inter bank or LIBOR rate from the implied yield of the STIR future and then dividing the difference by the magnitude of the expected rate movement.

For example, on 1 February 2006 the M6 Short Sterling contract was 95.38, implying a rate of 4.62% (100-95.38), and the 3-month inter-bank rate was 4.52% (UK base rates were 4.5%). Subtracting the 3-month inter-bank rate of 4.52% from the implied yield of the STIR future leaves 10 basis points (4.62%-4.52%), which is then divided by the magnitude of the expected rate movement (being 25 basis points). This results in 0.40, or a 40% probability of a 25 bps rate hike by the M6 expiry. Note that if the implied yield of the STIR future was less than the 3-month inter bank rate, a negative probability would be returned indicating the chances of a rate cut.

Liquidity considerations of the micro-curve

The micro-curve can be considered to be the local effects on a small segment of the yield curve. Although yield curves can extend to 30 years or more, STIR futures generally cover a liquid section of the curve to around 3 years and can exhibit small distortions along its own price curve. These distortions are unlikely to violate arbitrage channels to any significant amount but can create opportunities in certain trades such as spreads and strategies.

These distortions are based upon the concept of liquidity preference. Users of STIR futures often tend to trade the front, white months which reflect about a year's interest rate expectation. Consequently these months or contracts tend to have the highest traded volume and most liquid markets, in turn attracting new trade for precisely that purpose.

Table 1.9 shows the Short Sterling volume data from the close of business on 19 December 2005. The data includes the contract code, total traded volume and net change from the previous days settlement prices.

Table 1.9: Short Sterling volume figures for 19 December 2005

Contract	Volume	Net change
Z5	33,881	+0.01
H6	91,411	+0.10
M6	190,722	+0.14
U6	102,054	+0.14
Z6	73,634	+0.12
H7	36,378	+0.11
M7	28,499	+0.10
U7	10,590	+0.09
Z7	7,491	+0.08

It can seen be how M6 and U6 have the majority of volume and are the main points of liquidity on the STIR price curve – not the front month Z5 that is close to expiry. Volumes steadily decline from the U6 contract onwards, dwindling to a mere 7,491 contracts by Z7. A trader wishing to execute a large order would be more inclined towards trading M6 or U6 simply because the market is more able to accommodate the business.

The net change shows some distortions where the highest volume M6 and U6 contracts have gone up the most. Beyond U6, the upward performance diminishes again with liquidity. Often, the back months might be higher or lower than the front reflecting changing curve shapes but usually in progressive amounts. However, the incidence of a large trade in a particular month can sometimes differentiate prices, particularly intra-day. Traders can take advantage of these small kinks in the price curve with a variety of trades such as spreads and strategies.

Seasonal influences

Sometimes, the contracts covering the year-end, namely the December contracts can trade at a slightly higher yield than those surrounding them. This is put down to tighter credit conditions in the inter-bank money markets and hence a slight rate premium in the banking system over the Christmas and New Year period. It stemmed from a botched liquidity operation from the Federal Reserve Bank in the US during the 1980s and consequently became a pricing characteristic of the market structure, although its effects did diminish during the 1990s. The notion of tighter year-end rates was reinvigorated over the millennium when the December 2000 contracts of all major STIR futures contracts fell sharply on Y2K fears, which ultimately proved unfounded. On balance, the December contracts do tend to trade relatively cheaper to their adjacent expiries.

Turning to the other driver of STIR futures.

Price sensitive effects

Price sensitive effects are causes that influence the STIR futures price. They include economic data, interest rate sensitive comments by central bankers, influences of other markets and event and systemic risks.

Economic data

The yield curve, and so the STIR futures price curve, is heavily influenced by the interest rate outlook which, in turn, is dependent on the state of the underlying economy. Economic statistics, reflecting the state of the economy, are released on a monthly basis and some are eagerly anticipated by the markets looking for new direction. Banks, brokers and information vendors provide calendars of impending economic releases and their corresponding forecasts. Some are available free over the internet. [See the appendix for details.]

Economic releases are usually released at the following times:

UK	0930 GMT
US	1330 GMT and 1500 GMT (0830 ET and 1000 ET)
Euro zone	0700 0900 1000 GMT (0800 1000 1100 CET).

Economists provide forecasts of upcoming economic releases and financial markets can move significantly in reaction to figures that deviate from their consensus. Some figures are consistently more important than others and some are of more cyclical importance. Sentiment surveys tend to be cyclical indicators of economic turning points. Most international markets closely watch US economic releases since America is the world's largest economy and if America catches a cold – as they say – everybody sneezes.

Below is a list the main economic releases, see also Table 1.10 (page 43). This is not meant to be a comprehensive list, but includes the main and most consistent market movers. The figures relate to all three economic areas of the United States, Europe and UK unless a release is indicated as being country specific.

Employment

The US figure, Non-Farm Payrolls is probably the most closely watched indicator in world financial markets. It's usually released on the first Friday of each month and is a barometer of whether the economy is creating jobs or not, and so is a reflection of the health of the economy itself. The figure includes both the private and public job data and so needs to be analysed beyond the headline number to see whether the one sector has unduly influenced the figure. The private business sector payrolls will be most important. A lower than anticipated Non-Farm Payroll number will tend to cause the STIR futures prices to increase, reflecting the possibility of a slowing economy and lower interest rates and vice versa.

A weekly jobless figure is released every Thursday but has much less influence.

Domestic employment data for other countries will normally have a lesser, local effect.

Gross Domestic Product (GDP)

Gross Domestic Product is a national report measuring how quickly an economy is growing. It is issued quarterly and is a reflection of economic output. A weaker than expected figure will tend to cause the STIR futures prices to increase. However, bear in mind that the quarterly GDP lags other monthly indicators. This means that the market may well have already anticipated its effect. The figure is released in a series of estimates and then later revised. Watch out for the GDP deflator and price index constituents which are broad indicators of inflationary pressures.

Retail Sales

Retail sales are a monthly report of consumer spending. Retail sales account for approximately 30% of all consumer spending and that itself can account for up to 75% of economic activity. The figures are subject to large revisions in subsequent months. A lower than consensus number will tend to cause the STIR futures prices to increase, indicating economic weakness.

Consumer Price Index (CPI)

A very important number for financial markets, being the most popular measure of inflation in retail goods and services. It is released monthly and a lower figure will boost markets whilst a higher number will infer higher interest rates since the majority of central banks target inflation via the setting of interest rate levels. No monthly revisions.

Producer Price Index (PPI)

PPI, like CPI, is another price level indicator but measures the change in prices paid by businesses. It is a composite of several PPIs, but the most important component tends to be the finished goods PPI that can reflect price pressures in the manufacturing process. It will have the same effects on markets as CPI – some consider PPI changes to be a precursor for CPI changes. Watch out for the core PPI number.

Purchasing Managers Index (PMI)

The main US PMI is the Institute for Supply Management (ISM) Manufacturing Survey, important because it is a private survey issued on the first business day of the month and represents demand for manufactured products. This in itself is an indicator of economic activity.

PMIs are also issued by the Eurozone and the UK and have similar characteristics.

A number strongly above the median of 50 can cause STIR futures to sell off and a weak number well below 50 can have the opposite effect.

University of Michigan Sentiment

This US survey is a private indicator of consumer attitudes on the business climate, personal finance and retail, reflecting a sample of 500 individuals. It is regarded as being a superior consumer confidence figure and it is released at 0945 (ET) on the second Friday of each month. It tends to be a more closely watched number at turning points in the growth of the economy.

Consumer Confidence

Another indicator of consumer outlook. It differs from the University of Michigan figure in that it concentrates more on attitudes to employment and is drawn from a new sample each month.

Durable Goods

A monthly US figure based on future manufacturing activity. Important since it's a forward looking indicator gauging production in the months ahead. Durables are goods lasting three years or more. It can be one of the first numbers to indicate a forthcoming change in the state of the manufacturing economy.

Industrial Production

A monthly figure of industrial output, issued in the US, UK, and Europe in the main form of the German industrial production number.

German IFO Business Survey

An important figure issued by the largest economy in the Eurozone, and therefore closely watched by Euribor STIR futures traders. It is a predictive indicator of economic performance based upon survey answers from 7000 German business leaders in the main sectors of manufacturing, retail, construction and wholesale. The figure is presented in three forms: Climate, Situation and most the widely watched Expectations index The Expectations component is a forward looking indicator of industrial production and has a good history of forecasting changes.

It is issued monthly in the fourth week. A higher than consensus number will cause Euribor futures to sell off.

German ZEW economic sentiment indicator

The ZEW Economic Sentiment Indicator is released monthly, usually on the second or third Tuesday of the month. Up to 350 financial experts take part in the survey and the indicator reflects the difference between the share of analysts that are optimistic and the share of analysts that are pessimistic for the expected economic development in Germany over the course of six months.

Housing

Housing statistics are regarded as being a good indicator of the state of the economy. The US issues New Home Sales (sales of new single family homes), Existing Home Sales (sales of previously owned single family homes) and Housing Starts (numbers of new homes being built and future construction permits). The main UK figures are the Royal Institute of Chartered Surveyors (RICS) Survey (three hundred surveyors and estate agents in England & Wales are asked if they feel prices are falling or rising) and a monthly House Price Index issued by the Office of the Deputy Prime Minister. Other surveys are supplied by Nationwide, Halifax, Hometrack and Rightmove.

Table 1.10: Summary of the effects on STIR futures prices by economic releases

Economic release	Country	Higher than consensus forecasts	Lower than consensus forecasts	Market effect ranking
Non Farm Payrolls	US	↓	↑	High
US Weekly Jobless claims	US	↑	↓	Low
GDP	All	↓	↑	Med/Low
Retail Sales	All	↓	↑	High
CPI	All	↓	↑	High
PPI	All	↓	↑	Med High
PMI	All	↓	↑	Med
Consumer confidence	US	↓	↑	Med/High
University of Michigan	US	↓	↑	Med/High
Durable goods	US	↓	↑	Med
Industrial production	All	↓	↑	Med
Housing	All	↓	↑	Med

Central banker rhetoric

The main function of a central bank and its central bankers is the monitoring and regulating of interest rates in the economy.

An old joke goes:

How many central bankers does it take to screw in a light bulb?

Just one. He holds the light bulb and the whole earth revolves around him.

In financial markets, it's not so much light bulbs as comments on interest rate policy that the financial world revolves around. Announcements from central bankers are followed closely and every nuance examined for an indication of the future direction of interest rates. Central bankers have cultivated the art of sometimes saying a lot but revealing little. Speeches can be deliberately obtuse – rarely will bankers be explicit in their commentary.

However, central bankers do inform market participants when their behaviour is not consistent with that of the central bank, or when market expectations need guidance. Sometimes markets will price in a rate rise or cut too agressively and the bankers need to communicate this via speeches or interviews. This managing of expectations is done in the hope that markets can be smoothly guided to a homogenous viewpoint. The aim is to achieve this with the minimum of price volatility, but can often create price action in the STIR futures markets.

An example of managing expectations – November 2005

In November 2005, Eurozone central bankers were agreed on the need to raise rates from a historic low of 2% to combat inflationary threats from high money supply, credit and energy prices. However, differences were apparent as to the timing of a rate rise and financial markets were increasingly critical of the lack of guidance. The following depicts a sequence of ECB bankers and political comments and events over a period of nine days showing how, by the use of rhetoric, markets were guided to conclude that rates would be raised in December.

"The European Central Bank is ready to move interest rates at any time but is not committed to any timetable. We can act at any time, but are not fixed on any one meeting,"

9 November 2005, ECB Chief Economist Otmar Issing speaking to the German Sueddeutsche Zeitung newspaper.

"Nothing has been decided, I don't find it appropriate that statements or comments are made which, voluntarily or not, pre-empt future policy decisions that have not been made yet."

10 November, Lorenzo Bini-Smaghi, Member of the Executive Board of the European Central Bank

Both these comments made the likelihood of an interest rate rise increasingly clear, but provide no guidance as to the timing. Euribor H6 was trading 97.345 at this time. A few days later, ECB Chief Economist Otmar Issing provided further stimulus for a rate rise, which caused the Euribor futures to fall marginally lower to 97.320.

"We have a medium term orientation. We are not acting on data from month to month. We assess the situation very carefully and if we come to the conclusion that risk to price stability increase and endanger our objective again over the medium term, then we have to act."

14 November, Otmar Issing, Executive board ECB

However, not all observers thought the ECB should raise rates. There is quite often resistance from business and political leaders towards monetary tightening. Two days later, French politician, Pervenche Beres said,

"ECB rate rise would be big risk to growth"

16 Nov 2005, Pervenche Beres, Head of the European Parliament Monetary Affairs Committee

The issue of the timing of an interest rate rise came to a head on Friday, 18 November at the Frankfurt European Banking Congress. The managing director of the International Monetary Fund[2] (IMF), Rodrigo de Rato, met with the Executive board of the ECB. The financial markets had been critical of the ECB's poor communications policy that had made the timing of a rate increase unclear. Rato announced at 1300GMT that,

"Central Banks must signal monetary policy plans clearly to avoid market instability"

Furthermore, Rato, who had earlier said on 4 November that,

"actual monetary conditions should stay for the moment,"

declined to repeat his call for no interest rate change after meeting with the ECB Executive Board. It is likely that ECB board members, meeting the previous day for the second of the ECB's twice-monthly meetings (where monetary policy issues are discussed but interest rates are not generally announced until the first meeting of the month), decided that a rise was imminent and this would have been conveyed to Rato to avoid any embarrassment of conflicting messages.

The ECB president, Jean-Claude Trichet, then made the following statement at 1348GMT on the same day,

"After two and a half years of maintaining interest rates at a level historically exceptionally low, I would consider that the Governing Council is ready to take a decision to move interest rates, and to moderately augment the present level of ECB rates in order to take into account the level of risks to price stability that have been identified. We would thus withdraw some of the accommodation which is embedded in the present monetary policy stance, while the policy would remain accommodative."

Euribor H6 futures immediately fell to 97.23, interpreting this as a clear sign that interest rates were to be increased by 25 basis points at the December meeting, which they duly did on 1 Dec 2005.

---

[2] IMF is an organization of 184 countries, working to foster global monetary cooperation, secure financial stability, facilitate international trade, promote high employment and sustainable economic growth, and reduce poverty.

Central bankers rhetoric is not always clear. Quite often it can appear conflicting, and political and business interests can muddy the waters further. However, it is the bankers' comments that carry most weight and it is in these that the clues must be sought.

In the above example, it is apparent, with analysis, that the ECB were unanimous in their calls for an interest rate increase, but were uncertain over the timing. The European Banking Congress, meeting a day after the ECB's own meeting, provided an opportunity to update markets on the Board's consensus of opinion. Rato gave a clue by declining to repeat his earlier call for unchanged interest rates and gave the ECB President a cue by indicting that central banks needed to clearly signal their intentions. Trichet duly took this opportunity and the markets reacted accordingly.

Interest rate announcements

Interest rate announcements by the main central banks are of great importance to the STIR futures markets. They are made at regular intervals and are eagerly awaited by the markets. Central bankers do not decide in advance of a meeting as to whether interest rates should be increased or decreased. Instead they analyse the latest statistics and reports, discuss, and then decide. Market expectations are usually guided by central bankers rhetoric to align the consensus with the outcome.

U.S. Federal Reserve ('Fed')

The Federal Open Market Committee (FOMC) consists of the seven-member Board of Governors and five of the 12 regional Fed presidents. They vote on monetary policy by simple majority. The FOMC holds eight regularly scheduled meetings during the year, and other meetings as needed. They release the result of the vote, along with names of how each person voted, at the same time as they announce the interest-rate decision. The Federal Reserve releases its meeting minutes three weeks later and these are eagerly awaited for indications of future interest rate expectations.

European Central Bank (ECB)

The Governing Council of the ECB meets twice-monthly, but interest rate decisions are usually taken at the first meeting, usually the first Thursday of the month. The ECB decides by consensus, rather than formal vote, of its 18 Governing Council members and a majority carries decisions. However, if there is a tie, the President has the casting vote.

No detailed information is available about how decisions are taken, since no minutes are released and no breakdown of a vote provided.

Bank of England (BOE)

UK interest rate decisions are made by the nine-member Monetary Policy Committee comprising the Governor, the two Deputy Governors, the Bank's Chief Economist, the Executive Director for Markets and four external members appointed directly by the Chancellor. The interest rate decisions are announced at 12 noon on the Thursday of the first or second week of the month. Decisions of the Monetary Policy Committee are made on a one-person one-vote basis, with the Governor having the casting vote if there is no majority.

BOE policy meeting minutes are usually released on the third or final Wednesday on the month of the policy meeting and are eagerly received by the markets. Policy meeting minutes can be one of the most influential releases for shaping market interest rate expectations.

Correlated markets

It has been shown how STIR markets are influenced by yield curve effects, economic news, central banker rhetoric and interest rate announcements. However, the movements of other STIR futures can also affect them and this effect can be observed by the use of the statistical measure: correlation.

Correlation is the causal relationship between two comparable entities. It is expressed as either being positive with a value between zero and one, or negative between zero and minus one. An example of a positive correlation is the relationship between smoking and lung cancer, whilst a negative correlation could be that between age and normal vision. The relationship, either positive or negative, is strongest closest to the respective boundaries of 1 and –1.

International STIR futures markets are highly correlated because of their interest rate parity relationship. Simply put, this means that an equilibrium must hold between the interest rates of two currencies if there are to be no arbitrage opportunities.

Table 1.11 opposite shows the correlation coefficients between the four main STIR futures representing the currencies of the US Dollar, British pound, the Euro and the Swiss franc.

Table 1.11: Correlation matrix between M6 contracts based on 6 months daily data (1/5/05 to 1/11/05)

	Short Sterling (£)	Euribor (€)	Eurodollar ($)	EuroSwiss (CHF)
Short Sterling (£)	1.0	0.47	0.13	0.52
Euribor (€)		1.0	0.81	0.91
Eurodollar ($)			1.0	0.75
EuroSwiss (CHF)				1.0

It can be seen that most markets have a good positive relationship to each other. As one moves the others tend to move in line, with the Eurodollar and Euribor being the main drivers. The Euroswiss tends to follow the Euribor very closely, since its currency and economy are inextricably linked to the Euro. There is a lower correlation between the Short Sterling contracts and other contracts, notably the Eurodollar, perhaps reflecting the closer economic allegiance with Europe and a different stage of the interest rate cycle (the UK had recently cut rates in August 2005 whereas the US continued a policy of gradual rate rises).

Foreign public holidays, particularly those in the United States, can cause particularly quiet trading sessions in other international STIR futures markets.

Since the advent of electronic trading, trading correlations between contracts has been made easier since most trading software packages allow multi-exchange connectivity from one platform, making it comparatively easy to click and trade, for example, Eurodollar and Euribor. The popularity of these trades tends to reinforce the correlations.

Uncorrelated markets

The influences of correlated markets are quite clear; they tend to be intrinsically linked by their currencies and interest rates. Other markets, such as equities and oil, would appear at first to have little to do with STIR futures and have meaningless correlation coefficients to each other. However, in uncertain times, such as stock market volatility or oil price shocks, STIR futures can focus very closely on a particular agent such as stock index futures or oil prices.

Equities

Over a three year period from 1 Jan 1999 to 1 Jan 2002, the FTSE100 index had a correlation of – 0.63 to the then near month Short Sterling Z2 STIR future. This meant that, as the FTSE100 rose, the Z2 Short Sterling future might be expected to fall, but not precisely in line. The causal relationship wasn't that close. In May 2002, the stock market started to fall, increasing momentum until reaching a low in late July. Chart 1.4 shows the movement of the Short Sterling Z2 STIR future against this stock market movement. It can be seen to be almost the mirror image of the FTSE100. As the stock market fell, interest rates implied by the STIR future also fell and so the Short Sterling Z2 future rose.

Chart 1.4: FTSE100 v Short Sterling Z2 January 2002 to October 2002

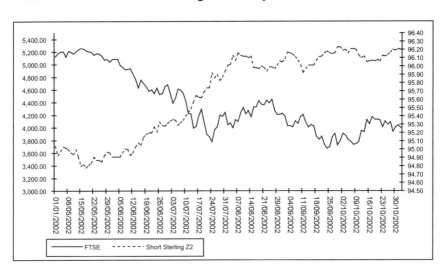

This is where STIR futures are driven by a 'flight to quality' effect. Investors were perceived to be selling more volatile equities and placing their money in a safer environment, namely on deposit in banks or invested in government bonds. Investors will always tend to seek out safer refuges for their money in times of stock market turbulence, political uncertainty, disaster and war. This effect is also exacerbated by the economic principle that rapidly falling stock markets or event risks tend to be countered by interest rate cuts from central banks to bolster the financial system.

The chart shows that even after the lows of late July 2002 each stock market movement was mirrored by the STIR future. A market rally would cause the Short Sterling Z2 STIR future to sell off and vice versa. During the period shown on the chart, the correlation changed to –0.92 from the previous 3 year period of –0.63, quantifying this causal relationship between cause and effect.

Oil

Chart 1.5: Brent Crude Oil v Eurodollar Z5 Jan 2005 to Oct 2005

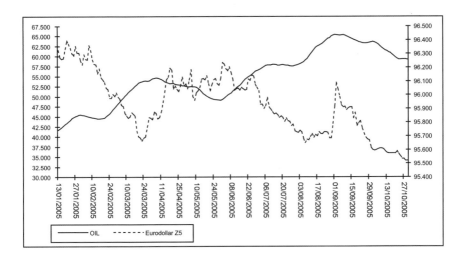

Chart 1.5 shows a similar effect between the Eurodollar Z5 contract and the price of oil, which reached an all time high in September 2005. Unlike the stock market though, this causal effect of the Eurodollar falling as oil price prices rose, is not a consequence of a flight to quality. Rather, it is the economic argument that high oil prices could be inflationary and so interest rates should rise and Eurodollars fall.

Economic arguments are not always clear in their causality and so movements are not mirrored to the extent that flight to quality shocks are. Indeed, it would be quite possible to argue that a high oil price might be recessionary for energy dependent economies such as the United States, hence causing Eurodollar futures to rally.

What is the market focusing on?

It's important to perceive what the market is focussing on and what the driver of the causal relationship is and how tenuous it might remain.

This phenomenon can be observed in the Eurodollar Z5 price spike in September 2005. Up until that time, there had been a clear inverse relationship between oil and STIR futures. As the price of oil escalated, Eurodollars sold down as underlying yields fell in response to the potential of higher inflation. The causal relationship was good and working well. Then along came Hurricane Katrina, which annihilated New Orleans and seriously impacted the oil refining capacity of the United States. Oil continued to rise, but the Eurodollar reversed trend and also rose sharply. The driver behind that move was now that Katrina might prove to be recessionary or that, at least, it might cause the Federal Reserve to pause on its policy at that time of regularly increasing interest rates. This causal relationship soon broke down when none of these fears materialised and Eurodollars sold back down.

These examples have shown how STIR futures markets can focus and move on rapidly shifting variables. It's very important to be able to interpret what is driving the markets at any particular time, whether it is rate expectations, a forthcoming central bankers speech or hurricanes. Sometimes the causal effects are short lived but they often yield trading opportunities to the aware.

Event risk

Event risk is the term applied to the effect of unforeseen events on the STIR futures price. The example of Hurricane Katrina in the previous section is an event risk. However, its effect on the STIR futures price was more of economic consequence, the threat of recessionary influences, than the flight to quality of funds.

Chart 1.6: Short Sterling M6 Jun 2005 to Jul 2005

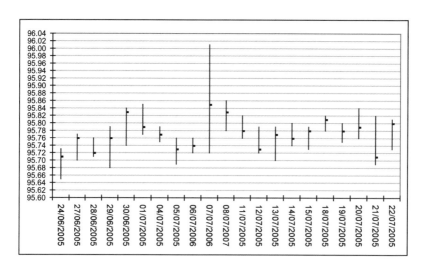

Ever since, the World Trade Centre attack of 11 Sep 2001, event risk premium due to the flight to quality has become more prevalent. Events or rumours of events will rally STIR futures prices as investors seek out safe havens and less volatile environments for their funds. Speculators also magnify this effect, trading instruments like STIR futures and bonds that will benefit from central bank intervention. Both the European Central Bank and Federal Reserve cut interest rates in the aftermath of 9/11 to restore confidence to financial markets and ease credit.

Event risk premium tends to be short lived and its influence is usually restricted to the period of perceived threat. In past years, 9/11, the Madrid train bombing and the London Underground bombings have all affected the STIR futures markets.

Chart 1.6 shows the effects of the London bombings on 7 Jul 2005 on the Short Sterling M6 STIR futures. A 25-tick spike on the day, driven on a flight to quality sentiment, was soon corrected as traders soon realised that there was unlikely to be any significant knock-on economic effects. Sentiment driven markets tend to become pragmatic rather quickly.

It should be noted that usually only acts of global terrorism affect the STIR markets – domestic terrorism such as the British IRA or Spanish ETA have little effect.

Systemic risk contagion

STIR futures can also influence each other via systemic risk. This is the risk that a localised problem in a financial market could cause a chain of events that has a knock-on effect to other markets. For example, a default by a major market participant, such as the bankruptcy of hedge fund Long Term Capital Management in 1998, can cause liquidity problems for a number of the counterparties to those funds. This can cause those counterparties to fail on their own obligations, prompting a liquidity crisis in the financial markets. This is usually countered by interest rate cuts and so STIR futures rise on a global basis.

Conclusion

In conclusion, the reader should now hopefully be aware of what STIR futures are, how they are priced and what influences cause them to move. They might also have awareness that they are unlike most other kinds of financial instrument and can offer a myriad of different trading approaches and risk profiles. The next section deals with the mechanics of STIR futures markets, which includes clearing and settlement, and how the markets are accessed.

2

Mechanics of STIR futures

Accessing The Markets

Most financial markets require the individual trader to transact through an intermediary, such as a broker or bank, who are members of a particular market. Exchange-traded financial futures markets are almost unique in that they permit individuals or smaller entities to trade and compete at a professional level, on the same terms and at similar cost to that of a bank or institution. An individual can post bids and offers and transact with all other participants in exactly the same way as a trader employed by a major bank or broker. There are no layers of intermediation and no tiered access levels or cost structures, favouring one class of participant over another. It is as level a playing field as can be found in the financial markets.

The exchanges have long recognised the importance of the smaller market participants as liquidity providers. Capitalised individuals or small groups assume the risk of other traders by taking on the other side of their trades in return for the prospect of financial gain. Their activities promote liquidity, particularly in areas such as further dated contracts or spreads and this is attractive to other market users. Clearly, there is an issue of counterparty risk. A small trader trading with a bank might not be worried about the bank's ability to settle the trade, but the bank most certainly will be. This is where the clearing structure removes the counterparty risk and guarantees the settlement procedure.

Clearing and settlement

[This section is written for beginner traders who are not familiar with the margining and settlement of futures contracts. Experienced traders may wish to skip this section.]

The clearing and settlement procedure is the trade matching and processing part of a trader's business and this is usually outsourced by the trader. There are several types of institution involved in this process, including Clearing Members and the Clearing House.

Clearing Member

Clearing Members are normally full members of the futures exchanges and fully regulated by the local financial regulatory body, who ensures that they are fit and proper to conduct business. Clearing Members tend to be banks or well-capitalised clearing companies, which specialise in processing and settling trades and they have all the necessary trade processing systems to match and settle a traders business. Each trader or market participant who is not a Clearing Member must appoint one and their trades will be processed, matched and settled by them in return for a commission. The Clearing Member will usually offer a fully integrated service, offering the trader office space, trading systems and trade settlement. The Clearing Member is effectively attaching their name and capital to the activities of the trader and so they must ensure that they cover their own risks by demanding a capital deposit from each trader that is consistent with their activity level and risk profile. The Clearing Member will also utilise risk management software to monitor trader activity.

Clearing House

The Clearing House is the institution to which the Clearing Members submit all their trades, and here they are guaranteed against default. Clearing Houses are also known as Central Counterparty Clearing Houses (CCP) since they remove the counterparty risk from the trading process. Once a trade has been matched and cleared by a Clearing Member and submitted to the Clearing House, there is no risk attached to the position of a default by any party to the trade.

Clearing houses such as LCHClearnet, which acts as CCP to the Euronext.liffe markets, also acts as CCP to other Exchanges, and cash markets such as swaps and equities. They are invariably substantial institutions and tend to be owned by their members, who themselves are exchanges, Clearing Members and banks. They are all required to deposit substantial sums of money with the Clearing House as collateral. The Clearing Houses are responsible for setting the margin levels for financial futures, which is a deposit reflecting the risk of a traders position. These margins will be enforced by the traders Clearing Member.

Clearing process

Figure 2.1: Clearing process

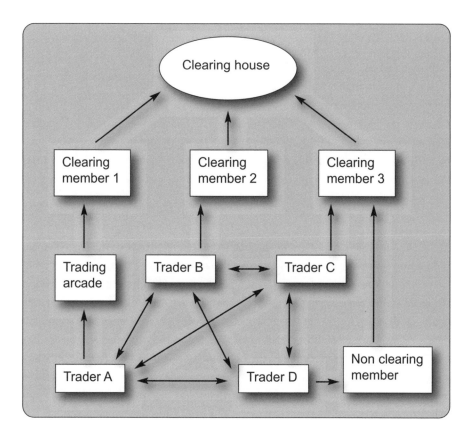

The diagram illustrates the trading, clearing and settlement process. Traders A, B, C and D can trade with each other via the exchange mechanism without fear of default by a counterparty. Since none of these traders are Clearing Members, they have appointed Clearing Members 1,2 and 3 to clear and settle their business. The terms and conditions of their relationship with their Clearing Member will be set out in a Clearing Agreement document that will define the amount of capital they need to deposit with the Clearing Member. Usually, this is a minimum of £25,000 and is considered a minimum liquidity balance that must be maintained at all times. The Clearing Member will also process and settle trade transaction in return for a commission usually expressed as an amount per lot (buy or sell one contract). This amount varies according to trade volume and further amounts for exchange fees and a Clearing House fee are added. There can be many Clearing Members offering this service to traders but only one Clearing House. [See the appendix for a list of Clearing Members.]

Non Clearing Members

Trader D has opted to process their trades through a Non Clearing Member of the exchange and the diagram shows how this adds an extra layer to the process. The Non Clearing Member still has to appoint a Clearing Member to process their business but might benefit from economies of scale if they have several traders attached to their company. This structure is common where smaller trading companies might be Clearing Members of one exchange but might only qualify for Non Clearing Status on another exchange. They will accept this arrangement in order to facilitate business for their customers who might want access to both exchanges.

Trading arcades

Trader A is trading via an intermediary called a trading arcade or bureau. This is a facilitation-based organisation that provides the technological access and trading support, sometimes in the form of training, to traders. They have a similar clearing structure to the Non Clearing Member in that they also need to appoint an exchange Clearing Member, but do not have the exchange membership or regulatory approval of the Non Clearing Member. Trading arcades are useful organisations for traders seeking training or support or financing, or for those traders looking to trade remotely from the Clearing Members facilities, perhaps closer to home or in a lifestyle enhancing or taxation beneficial foreign domicile. Several trading arcades run recruitment schemes. [A list of trading arcades is given in the appendix .]

There are some important considerations in the decision to use a trading arcade. Some are structured so that the trader can open an account directly with a Clearing Member and just use the services of arcade to access and execute their business. The arcade will usually have a wholesale commission deal with a Clearing Member and might be able to offer a more advantageous deal, plus they might be more adapted at servicing the needs of the trader, from technological support to creating the right atmosphere. However, a lot of trading arcades will require the trader to become their client or trainee, especially if taken on as part of a recruitment drive. This is fine if no capital is required, but if a trading deposit is necessary, it might be considered as part of the assets of the arcade, which will usually be a much less substantial organisation than the Clearing Member. This type of trading arcade might be considered a single account by their Clearing Member and their deposit with the

Clearing Member will cover the activities of several traders at the trading arcade. If one trader has a bad day and loses everything, it could possibly take the rest of the account and hence the trading arcade with it. It has happened in the past and might happen again. Even though the counterparty risk has been removed between traders, credit risk can still exist in the clearing structure. Sometimes it might be more prudent to accept a less favourable commission deal from a large international Bank acting as Clearing Member rather than a great deal offered by a newly established arcade.

Margin requirements

Each futures contract held from one day to another will require a deposit, reflecting its inherent value and risk. This deposit is called *margin* and is posted by the Clearing Member to the Clearing House for futures positions carried overnight (sometimes, in times of market volatility, intra-day margins can also be requested by the Clearing House). The futures contracts margin requirements are also used by Clearing Members to impose a traders' trading limits based upon the amount of capital a trader has in their account.

SPAN

The most popular method of calculating margin requirements for STIR futures is called SPAN. This stands for Standard Portfolio ANalysis of Risk and was developed by the Chicago Mercantile Exchange (CME) in 1988 and adopted by Euronext.liffe (LIFFE) in 1990. It is a margining system that calculates the effects of a range of possible changes in price and volatility on portfolios of futures and futures based options. The worst possible loss calculated by the system is then used as the margin requirement.

SPAN replaced an older system of charging a pre-determined initial margin for each contract and then a variation margin, which was essentially the profit or loss of the position when marked to market. SPAN calculates an initial margin by quantifying the risk and the potential for loss for all futures positions in a portfolio but also takes into account the offsetting effects of intra-contract and inter-market products. This means that portfolios that incorporate a futures position that partially offsets the risks of another futures position are fully recognised by the system and the trader is not burdened with margin overlap or duplication.

SPAN calculates its margin requirements by constructing a series of sixteen scenarios of changing underlying prices and volatilities to produce a risk array. This risk array will contain a number of probable outcomes based on the price and volatility factors over time. The Clearing House will determine on a daily basis, which range of outcomes is most appropriate and it will use the worst outcome as its margin figure or scanning loss for a particular product. Furthermore, a charge, termed an *intra-contact* or *inter-month spread charge* will be added to the margin where, for example, a long Euribor for March expiry is partially offset by a short position in the Euribor June contract. Where an inter-contract position reduces the overall risk, a credit to the overall margin call is added. For example, a future with similar risk characteristic such as a Swapnote future included in a portfolio of Euribor STIR futures will reduce the overall risk profile.

At present,

* A single Short Sterling future would attract an initial margin of £225.

* A single Euribor future would be €475.

* Inter-month charges are tiered according to the expiry month. A Tier 1 spread comprising, for example a long Short Sterling H6 contract and a short Short Sterling M6 contract would attract a charge of £50.

* A portfolio of different products would be margined as above but will benefit from an inter-contract charge. A portfolio including a long Euribor future and a short 2 Year Swapnote future would attract margin of €475 and €370 accordingly. However, both would benefit from a 75% credit per leg in recognition their offsetting risk characteristics.

SPAN is used by the Clearing House to set margin levels and the Clearing Members will be required to post margin to that amount on a daily basis for the cumulative position of its traders. Clearing Members will also use a PC software version of SPAN to manage their overall risk position for a range of traders. They might use the Clearing House margin requirements as a basis for their own, either increasing them if appropriate or allowing a leverage effect. A Clearing Member will sometimes allow traders to trade a multiple of their maximum overnight margin facility on an intra-day basis. This recognises the fact that traders can buy and sell many contracts per day and the inherent liquidity of short term trading can support larger transaction sizes.

Comparison of futures settlement with equities and CFDs

An investor buying a share through a traditional stockbroker experiences a different clearing and margining procedure to that of the futures trader. An equity trade is usually settled in full a few days after the trade and the total monetary consideration of the deal has to be delivered. For example, an investor buying 1000 shares of Vodafone at £1.80 will have to pay a total consideration of £1800 plus expenses when settlement is due.

Contracts For Difference (CFD) on equities introduce a futures type settlement procedure which is much more capital efficient than buying shares outright. An investor could buy 1000 shares in Vodafone at £1.80 and only have to post a small margin amount, reflecting the risk of the position. This margin requirement will increase if Vodafone shares decline in value from the purchase price of £1.80 but, ultimately, the investor is only financially responsible for the difference between the purchase price and the selling price of the shares.

STIR futures (and futures in general) are very similar in their settlement procedure to CFDs. Once a position is established, an initial margin is payable and then the difference between the traded price and the current price is added or subtracted from the margin account, depending on whether the trade is in loss or profit.

Although there are similarities between the way futures and CFDs are settled, there are also some notable differences:

- Futures and shares are traded on recognised and regulated exchanges, whereas CFDs are traded within the activities of a regulated financial broker or bank.

- Futures are matched by a central Clearing House which acts as a guarantor of the position, thereby removing counterparty risk. In contrast, a CFD is a contract between the investor and a financial broker or bank and is subject to the credit risk associated with that institution.

- The Clearing House is totally impartial in its decisions regarding margin levels as to the positions held by market participants, whereas the CFD broker might have an opposite position to that of its traders.

Fixed and variable costs

Traders face two types of cost structures:

- **fixed costs** are made up of regularly repeating costs such as software, communications and office space rental,

- **variable costs** are the transaction fees, including exchange fees and commissions.

Fixed costs

Software costs vary according to the level of sophistication of the software package and its connectivity. A base cost for a one or two exchange trading software package will vary from £250 to £500 per month, with connectivity to four or more exchanges and more advanced trading features raising this to £900 to £1250 per month. Communication charges will normally be included in an overall desk or administration charge if using the office facilities of a Clearing Member or trading arcade. They only really become a stand-alone factor for a remotely based trader; usually working from home, and costs can vary from £25 per month for a simple broadband connection to approximately £750 per month for a leased telephone line depending on location and distance. The desk or administration charge for a Clearing Member or arcade-based trader will amount to approximately £350 per month but can be incorporated into a single overall charge, including everything but will usually equate to similar amounts.

Variable costs

The variable costs are made up of commissions and exchange fees, usually quoted as a single rate by the Clearing Member or arcade. They are negotiated either as a flat rate based on estimated volumes or on a sliding scale, starting quite high and rapidly dropping as volume thresholds are reached. Note that all business for the month is usually put through at the lowest rate for the volume achieved. The total amount payable per transaction will incorporate an exchange fee, which is the portion charged by the futures exchange, a Clearing House fee, which is the amount charged by a Clearing House such as LCH Clearnet who guarantee and margin the futures traded on Euronext.liffe and a Clearing Member commission.

STIR futures traded on Euronext.liffe attract exchange fees of £0.25 per lot and a Clearing House fee of £0.03 per lot. Commissions for an active trader will vary from £0.03 to £0.25 per lot. Commissions for international exchanges might be higher than for those trading in the country of domicile, reflecting the higher cost of communications and international clearing procedures.

Like any business, everything is negotiable. Clearing futures is a competitive business and Clearing Members are eager for business especially from volume players. For those traders or collective groups of traders offering a significant transaction based revenue stream, a Clearing Member might waive a substantial portion of fixed costs in expectation of larger fee income. Smaller, new traders might be offered lower fixed costs in return for higher commission levels. Whichever way a clearing deal is structured, most traders will have to base their cost structure on an estimated monthly spend of approximately £1000, with commissions adding several thousand pounds to this amount.

Liquidity and rebate schemes

The previous section has highlighted the potential expense of futures trading. Fixed costs are high but it is exchange fees and commissions that make up the bulk of a traders costs.

The largest portion of the traders variable costs go to the futures exchanges in the form of exchange fees. The exchanges have a large cost structure themselves, having to provide and support the market infrastructure but they are mindful of the benefits to the liquidity of their markets of short term trading by speculative traders. Some exchanges address this issue by offering rebate schemes for volume trading or attempt to attract liquidity to less popular areas of the markets or products by offering incentives. Rebate and incentive schemes vary from time to time, but at present Euronext.liffe offers three schemes of interest to the STIR futures trader.

Individual Liquidity Provider (ILP)

The first is the Individual Liquidity Provider (ILP) scheme. This is designed to promote liquidity in the back or deferred expiry months of Euribor, Short Sterling, Euroswiss and Eurodollar STIR futures products and is available to registered[3] individuals trading futures on their own account or for an employer in whom they have an interest. There are no volume thresholds, only a tiered fee schedule. This starts in the red months with a saving of up to £0.10 per lot, increasing to £0.15 and £0.20 per lot for the green and blue months respectively.

---

[3] www.euronext.com > STIRS > liquidity schemes.

STIR Liquidity Provider (SLP)

The second scheme is the STIR liquidity provider (SLP) scheme. This is available to all registered traders who exceed 20,000 lots of propriety business in any one calendar month in the Euribor, or 12,500 lots in Short Sterling. A Clearing Member or Non Clearing Member may also join this scheme but will have a minimum threshold of 150,000 lots. This scheme builds on the ILP scheme by offering further volume based discounts based on the already reduced ILP scheme rates. For example, a trader trading back red Euribor futures will initially save £0.10 per lot on any business via the ILP scheme. With the inclusion of the SLP scheme, any further volume beyond 1201 lots will reduce the exchange fees to £0.11 per lot. The volume thresholds and exchange rate fees are variable according to contract and volume and details are available at www.euronext.com.

Both of these schemes will favour the high volume back month trader and the savings can be considerable, particularly for spread traders who usually face double fees for the two sides of a spread trade.

Table 2.1 shows the potential benefits. A trader trading 25,000 lots of the front white Euribor contracts would gain a total rebate of £350 from a fee spend of £6250. If the same 25,000 lots were traded in the green months, the same £6250 fee spend would apply but a total rebate of £5058 would be received, meaning that the trader pays an average exchange fee of £0.047 compared to a standard rate of £0.25.

Table 2.1: Rebate schemes for Euronext.liffe Euribor.

EURIBOR	Standard fee rate	ILP rebate	SLP rebate
White	£6250	£0	£350
Front red	£6250	£1250	£1175
Back red	£6250	£2500	£1412
Green	£6250	£3750	£1308

Source Euronext.liffe

This is quite significant because although the Clearing House fee and the Clearing Member commission will be unaffected, the overall cost of buying and selling back month STIR futures can be reduced by approximately one third to a half. This means that trades which the trader might have previously considered prohibitive due to high fees or marginal due to uncertain profitability can now be considered as part of a trader's repertoire.

The total savings available to a trader willing to concentrate on back months are shown in Chart 2.1 which illustrates the total percentage savings provided by both schemes for the Euribor contract.

Chart 2.1: Percentage saving in total exchange fees for Euronext.liffe Euribor, based on variable monthly volumes

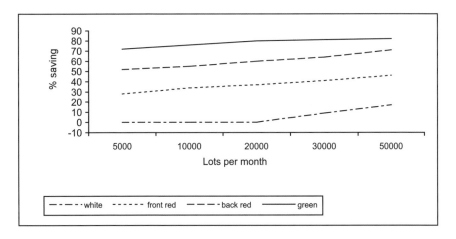

Source Euronext.liffe

It is clear that an even relatively small monthly volume in anything but the front white contracts quickly attracts large percentage savings over the standard fee schedule. As volumes increase the savings rise proportionally. The Short Sterling contract has a similar but slightly better profile than the Euribor and so has the same attractions to back month traders. The blue months onward attracts a 100% rebate in both contracts.

New Market Participants Scheme (NMP)

The Euronext.liffe NMP scheme is aimed at new trainee proprietary traders with no prior trading experience. Participants benefit from fully rebated exchange clearing fees, subject to a monthly cap for a maximum period of six months.

European Incentive Program (EIP)

The CME operates a European Incentive Program (EIP) scheme for European based traders trading on their electronic Globex market. Presently, individual non-member accounts are assessed at different rates from institutional and member accounts. This can result in unregistered Eurodollar traders paying exchange fees as high as $1.19 per lot. This reduces to $0.44 per lot on the EIP scheme and further discounts are available for volumes in excess of 25,000 lots per month for any contract month. See www.cme.com or contact the European Representative Office[4] for more details.

The choice of clearing member or trading arcade

The well-capitalised aspiring trader has the choice of several Clearing Members and trading arcades. The main selection criteria are:

Customer classification

Futures traders are usually regarded by the financial regulatory authorities as being professional traders who do not need to be directly regulated but must have a certain level of relevant experience before being allowed to open an account with an exchange Clearing Member. A trader with prior experience, perhaps working for someone else, would be deemed 'expert status' by the Financial Services Authority, the UK financial regulator, but this might vary according to international regulations. Those aspiring traders with no prior futures experience might be directed to training or mentoring schemes, or perhaps have to accept a retail client contract rather than a professional trading contract The compliance department of the Clearing Member has the responsibility of ensuring that traders have this level of experience and status and will make enquiries accordingly at the account opening stage. Aspiring traders should check with the Clearing Member or trading arcade to determine their potential classification.

---

[4] CME Europe, Pinnacle House 23-26 St. Dunstan's Hill, London EC3R 8HN Phone: 020 7623-2550 email: cmeeurope@cme.com

The criterion for an experienced trader is governed by the compliance department of a Clearing Member and is based on guidance from the Regulatory Authority. As a guide, there follows typical requirements for acceptability, as might be specified by a UK based Clearing Member.

- The trader would need to have a general knowledge of the products that they intend to trade, and they should show that they have read the relevant information regarding contract specification and mechanisms.

- The trader should have a general overview of the exchanges that they intend to trade on. They should know where the exchanges are based, how they are run and the exchange trading rules.

- The trader should have knowledge of the FSA code of conduct and relevant sections for trading.

- The trader should have sufficient training on the trading system that he intends to use so that they understand how to place outright trades, spreads and how to pull orders.

- The trader should be able to trade in single lots under the supervision of an experienced trader. This can be achieved by the experienced trader having a sub account, which the trainee can trade in single lots and therefore provide an audit trail ascertaining the trader's ability to place and pull orders and the profitability/loss over the training period.

- The trader should have a fundamental knowledge of economic figures and how they will influence the products he is trading.

- The trader should be able to explain why they have taken a position and why that position should make money and the same when the position is closed. If this results in a loss the experienced trader should determine if the logic applied to the taking of that position was correct.

Financial probity

The trader needs to assure himself or herself of the financial standing of a Clearing Member or, more importantly, a trading arcade. The Clearing Member will have to have met certain criteria to qualify for regulation by the local Financial Regulator in order to qualify for exchange membership. A trading arcade only has to meet the financial requirements of the Clearing Member. That's not to say that trading arcades should be avoided. Many provide a very high level of service and are run by traders for traders.

The largest institutions are not always the most secure, Refco[5] being a prime recent example.

Usually it's a question of meeting the people, talking to their traders, others in the market and using judgement. The internet can be useful for opinion. There are several traders' forums[6] where participants are not reluctant to share their views.

Financial protection

Futures traders are normally considered professional traders by the regulatory authorities and so do not benefit from segregated funds protection offered to the retail investor. This means that futures clients' money can be pooled and can be at risk in the case of Clearing Member default. It can be useful to be aware of how funds are regarded and to enquire whether any protection or guarantees can be put in place.

Capital requirements and commissions

Cheapest is not always best and this should not be the sole factor in determining choice. Commissions on futures will always be on a per lot or per round trip basis (buy and sell one lot) and never on capital value. Look out for hidden charges such as tiered commission schedules not defaulting to the lowest tier for all business at the end of the trading month, no (or low) interest being paid on capital deposits, or punitive financing for traders requiring financial backing.

Check to see if interest is paid on margin deposits. This can be significant for spread traders carrying large inventories. Clearing Members effectively receive interest from the Clearing House by posting bonds as security and so they are in a position to pay interest to clients, but this tends to be by negotiation.

---

[5] Refco was one of the world's largest futures brokers, a Clearing Member of several Futures Exchanges and a public company quoted on the New York Stock Exchange. It was bankrupted in October 2005 by a $430m securities fraud committed by its Chairman and Chief Executive, Phillip Bennett. Refco's futures businesses were sold to Man financial and Marex with client/traders funds intact.

[6] For example, www.elitetrader.com, www.trade2win.com

It's also worth checking to ensure that any eligible rebate and liquidity schemes are passed on in full to the trader.

Technological ability

Speed can be everything in futures trading. A poorly constructed or overcrowded network can cause slowdowns and outages.

Trading arcades

Trading arcades usually offer training schemes for new traders and financing for suitably qualified traders.

Training schemes operate by a crop of trainees being recruited from web sites[7], newspaper adverts and referrals. They may or may not be paid a salary, but they normally should not be required to provide capital. They are placed on a training scheme and paper trade for a time, which involves trading a simulated market and their performance monitored. Those showing promise are retained and the rest let go – a process of selection that continues into the graduation to trading real markets.

Those who graduate are placed on contract defining the terms of their deal and these are regularly renegotiated as the trader's star rises or falls. Many trainees chose to stay with their original trainers and several have gone on to become major players in the futures markets.

Financing deals are variable and normally involve a profit share deal defined by how much capital is provided. They are usually offered to experienced traders looking for more capital to trade bigger size or other more capital-intensive markets, but some arcades will offer financing deals for those with less capital. Such deals are not always attractive to either party. The arcade will be asking why an experienced trader is in need of financing – are they any good at the job? The trader seeking financing will need to ensure it is an equitable deal.

---

[7] For example, www.efinancialcareers.com, www.cityjobs.co.uk, www.monster.co.uk

Software and hardware

The two main STIR futures exchanges operate two similar trading systems. Euronext.liffe call their electronic trading system, *Connect* and the CME platform is called *Globex*. Both are based on open host system architecture with an application program interface (API) that allows users to build trading applications directly to the exchange trading platform. Some larger users such as banks have built their own propriety front end trading applications. But the most popular way of accessing the markets for the smaller trader is by commercially built software developed by independent software vendors (ISV). This integrates trading, settlement and risk management in one off the shelf package.

Figure 2.2: Trading system architecture for Connect and Globex

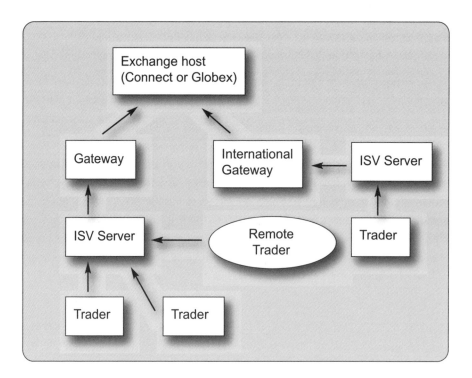

The system architecture is shown in the above diagram. Multiple traders using the same ISV software will connect directly to the ISV server, either by internal network, if situated in the same offices, or remotely via an external network such as a leased line or by the internet. The server connects directly into the exchange gateway, which is usually a server-based exchange network hub. This can be located in a Clearing

Members office or as a designated hub on an international network, allowing quick access for traders based in foreign countries. The gateway connects directly to the exchange host where orders are matched or placed in the market according to price level and priority as determined by the trading algorithms.

Trading algorithms

These are controlled by the exchanges and usually operate on a time priority or pro-rata basis. A

- *time priority* based algorithm (also known as first in first out, FIFO), will give precedence to the earliest placed orders at a given price, and a

- *pro-rata* algorithm will give an equal preference to all orders, irrespective of when they were placed.

Both Euronext.liffe and CME operate a similar pro-rata algorithm for STIR futures, but they can both be altered, with notice, to accommodate different preferences. Such preferences can include a top order priority, where an order, of any or a maximum designated quantity, is placed at a price before all others and so is given preference over all other orders. Another is a preference recently introduced by the CME to their algorithm that gives an element of FIFO to their pro-rata algorithm for trades allocated after the top order.

Algorithms can be modified frequently by the exchanges to enhance host performance, give preference to a certain class of trader such as those fulfilling a market-making obligation or to attempt to gain a competitive advantage over another exchange's products in the case of a dual listing. Consequently, it is advisable to check the current algorithm in use from the exchanges' websites and notices.

Implied pricing functionality

The exchange host trading platforms on both Connect and Globex supports functionality called *implied pricing*. This is where the prices from outright futures contracts can be used to imply prices for a spread or similar trading strategy, and vice versa.

Strategies such as calendar spreads and butterflies are quoted as instruments in their own right, rather than just being a by product of the futures strip. The concept of implying prices into these strategies directly from the futures prices was pioneered by Euronext.liffe during the development of Connect. Implied prices help promote liquidity into the order books and the exchanges guarantee the fill of all sides of a transaction involving implied prices.

There are two types of exchange-supported implied pricing:

1. *implied-in pricing* – where prices are implied into the spreads from the outright futures

2. *implied-out pricing* – where spread prices are used to imply prices into the outright futures.

There is a third kind which is *implied upon implied pricing*, where prices are created based upon implied prices elsewhere. The exchanges do not support implied upon implied prices and do not guarantee execution of all component positions of this kind of trade. Implied upon implied functionality is usually a feature of ISV trading software and can be useful to the trader in that it can indicate additional liquidity, provided they are aware of the inherent execution risk. Euronext.liffe only supports implied out pricing to calendar spreads whereas CME extends this to cover butterfly spreads.

Examples

Table 2.2 illustrates the implied in functionality. Three outright contracts, H6, M6 and U6 are quoted in quantities of 100 lots on both bid and offer. The quoted bid/offer spread is one tick for the first two contracts but two ticks for the U6 expiry. All of these prices are used by the exchange host computer to calculate implied-in prices to populate the strategies, in this case the H6M6 and M6U6 spreads.

Table 2.2: Implied-in functionality for STIR futures. (Implied prices are shown in italics)

Contract	Bid Qty	Bid	Offer	Offer Qty
H6	100	98.78	98.79	100
M6	100	98.55	98.56	100
U6	100	98.37	98.39	100
H6M6	100	*0.22*	0.23	50
M6U6	50	0.17	*0.19*	100

Table 2.3: Implied in and out functionality for STIR. (Implied-in prices are shown in italics and implied out prices are in bold.)

Contract	Bid Qty	BID	OFFER	Offer Qty
H6	100	98.78	**98.79**	150
M6	150	**98.55**	98.56	100
U6	100	98.37	**98.39**	150
H6M6	100	*0.22*	0.23	50
M6U6	50	0.17	*0.19*	100

Since spreads are a function of the bid/offer prices of the component outright futures, the implied-in price for the H6M6 will be 0.22 bid and 0.24 offered as shown by:

Figure 2.3: H6M6

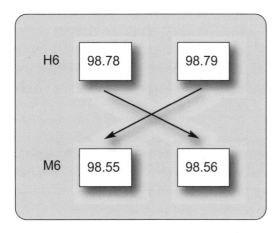

The spread H6M6

- **bid price** is given by the bid of H6 subtracting the offer of M6 (98.78-98.56 = 0.22), and the

- **offer price** is given by the offer of H6 subtracting the bid of M6 (98.79-98.55 = 0.24),

making an implied in quote of 0.22 bid and 0.24 offered in 100 lots per side (since that is the quantities available in the outright futures).

However, the spread implied bid and offer price has been improved upon by a market participant who has placed an offer to sell 50 lots at 0.23. This then creates a true spread price of 0.22 bid in 100 lots which is all implied-in and a trader's offer of 50 lots at 0.23.

A similar situation occurs in the M6U6 spread which has implied-in price of 0.16 bid and 0.19 offered, again a function of the component outright futures bids and offers. The three tick wide implied-in price reflects the totals of the bid/offer spreads in the M6 and U6 contracts, the U6 having a two tick wide spread, perhaps reflecting less liquidity. A market participant has improved this three tick wide implied-in spread quote by bidding 0.17 for 50 lots making a true M6U6 spread price of 0.17 bid and 0.19 offered, which is all implied-in.

If the market participants had not improved upon those spread prices, then the market prices available would be the outright futures, as quoted in price and size in Table 2.2. The spreads would all be implied-in and quoted as the function of their component outright futures bids and offers. All the outright futures and spreads would have a quoted size of 100 lots. However, the presence of those two trader orders, to sell 50 H6M6 at 0.23 and buy 50 M6U6 at 0.17 have the effect of implying out additional quantities into the outright futures. The offer to sell 50 H6M6 at 0.23 will imply out an offer to sell 50 H6 at 98.79 against buying the M6 offer at 98.56 (98.79 – 98.56 = 0.23). This adds an additional 50 lots to the existing offer of 100 lots, making a total of 150 lots available at 98.79, of which 100 lots is a trader order and 50 lots is implied-out. This is shown in Table 2.3 and is represented by bold font.

The offer to sell 50 H6M6 at 0.23 can also work the other side of the spread as well. A bid to buy 50 lots of M6 at 98.55 is implied out against the trader bid in H6 to buy 100 lots at 98.78 (98.78 – 98.55 = 0.23). This will add an additional 50 lots to the existing trader's bid of 100 lots.

The order to buy 50 M6U6 at 0.17 will imply out another 50 lots of U6 at 98.39, making a total of 150 lots at 98.39, against buying the M6 offer at 98.56 (98.56- 98.39 = 0.17). However, it will not be able to imply a bid into the M6 since it would need to purchase at a price of 98.54 against the U6 bid of 98.37 (98.54 – 98.37 = 0.17) but the M6 is 98.55 bid already.

Implied prices – traders friend or foe?

The good

The development of implied pricing was an inspirational enhancement for the trading of STIR futures. It immediately created liquidity from the outright futures contracts into the strategies markets, which were traded as separate instruments. It also defined arbitrage boundaries for all types of spreads that prevented the possibility of trading a spread or similar strategy at prices outside of those implied by the component outright futures. The implied out prices returned a lot of the liquidity from the more stable and liquid spreads such as the 3-month calendar spreads into the outright futures strip, creating a more liquid market all round. Traders also had the assurance that if they traded a spread based upon implied prices, they were guaranteed a fill of all sides of the trade at the required prices. This effectively removed execution risk from transacting a spread trade in the outright futures.

The bad

However, these benefits of implied prices can also prove to be its Achilles heel in that the market has become very efficient in its pricing and hence reducing the opportunities for traders. On the other hand, implied pricing can help traders in that trades can be triggered by price action elsewhere. A spread seller might inadvertently trigger two outright futures trades if that spread price were made up of only implied in prices.

It is important to be aware of where the implied prices are and how much of the outright or spread bid or offer quantities it makes up. Implied prices can disappear instantaneously if the providing bid or offer is removed. Consequently, care must be taken if legging spreads, particularly in the back months of STIR futures where incidence of implied pricing is higher.

Selecting an ISV

There are many ISV software packages commercially available, of which about seven are most popular [see the appendix]. Some specialise in different products, such as options, but to a large extent they are similar in design and functionality. The choice of ISV might be limited to those offered by the trader's Clearing Member or trading arcade but usually the trader will have a choice of around two to five different ISVs.

The majority of ISV software will offer similar features, with the majority of resources having gone into the design of the trading functionality. Some ISV software includes more advanced features such as stop losses in their order management programs and links into Excel for automation, but all will share common trading features such as trade history, position management and working order books, as well as additional information sources such as exchange tickers and messaging.

- The **trade history** is an audit of all completed trades with relevant order numbers and execution time.

- **Position management** indicates the open futures positions currently held, displayed as a total and detailed by individual contract or expiry. The position management function often incorporates a real time profit and loss on open and closed positions.

- The **order book** shows all futures orders currently being worked in the market and indicates whether part of the order has been filled or not.

- **Exchange tickers** are price and time histories for futures contracts.

- **Messaging** is an information flow indicating market and software status.

But it is the price display functionality that is of most importance to the trader. This is where the futures price action is observed and trades entered and deleted. Every trader probably has their own idea of how they would ideally like to view the markets, but some commonality is unavoidable. The essential requirements are an economic use of screen space, easy and quick order entry and deletion, and clearly viewable information

Price displays

STIR futures traders tend to look at several delivery months at once, as well as strategies such as spreads, and so a market grid layout is a popular choice for the price display functionality.

Table 2.4: Market grid display of STIR futures and strategies

Product	Bid qty	Bid	Offer	Offer qty	Last trade	Last Qty	Volume
S H6	1171	**98.79**	**98.80**	3758	98.80	1	1692
S M6	23	**98.59**	**98.60**	6208	98.59	10	7124
S U6	1695	**98.40**	**98.41**	100	98.41	100	3507
S Z6	43	**98.23**	**98.24**	717	98.24	53	1416
S H6M6	3260	**0.20**	**0.21**	349	0.20	18	937
S M6U6	2054	**0.18**	**0.19**	63	0.19	28	1206
S U6Z6	121	**0.17**	**0.18**	3269	0.18	1	428

Table 2.4 shows a typical market grid layout.

Product column

In the left column, the products are titled and usually presented in a user defined order, the most popular approach being to have the outright futures in descending sequential order followed by a similar display of the strategies. The strategies shown here are the 3 month calendar spreads, but any combination or other strategies can be included as well as other futures contracts. The S is the contract code; in this case the Euronext.liffe EuroSwiss STIR futures.

Bid and offer quantity columns

The bid and offer quantity columns shows the amount of futures contracts bid and offered for purchase and sale by market participants. These quantities will normally include implied pricing as well as the trader bid and offers. Usually it is possible to see exactly how much implied pricing is present by a variety of methods, including a mouse tool tip display, a check box that turns the implied prices on or off, an indicative colour display or the implied prices additionally displayed in separate columns, as shown in Table 2.5.

Table 2.5: Implied price functionality of Short Sterling 10 Feb 2006, 10.01am

Product	Bid qty	BID	OFFER	Offer qty	Implied Bid Qty	Imp. Bid Price	Imp. Offer Price	Imp. Offer Qty
L H6	21996	95.42	95.43	23232	887	95.42		
L M6	11869	95.48	95.49	8241	125	95.48		
L U6	8068	95.48	95.49	856	2660	95.48		
L Z6	1607	95.44	95.45	5656			95.45	1117
L H6M6	887	-0.06	-0.05	13969			-0.05	11869
L M6U6	17769	-0.01	0.00	761	856	-0.01		
L U6Z6	3724	0.04	0.05	30627			0.05	856

Here it can be seen from a real-time snapshot of Euronext.liffe Short Sterling STIR futures that the bulk of the front months are made up of outright trader orders. In the H6 contract, out of the total of 21,996 contracts on the bid, only 887 are implied out prices. However, the H6M6 spread has a very high proportion of its offer quantity (13,969) as implied in (11,869), generated by the bid for 11,869 lots in M6. This means that the spread, although seemingly very well offered, could lose the majority of its offer quantity if sellers sold out the M6 bid. If this happened, the H6M6 would be left with a trader offer quantity of only 2100 lots. Not as liquid as it first appeared!

The trader offer of 856 U6 at 95.49 is implying in a M6U6 spread bid of –0.01 for 856 lots, adding to the 16,913 lots already bid by traders. It is also implying in an offer in the U6Z6 spread at 0.05, adding to the 29,771 already there.

To take things further, the combination of these two implied in spread bid and offers could imply out a bid of -0.06 for 856 lots (-0.01 – 0.05) for the M6U6Z6 butterfly spread. In this case, the butterfly would be -0.06 bid for thousands anyway, because of the existing trader bid of –0.01 in the M6U6 spread and the existing 0.05 offer in the U6Z6 spread, but it highlights the extension possibilities of implied pricing.

Although these implied in spread prices could imply out a butterfly price of –0.06, this functionality is not supported by all exchanges. Euronext.liffe does not support implied out pricing on any strategy other than calendar spreads, whereas CME does support implied out pricing on butterflies. However, it is all slightly academic since the butterfly spread would be well –0.06 bid anyway since that would permit traders to effectively buy the M6U6 spread on the bid and sell the U6Z6 spread on the offer. In fact, bidding –0.06 for the M6U6Z6 butterfly would be so attractive that there was actually a better -0.05 trader bid in the market at the time of writing!

Finally, there is a big implied out bid for 95.48 in U6 for 2660 lots created partly by the 0.00 offer in 761 lots in the M6U6 spread (bidding 95.48 in the U6 against selling 95.48 in the M6) and the 0.04 bid for 3724 in the U6Z6 spread (bidding 95.48 in the U6 against selling Z6 at 95.44).

It must be apparent by now that the concept and identification of implied pricing can be tricky but its worth taking the time and using an ISV package where inter dependencies on implied prices can be spotted with a bit of practice. Implied prices will often lean against trader prices and are easily triggered by price action elsewhere. Again it is important in back months, where the liquidity is less than the front month examples shown above, to be aware of what is generating the implied price and gauging how reliable it might be.

Two or one click dealing

Going back to the market price grid display of Table 2.4, the price bid and offer shows the current market prices. Most ISV packages allow the trader to mouse click the price and execute the order. This is done by either a two-click approach, where for example, clicking the offer price will bring up a buy ticket, usually colour coded blue, with the trade price and a pre-defined quantity and a second click will send the order to market. Some ISV's have one click trading functionality for speed advantage.

From this display, traders can normally view a depth of market by a drop down function within the software. This will show the prices and quantities above and below the current market prices as shown in Table 2.6.

Market depth

Table 2.6: Market depth display of STIR futures

Product	Bid qty	BID	OFFER	Offer qty	Last trade	Last Qty	Volume
S H6	1171	**98.79**	**98.80**	3758	98.80	1	1692
	567	*98.78*	*98.81*	*1256*			
	245	*98.77*	*98.82*	*768*			
	43	*98.76*	*98.83*	*435*			
	85	*98.75*	*98.84*	*324*			

The top price is the same bid/offer price and quantity as shown for the H6 contract in Table 2.4 but underneath a drop down shows the market depth depicted in italics. These are the prices either side of the bid and offer and are tradable in the same way as the top-level prices. This is a useful function in faster moving markets where it might be necessary to click above or below a current price in order to stand a better chance of being filled on the trade.

Most exchanges employ a price match function where an order will always be filled at the best price within its limit confines. For example, if the market were rising quickly and a trader clicked to buy 200 lots at 98.82 in the market depth, the order would be filled at a better price of 98.80 or 98.81 if those offers were still available. The exchange host algorithms will not normally allow a trader to be filled at an off-market price.

Note: implied prices will not be a constituent of the market depth liquidity; they will only be generated for top-level best market prices only.

The market depth can also be useful as a technical indicator to determine order flow. Should there be much larger offers than bids in the market depth then it might indicate some reluctance by the market to go up since it is likely that resistance will be met from sellers. Often key technical levels attract market depth volumes and this can be useful to the trader.

The popularity of trading in the market depth for faster moving products such as bond futures have led to the development by ISV of trading applications specifically tailored to fast execution within the market depth. These can be of interest to the STIR trader for outright trading in times of volatility.

Table 2.7: ISV market depth display

B. QTY	BID	OFFER	O QTY
		98.84	324
		98.83	435
		98.82	768
		98.81	1256
1171	**98.79**	**98.80**	3758
567	98.78		
245	98.77		
43	98.76		
85	98.75		

Different ISV presents such trading tools in a broadly similar format. Table 2.7 illustrates a typical layout. They tend to be single contract displays showing the market depth in a permanent vertical profile that automatically re-centres as the price moves. Orders are executed by fast one click trading in a pre-determined quantity, usually on the blank space to the side of the price. Orders to sell an offer or join a bid are normally done by single clicking the price. Additional functionally such as drag and drop order movement, cumulative traded volumes and quick delete of all order or all bids or all offers vary from different ISV and make for a fast trading interface.

Last trade and volume

Finally, the remaining columns on the market grid display shown in Table 2.4 are the market information displays of last trade and quantity, total volume traded and can be expanded to include additional columns such contract highs and lows, previous settlement price, net change of the day and open positions. All columns and rows in the market grid display are usually user-customisable and moveable to the trader's specifications.

Spread matrix

Most ISVs include a spread matrix as part of their software. This is a display where all the permutations of calendar spreads for a STIR future are shown in a tradable matrix as shown in Table 2.8.

Spread Matrices are presented in slightly differing format depending on the ISV. Some are a fixed display mechanism and some are highly customisable so that the user can configure the display to their own liking, with prices and quantities presented horizontally or vertically.

Generally, all matrices will be the same in that they will be a two axes display, with the sequential futures quarterly expiries displayed along each side. The prices of the outright futures are normally portrayed and will be click and tradable in the usual manner. Here, they are shown on the top row in a vertical format where the bid price and quantity is on the lower cell and the offer price and quantity is on the higher cell. Implied prices can be shown either by colour coding, mouse tool tip or by a check box that turns the implied prices on or off.

Table 2.8: Euronext.liffe EuroSwiss spread matrix – 10th February 2006

Price	Qty	Price	Qty	Price	Qty	Price	Qty
98.79	3060	98.58	1569	98.40	2453	98.23	275
98.78	601	98.57	692	98.39	409	98.22	319
H6		**M6**		**U6**		**Z6**	
H6		*0.22*	1779	*0.40*	409	*0.57*	*319*
		0.21	478	*0.38*	*601*	*0.55*	*275*
		M6		*0.19*	1507	*0.36*	598
				0.18	684	*0.34*	379
				U6		0.17	302
						0.16	1465
						Z6	

The spread prices are generated against the relevant futures, so that the first spread, the H6M6 spread, is quoted as 0.21 bid for 478 lots and 0.22 offered in 1779 lots. Following down and across the matrix returns the other 3-month spreads, the M6U6 and U6Z6. Going up one level gives the 6-month calendar spreads, the first one being H6U6 and then M6Z6. Another level higher returns the 9-month spread which is the H6Z6 spread.

The implied pricing in this example is shown as italics on the price where the implied pricing is only a part of the total order quantity and shown as italics on both the price and quantity when it is all an implied price. It can be observed that implied pricing is present as part of a larger quantity in the 3-month spreads but can be the sole price and quantity in the less liquid and traded 6-month and 9-month spreads. The 9-month H6Z6 is a purely implied in price of 0.55 bid, 0.57 offered and its quantities are limited to the quantities available in the outright Z6 contract.

Auto-spreaders and price injection models

Some ISVs offers *auto spreaders* and *price injection* models. These are usually optional extras and can be expensive additions.

Auto-spreader model

The auto-spreader is a simple concept to understand, but a complex piece of software. It works by creating its own spread or similar strategy based upon the contracts entered by the user. It can work spreads based on existing strategies, such a calendar spreads, or hybrid spreads such, as a bond future against one or more STIR futures. Most auto-spreaders are customisable so that several spread legs can be entered and worked at once. For example, the three legs of a butterfly can be worked simultaneously or more complex multi leg trades such as packs and bundles against swap or bond futures. Some auto-spreaders even permit strategies such a calendar spreads to be entered so that a butterfly spread could be worked as the two component spreads as well as the individual outright legs.

The auto-spreader will effectively create an implied in price for a spread or strategy based upon the inputted component legs. But this is not an implied in price like those generated by the exchange host, and there is no guarantee of execution of both sides. The auto-spreader can be configured to work one or all sides of the spread or strategy by showing a bid or offer to the market in those selected contracts. It can also look for a certain amount of volume on the other side to the trade or to avoid leaning against just implied prices to reduce the risk of being legged out. This is where one side of the spread or strategy is completed but the other side is missed, usually by another trader beating you to it or, more commonly, by an exchange implied price being used preferentially to guarantee the fill on an exchange spread or strategy that is trading at the same time.

Auto-spreader example

Using the prices from spread matrix with Euronext.liffe EuroSwiss as shown in Table 2.8, a trader decides that they wish to buy 50 lots of M6U6 spread at 0.18. They could join the bid of 684 lots with everyone else be guaranteed a fill on both sides in a pro-rata allocation when that price traded. Alternatively, they could use an auto-spreader to inject prices into the outright futures. This would effectively bid 98.57 in the M6, against selling 98.39 in the U6 if partially or fully filled on the M6. It could also simultaneously offer 98.40 in the U6 against buying 98.58 in the M6 if partially or fully filled on the U6. If the outright prices were to change, the auto-spreader would automatically re-submit the orders at revised prices. The auto-spreader could be configured to look for a multiple of more than one times the order size before entering the leg order. If it were set to two times, it would ensure that the U6 bid of 98.39 was at least bid for 100 lots before submitting its order to bid 98.57 for 50 lots in the M6 and do the same on the other working side of the order. It might also be programmed to ignore any implied prices that were part of the total quantity. However, if the figure is set too high, the auto- spreader might be unable to enter the order since insufficient size would be available on the other side.

The astute reader who has fully understood the concept of implied out pricing might be wondering what the point of the auto-spreader is. It's effectively doing exactly the same as the implied out functionality of joining the M6U6 spread bid at 0.18. The exchange host will imply out a bid into the M6 and an offer into the U6 at the same prices but with no execution risk. It's a fair point in this case, which is using the less liquid EuroSwiss as an example, but busier contracts such as Euribor and Eurodollar can commonly have 3-month spreads bid or offered in 10,000 or more lots per side whereas the outright futures might only be bid and offered in quantities of perhaps a thousand. In this scenario, joining a large spread bid would yield proportionally less fill than working the orders in the outrights and particularly so if the exchange host algorithm gives a preference to the outright prices rather than the implied out prices.

Price injection model

Price injection models are very similar to auto-spreader and work on similar logic but might be tailored towards option hedging or market-making. Market making might just require the constant injection of prices to fulfil a market-making mandate but will not necessarily require a fill to spread off against another contract or expiry. Both auto-spreaders and price injection models can create a lot of network traffic and demands upon the exchange trading host. It is common to have to be registered to use such an application and the traffic levels of the trader will be monitored. If too many auto-spreader orders are being placed in the market, perhaps at price levels, which are not close to being filled, then the exchanges can take punitive measures. Most ISV auto-spreaders have some functionality to minimise order change traffic.

The use of auto-spreaders requires the acceptance of the additional risk of being legged out. It does happen frequently, the usual causes being the entire bid or offer being traded in one clip causing a fill on one side but the other being missed due to implied order preference or technical issues such as system slowdowns. They are useful tools but should be used cautiously and not in times of volatility.

Auto-traders

Auto-trading interfaces are available on a few ISV trading platforms. They usually take the form of a Dynamic Data Exchange (DDE) or more recently a Real Time Data (RTD) protocol in Microsoft Excel or directly writing to an Application Programming Interface (API). These allow the programming, usually in Visual Basic or C++, of a fully user customisable automated trading model. These tend to be technically driven models, sometimes referred to as 'black boxes', which base their trading decisions on a range of user defined variables. They can also be used to automatically trade economic releases when linked with Bloomberg or Reuters content into Excel. No wonder someone else always seems to beat us to it!

Risk management considerations

All ISV software will have a risk management solution that provides both pre-trade and post-trade risk management for the trader.

Pre-trade risk management

Pre-trade risk management is determined by the risk manager and partially by the trader. Futures position limits are based on the traders experience, their capital, the futures margin requirement and an intra-day multiple, if offered, based on the current market volatility. These limits will be entered into the ISV risk management software and then will relate to a specific trader, only allowing them to trade a maximum clip size or build an inventory of a maximum amount. The system will check each order before it is allowed to market to ensure it conforms otherwise it will be rejected. The trader can adjust these amounts downward, so that their clip size might be less than their maximum permitted.

Post trade risk management

Post trade risk management is the analysis of a trader's open futures position that have already been traded and permitted by the pre-trade risk management. Most systems mark positions to market based upon either the last traded price, the current bid or offer price, or settlement prices if the market has closed, and operate a warning system if absolute levels of loss or cash balances are breached. Some post-trade risk management systems can be more sophisticated and use a correlation, SPAN or VAR[8] type discipline and some are capable of analysing firm wide risk for larger Clearing Members, who might have several ISV packages.

Many ISV risk management packages operate on the principle that all working orders can be executed simultaneously. That is to say, for example, if ten orders were being worked then in theory all might be instantaneously filled in times of severe market volatility. That would be true if all ten orders were all bids or all offers since volatility tends to manifest itself directionally but unfortunately many ISV risk management systems include both bid and offer orders as part of their calculation. This means that the trader with a pre-trade position limit of 100 lots could enter ten orders of 10 lots, either bid or offered and run the possibility that all could be hit, but only enter five bids and five offers before reaching their maximum threshold. It is very difficult to envisage a situation where both bids and offers are executed almost simultaneously and would not the trader be pleased with that outcome? However, for lack of a better model, many ISV risk management software programs run on that principle and traders should be aware of the constraints that it can impose

Limitations of some ISV risk management system

Some ISV companies have put most resources into their trading applications and given little further consideration to their risk management solutions once they are proven and robust. Consequently, some contain risk management principles of dubious merit. An example that affects STIR futures traders is the inclusion of strategies as outright futures risk. For example, a trader with a pre-trade position limit of 100 lots might not be able to enter an order into a calendar spread for 100 lots since the risk management software will consider it to be two 100 lot positions (long/short 100 lots of one expiry, short/long 100 lots of another expiry). This is despite there being no execution risk, being guaranteed by the exchange algorithm and the Clearing House SPAN margin system regarding a spread strategy as having approximately only 22% of the risk of an outright future (a front month Short Sterling spread currently having a margin of £50 compared to £225 for an outright future). This can result in the dichotomy of the trader having to request higher than usually allowable position limits from their risk manager to facilitate their business at normal levels. Accordingly, spread traders should check to see how their ISV risk management system manages strategy based trading.

---

[8] VAR – Value At Risk. A technique used to estimate the probability of losses within a portfolio of securities based on the statistical analysis of historical price trends and volatilities.

Rogue traders – when risk management fails

Virtually all risk management software packages and procedures are proven and robust nowadays, after about five years of continual use and refinement. It hasn't always been like that though; particularly in the early days of electronic trading and the case studies below serve as a reminder that software, people and arcades aren't infallible.

Griffin Trading Company[9]

Griffin Trading Company was a Chicago incorporated company specialising in providing clearing services to futures traders. It was a non-Clearing Member of Eurex and had in place an arrangement with a Clearing Member of Eurex to clear the trades of GLH Derivatives Ltd, which comprised a number of traders, trading on Eurex and Euronext.liffe, including a John Ho Park.

John Ho Park had been in breach of his pre-trade position limits several times from July 1998 to December 1998 by trading positions up to twenty times his permitted daily trading limits. Griffin and GLH had inadequate risk management software and procedures, and John Ho Park was aware of this and exploited it. Although being warned about his position limit breaches, Park continued to over trade and on 21 December. 1998 had an intra-day position of 10,176 Eurex futures when his allowable position limit was restricted to 978 lots. His overnight position limit was 50 lots but he actually carried 10,128 lots over the night of 21 December resulting in a loss of £6.3m on 22 December as prices moved against him.

The failure by Griffin and GLH to meet margin calls from their Clearing Member resulted in default and ultimately the liquidation of Griffin.

Sussex Futures Ltd[10]

Sussex Futures Ltd acted as an arcade for traders trading Eurex and Euronext.liffe. On 6 Aug. 1999, a trader called Stephen Humphries, trading as SPH Futures Ltd., exceeded his 10 lot intra-day position limit in the Euronext.liffe Gilt future by building a position of 1129 lots, and which resulted in a loss of £743,000. Sussex Futures Ltd had an automated risk management system but on that day it had been disconnected due to malfunctions and there were insufficient staff available to adequately manually monitor his activities.

---

[9] Securities and Futures Authority (SFA), now part of the Financial Services Authority (FSA), Board notice 574 – 19th February 2001.

[10] SFA Board notice 579 – 20th March 2001.

Sussex Futures Ltd ceased traded but no other customer was disadvantaged since the owner made arrangements to cover all the losses by making a substantial personal financial contribution. Stephen Humphries of SPH Futures Ltd served a prison sentence for fraudulent trading.

Influences regarding the trader's choice of markets and contracts

STIR futures traders have the choice of several exchanges and contracts to trade, but there can be advantages or incentives that can influence the decision.

There are two principal STIR futures exchanges, Euronext.liffe in London, offering Euribor, Short Sterling and Euroswiss, and Chicago Mercantile Exchange (CME) in Chicago offering Eurodollars. There is also Euroyen STIR futures traded on Tokyo Financial Exchange (TFX) in Japan, but difficult and expensive access, plus anti-social trading hours (for western traders), rule this out as a viable choice.

The majority of traders tend to stay close to home in their choice of markets and contracts, usually for reasons of domicile, time zone and connectivity, but the more mobile trader can choose to trade from different locations for reasons such as lifestyle and taxation considerations.

Domicile and time zones

The exchanges operate their electronic trading platforms on a global network with access points in most countries and major cities. Euronext.liffe, for example, operates Connect in over 831 sites covering 31 countries and all time zones.

This makes connectivity and market access relatively easy and the trading hours of the major STIR futures contracts tend to overlap with time zones of other major financial centres to facilitate business. CME Eurodollar is available 23 hours of the day and Euronext.liffe Euribor is traded from 0700hrs until 2100hrs (local London time), which coincides with the close of the US markets. Smaller, indigenous STIR futures contracts tend to have trading hours matching the usual local working day. However, despite around the clock and extended trading hours being available in the larger global contracts, the vast majority of business is conducted during their domestic time zone. Eurodollar is relatively inactive during the Far Eastern trading day (US night), moderately active during European trading hours (US very early morning), as traders might trade or spread Eurodollars against moves in Euribor.

However, the bulk of business is transacted during the US working day (the European afternoon and evening). Euribor is also usually quiet after European working hours despite being available to US traders during their afternoon.

Consequently, it is not unusual to find mobile US traders relocating to London or Europe to access those markets, and vice versa, despite the markets being available globally.

Taxation considerations

Most futures trading will either attract taxation for the country of residence or by a double taxation agreement with the original domicile. However, some international futures trading locations have become very popular for their favourable taxation treatment of futures trading. Not all tax shelters are suitable as trading locations. It is important that they have a first class technological infrastructure and ideally be a hub on the exchange's global network.

Gibraltar

Gibraltar has become a popular trading location in recent years, as much for its taxation benefits as for its lifestyle advantages, technological infrastructure and British colonialism.

Gibraltar based trading arcades operate as tax-exempt companies, a status granted subject to certain conditions, the main one being that no resident of Gibraltar has a beneficial interest in the shares of the company. Once taxation exempt status has been approved by issuance of a tax exemption certificate, in return for the payment of a fixed annual fee (between £200 and £300), the company is exempt from further taxation in Gibraltar including corporation tax and withholding tax.

Individual traders relocating to Gibraltar are designated Qualifying Category 3 Individuals. These are deemed expatriates possessing specialist skills not available in Gibraltar. They can apply to the Financial Centre Director[11] and obtain a certificate, which sets the tax payable by the individual at £10,000 irrespective of their income.

---

[11] Government of Gibraltar Finance Centre, Suite 761, Europort, Gibraltar.

Ireland

Several trading arcades set up in Dublin's International Financial Services Centre (IFSC) to take advantage of the special 10 percent corporation tax rate accorded to companies located there. However, from 1 Jan 2006, companies in the IFSC will pay corporation tax at the normal Irish rate of 12.5 percent which, although low by European standards, has removed the prime incentive to be located in that particular part of Dublin. Consequently, the attractions of Dublin as a trading location have largely been surpassed by the warmer appeal and tax efficiencies of Gibraltar.

Remote trading

Remote trading includes any trading outside of the Clearing Member's internal network. It can include most trading arcades, either located locally or abroad, and individual traders working from home or a small office. All remote trading organisations or individuals will need to have some form of connectivity to connect to the internal network of the Clearing Member, unless they host their own exchange gateways or hubs.

Internet

The simplest form of connectivity is via a simple broadband internet link – popular with home based traders because of the low cost, short contract period but relatively fast performance. Larger futures brokers such as GNItouch[12] tend to offer ISV trading software with internet connectivity for the remote based trader.

It should be remembered that all broadband internet connections are Asymmetrical Digital Subscriber Line (ADSL) which means that although a service might be advertised as having a 1MB (megabyte) or 2MB bandwidth, that only applies to its downstream capability. Its upstream bandwidth will normally be limited to just 384k which might be fine for a single user connecting to one or two exchanges but will not have surplus upstream capacity for more users. Symmetrical Digital Subscriber Line (SDSL) are being rolled out in urban areas and offer the same upstream and downstream bandwidth but are many times more expensive.

---

[12] www.gnitouch.com

Virtual Private Network (VPN)

A variation on the internet connection is the Virtual Private Network (VPN) which is a secure internet connection by the use of encryption. VPN will be a more secure method of trading via the internet but might be fractionally slower due to the encryption process. Both internet and VPN users should be aware of their contention ratio, which is the ratio of total bandwidth available that is shared amongst subscribers. A residential internet connection might have a contention ratio of 40:1 meaning that there can be up to 39 other users sharing the service. This can be fine if there are only a few other daytime users competing for your bandwidth over Non-Farm Payrolls, but if music downloaders and file sharers surround you, then slowdowns are a likely possibility. Business broadband services are better options, being a little more expensive but offering lower contention ratios, better service back up and usually a little more upstream bandwidth.

Digital Private Circuit

Top-level connectivity is via a Digital Private Circuit such as British Telecom's[13] Kilostream and Megastream services or by an Application Service Provider (ASP) such as Radianz.[14] These are the most expensive methods of connecting a remote office or arcade, but also are the quickest and most reliable. ASP connections tend to be fully managed with redundancy (back-up), meaning that the entire connection is supplied and managed including the network, routers (device forwarding data between networks) and back up in case of a partial failure. Some ASP connections use a network protocol such as Network Address Translation (NAT) that is not supported by all ISVs, so it is necessary to check in advance to entering into a contract, which are usually of one years duration, although discounts might be offered for longer commitments. Digital Private Circuits such as the Kilostream and Megastream services can be supplied on a network only basis, where the client is responsible for supplying and configuring the routers. They usually involve a connection fee and annual rental charge dependant upon location and distance to point.

---

[13] www.bt.com

[14] www.Radianz.com

Connectivity speed

Connection speed is always of vital interest to remote traders. There can be several influences upon speed to market, the main ones being distance and quality of connection and network infrastructure integrity.

Connection speeds can be tested by Ping tests and Traceroute (tracert) commands, if the destination Internet Protocol (IP) address is known.

Ping

On Windows machines, ping tests are run in the MSDOS or command window[15] of the operating system and will have the following syntax.

C:\> ping xxx.xxx.xx.xxx

Where xxx is the IP address of the remote server.

The ping test sends a data packet to its destination and measures how long it takes to come back, rather like an echo or sonar. Its round trip is measured in milli-seconds (thousandths of a second) and ping speeds are governed by network traffic, distance and bandwidth constraints. Very generally speaking, a remote trader based in the same city as their destination host should consistently ping at between 8ms and 20ms. Further distances such as London to Chicago might ping up to 100ms and trans world can be approximately 300ms.

Not all networks can be pinged, since firewalls often block them as being intrusive security threats.

Traceroute

The traceroute command has similar syntax except 'ping' is replaced by 'tracert'.

This command provides details of the path between the two hosts with the number of nodes involved. The less number of nodes or hops between nodes will mean a more direct, possibly quicker, connection.

There is also a pathping command that combines the ping and traceroute utilities. The difference is that each node of the connection is pinged as the result of a single command, and that the behaviour of nodes are studied over an extended time period, rather than the ping's default sample of four messages or Traceroute's default single route trace. The disadvantage is that it often takes more than five minutes to produce a result.

---

[15] START>programs>accessories>command prompt

Spread betting alternatives

Spread betting can offer low end access to the STIR futures markets, either by a quote driven service from a traditional spread betting firm or by using the platform of a specialised futures betting spread betting company[16]. These provide an ISV-like internet-based interface and permit eligible clients to trade futures in a similar way to how they would directly trade into an exchange. They tend to operate a spread around the existing bid/offer spread and charge commissions according to volumes. Since they are regulated as gambling entities, profits are not subject to tax.

They can be a consideration for the less capitalised trader since accounts can be opened for approximately £5000, compared to the £25,000 usually required by a Clearing Member but the trading spreads and higher commissions will be a disadvantage.

---

[16] www.futuresbetting.com or www.twowayfutures.com, who act as an introducing broker to the Gibraltar based futuresbetting.com

3

Trading STIR futures

Trading Opportunities: The Two Trades

There are two ways to trade STIR futures:

1. **outright trading**, which is the purchase or sale of a single contract only, and

2. **spread trading**, which is the trading of multiple contracts against each other. Spread trading (also known as *strategy trading*) can be either intra-contract, where trades are within the same futures contract or inter-contract, where one contract is traded against another correlated contract.

Outright trading

This is the simplest form of trading but also one of the most difficult. Someone once described futures trading as *"being the hardest way to make easy money"* and no doubt they were probably referring to outright trading.

On the face of it, trading outrights is fairly straightforward. You try to buy low and sell high, but it's a volatile form of trading and earnings can be erratic. It's possibly the area of highest failure amongst new traders, but it's also the arena of the trading legends.

Macro trading

Fundamentally based macro view

Outright trading can be considered in two forms. The first is macro trading where a considered view is used to justify a purchase or sale. This view might be based on an economic incongruity, such as the trader thinking that the STIR futures prices were too low, driven down by the market's inflationary expectations of high oil prices but against a background of a rapidly weakening economy and the possibility of future interest rate cuts. George Soros, one of the most successful traders of all time, employed this kind of trading with great success and he attempted to quantify this discrepancy between market participants' expectations and the actual course of events by a theory of reflexivity in his book *The Alchemy of Finance*. It's an interesting read, mainly to learn more about how these discrepancies can build up in markets, but it was difficult to quantify this phenomenon.

Technically driven macro view

Alternatively, the macro view might be technically driven where the decision to buy or sell is based upon chart patterns or trading indicators. Charts are graphical representations of price time series and indicators are mainly mathematically derived measures of relative price movements. Many books have been written about each but the subject is beyond the scope of this one. Most traders look at charts and familiarise themselves with price levels, either to generate trading ideas or to be aware of what other more technically driven traders are watching. It really depends on whether the trader believes that historical price trends can influence future trends or whether mathematics can interpret price action.

Trading example

In November 2005 market expectations of an interest rate rise by the ECB were being supported by increasingly hawkish central banker rhetoric and at their 1 December meeting the ECB duly raised interest rates by 25bps.

Chart 3.1 shows that, afterwards, the Euribor future was finding resistance at the 97.11 level, providing a good selling point in expectation that further interest rate rises would put downward pressure on the market. This view gathered momentum during December and the market fell to 96.90 on expectations that the Eurozone was at the start of a monetary tightening cycle.

Chart 3.1: Hourly chart of Euribor Z6 – November 2005 to January 2006

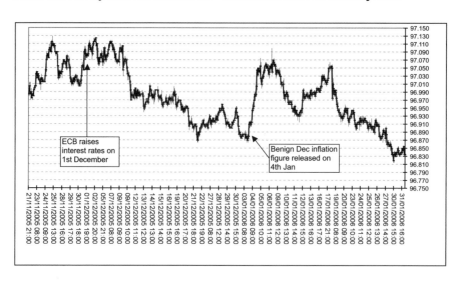

However, these expectations were temporarily reversed early in the new year when the December inflation figure released on 4 January was less than expected. This prompted a sharp inter day rally as shorts covered their positions. This provided further selling opportunities for the brave, believing that this rally was mainly technically induced and the upward pressures on interest rates remained. This view was subsequently correct as the markets sold lower in January.

Trading example – the money flows

On 7 December, a week after the ECB rate rise, the Euribor Z6 future had bounced back to the 97.11 level, a decision is made to sell 10 lots around this level with a view to further rate rise expectations driving the market lower. The trade is closed out five days later, on 12 December; the money flows are described below.

- **Commissions** are €2 per round trip (to buy and sell 1 lot), therefore totalling €10 to sell the opening position of 10 lots.

- The **initial margin** requirement is €475 per contract, totalling €4750 for the 10 lot position.

The market account will be marked to market with the closing prices of the position each day. If the position is showing a profit, then this will be credited to the account. If it is showing a loss, it will be debited from the account. The prices for the trade period are shown in the table below.

Date	Open	High	Low	Close
7 Dec	97.11	97.12	97.06	97.07
8 Dec	97.07	97.11	97.03	97.055
9 Dec	97.06	97.075	96.97	96.97
12 Dec	96.98	97.00	96.97	96.99

1. **7 Dec**

   Sell 10 Euribor Z6 at 97.06. Commission bill is €10. Initial margin requirement is €4750, but since the market settles higher at 97.07 than the traded price of 97.06, there is an unrealised loss on the trade of 10 ticks equalling – €250 (10 x 97.06 - 97.07 x tick value of €25). This amount is added to the margin requirement making a total of €5000.

2. **8 Dec**

   The market tracks a little lower, settling at 97.055. The margin account is now credited with the inherent profit on the trade, reducing the total requirement to €4750 - €125, equalling €4625 (10 x 97.06 - 97.055 x €25).

3. **9 Dec**

   Market breaks lower and settles at 96.97. Margin requirement is now €4750 - €2250, totalling €2500 (10 x 97.06 - 96.97 x €25). Now would have been a great time to close the trade but a decision is taken to run it over the weekend, in the hope of some rate rise commentary in the weekend press.

4. **12 Dec**

   The market opens it a little higher. The hoped for negative press didn't materialise and a decision is taken to close the position. 10 lots are bought at 96.99 making a profit of 7 ticks. The second part of the commission of €10 is now payable.

   The total profit equals:

   ```
   97.06 - 96.99 = 7 ticks x 10 lots = 70 ticks = 70 x €25 = €1750.
   ```

   Commissions equalled €20, making an adjusted return of €1730.

Trading size is purely dependent on account size and the position limits imposed by the risk manager. The above trade could equally have been done in 1 lot, 10 lots, 500 lots or 1000 lots. The liquidity is there in STIR futures, at virtually all times. Commissions would naturally be larger, being charged on a per lot or per round trip basis, but so would the accompanying profit and loss. For example, the commissions on a 1000 lot trade would total €2000 but the profit on the above trade would have been €175,000.

There is a funding cost of margin which is dealt with in different ways by different clearing members. Interest is usually payable on traders' accounts, but capital utilised as margin might not attract interest. However, for most STIR traders, these amounts are relatively insignificant given the trade's profit or loss potential.

Scalping

The second form of outright trading is scalping. This is short term intensive price action trading. Unlike macro trading where a position is established based on a view and looking for a significant movement, scalping is all about trading the bid/offer spread and trying to gain a quick tick here and there. Scalpers add liquidity to markets they operate in, acting in a market making capacity, providing price quotes almost continually. Scalping is usually involved in the more volatile bond and equity futures markets but can be used with success in the liquid front months of STIR futures.

Scalping examples would be exactly the same as above (under *Macro Trading*), except on a much shorter time scale. And since most scalping is intra-day, it would not involve overnight margin.

Losing money

The problem with outright trading is the risk of losing money; either absolutely or in a drawdown. Losing money absolutely is easily understood and very easy to achieve, especially when the odds are stacked against the trader. A trader needs to be right about 7 times out of 10 in order to make money after fees. No mean feat, but those traders who have a firm grasp of limiting their losses and getting their view right most of the time and at the right time, can get ahead.

Drawdowns are the unrealised losses on a position. For example, a trader might buy futures at 95.50 and sell it later for 95.55, making 5 ticks. If, however, whilst holding the position the price had dropped to 95.45 before going up to 95.55, the trader would have had a drawdown of 5 ticks.

Some traders can handle drawdowns, other can't. The legendary hedge fund trader Michael Steinhardt was renowned for *being able to see the mountain in the distance whilst ignoring the valleys in-between.* Others prefer to take the loss and start again.

In outright trading, most macro-traders tend to be hedge funds seeking higher returns whilst the scalpers tend to be independent traders using their own capital for smaller but more frequent profits. Perhaps it's easier taking drawdowns when it's someone else's money!

Trading considerations for outrights

1. Markets move between periods of volatility and inactivity. It is usually during the periods of volatility that the scalping and trading opportunities exist – but periods of extreme volatility are best avoided.

2. Economic releases often have big effects on the STIR futures markets. Trading just before the figure, or carrying positions over numbers, carries additional risk.

3. STIR futures can move quickly but not as quickly as the more volatile bond futures at the longer end of the yield curve. Scalpers use them as leading indicators for STIR futures.

4. Markets frequently move on false rumours, usually based on what is fashionable at the time. At present it is terrorism and they are identified by sharp, sporadic price movements. Normally, the trader will only hear about the rumour after the market price action, making them difficult to trade. Real events are usually identified by consistent large scale buying or selling.

5. Each STIR future has its own culture, which can change from month to month. At present, the Euribor and Eurodollar are the busiest and noisy; while Short Sterling and Euroswiss are quieter, but have their moments.

6. Price action is often a reflection of traders' cumulative positions. Sometimes, such as on Friday afternoons or before a bank holiday, prices can fall or squeeze higher as traders seek to square their positions.

Spread trading

Spread trading is the purchase or sale of one futures contract against an opposite position in another related contract. There are two classes of spread:

*   **intra-contract** – where one series is traded against another within the same STIR futures contract, and

*   **inter-contract** – which involves a spread between two or more different futures contracts.

Spread trading usually has a lower risk profile than outright trading, particularly intra-contract spreading. Table 3.1 shows the differences in average deviations and standard deviations[17] between The Euribor H6 outright futures and the Euribor H6M6 spread, which is essentially a differential between the H6 and M6 series.

Table 3.1: Average and standard deviations between Euribor H6 and Euribor H6M6 spread (3 Jan 2005 to 25 Nov 2005)

	H6 outright	H6M6 spread
Average Deviation	0.206	0.027
Standard Deviation	0.229	0.032

It can be seen that the outright is much more volatile than the spread, making the spread a lower risk method of trading. Spread trading offers a more controlled exposure to the differential between two futures contracts instead of trading a single futures and being fully exposed to its price action. Looking at both trades in absolute terms using the above data range, the high and low range between 3 January and 25 November for the H6 future was 82 ticks compared to only 12 ticks for the spread[18].

Spread trading offers a different kind of trading experience than outrights. There is less outright risk, numerous trade permutations, either within its own contract or against others and they can be traded electronically as single strategies where both parts of the spread are transacted simultaneously thus eliminating execution or leg risk.

---

[17] Average Deviation is the average of the absolute deviations of data points from their mean. Put another way, it's how much the outright or spread has moved on average away from the mean.

Standard Deviation is a more recognised statistic that states how tightly all the various examples are clustered around the mean in a set of data. In both cases, a higher figure denotes higher volatility.

[18] H6: high low 98.05, 97.23. Spread high/low of 0.16, 0.04

Spread Trading: Intra-Contract Spreads

There are basically three types of intra-contract spreads (which are those that trade within the same STIR futures contract):

1. calendar spread,

2. butterfly spread,

3. condor spread.

They are characterised by the fact that their total position will always net out to zero since the component legs will counter-position each other. An example could be the long calendar spread that comprises a purchase of a near dated future (+1) and a sale of a further dated future (-1), netting out to zero. All these spreads can be traded either as the component legs or as strategies or single instruments on the leading futures exchanges.

Calendar spread

The calendar spread is the simultaneous purchase and sale to open of the same underlying contract but in different delivery months.

It is simply the difference between two delivery months in the same futures contact. They are also known as *legs* and can be expressed as:

```
P₁ - P₂
```

```
where P1 is the price of the nearest delivery month in the spread
and P2 is the longer dated delivery month in the spread.
```

Example

If Z5 was trading 97.490 and H6 was trading 97.320, then the Z5H6 spread is the difference between the Z5 and the H6 or 97.490 – 97.320 = 0.170.

0.170 is the differential between these two contracts and is effectively 17 ticks or 17 basis points. This differential, or spread, can change as the two futures change in price since they are not perfectly correlated to each other because they represent different points on the yield curve.

Calendar spreads don't have to be limited to just P1 – P2, where there is only the difference of one delivery cycle or three months in-between. Another example might be:

```
P₁ - P₃
```

```
where P3 would be M6, making the Z5M6 spread with a six month
interval between expiries.
```

Calendar spreads are always priced by the convention of dealing the nearest month first so that buying the spread would involve buying the nearest dated series, selling the far dated series. Selling the spread would be selling the nearest dated series and buying the far dated series. Calendar spreads have a market bid/offer spread just like any single future. These can be determined by a simple process of using the bids and offers of the component futures:

- Spread **bid price** = bid price nearest future – offer price further future

- Spread **offer price** = offer price nearest future – bid price further future

So by using the following price quotes from the Euribor on 25 Nov 2005.

Table 3.2: Euribor futures prices on 25 Nov 2005

	Bid Price	Offer price
Z5	97.490	97.495
H6	97.315	97.320
M6	97.210	97.215
U6	97.160	97.165
Z6	97.105	97.110

The buying price (or offer) and the selling price (or bid) of the Z5H6 spread would be:

- Z5H6 **bid price** = 97.490 – 97.320 = 0.170

- Z5H6 **offer price** = 97.495 – 97.315 = 0.180

Continuing this process would give the following spread prices from the price table.

Table 3.3: Spread prices implied by the Euribor futures prices in Table 3.2

	Bid Price	Offer price
Z5H6	0.170	0.180
H6M6	0.100	0.110
M6U6	0.045	0.055
U6Z6	0.050	0.060

The calendar spread bid/offer spread will always be a maximum of the combined bid/offer spreads of the component futures. In this case, where Euribor has a half tick spread, the spread bid/offer will be 1 tick. It could possibly be wider if a more illiquid future was used with a bid/offer of more than half a tick but will always be the sum of the individual bids and offers.

This spread is also the implied price since it is generated by the outright futures. In practice, the spread bid/offer in the market is narrower than the implied prices. Table 3.4 shows the market prices of the Euribor spreads and, comparing these to those of Table 3.3, it can be seen that the spread bid/offer is the minimum permitted increment of half a tick. The implied prices make up one side of the price, but the other price is improved upon by market participants. Spread markets are usually tight and highly liquid since they have less volatility than outright futures. Traders are more willing to trade for the minimum increment on an instrument that has less movement and usually in larger size hence promoting liquidity.

Table 3.4: Market prices for Euribor spreads on 25 Nov 2005 (italics show implied prices)

	Bid Price	Offer price
Z5H6	0.175	*0.180*
H6M6	0.105	*0.110*
M6U6	0.050	*0.055*
U6Z6	*0.050*	0.055

The market examples in the table are the actual exchange traded strategies for the sequential 3-month spreads. These spreads, in this form, can be traded as instruments just like individual futures. It is also possible to construct and trade spreads consisting of component futures that start and end with any delivery month within the cycle. However, a number of characteristics need to be observed.

1. A calendar spread with a larger interval between component delivery months will be more volatile than one with a shorter interval.

2. Shorter interval spreads tend to be more liquid than longer interval spreads (although 1 year spreads are popular, for example, Z5Z6).

3. White pack spreads will be more volatile than red pack spreads, which in turn will be more volatile than spreads in the green pack.

3. Margin requirements will be higher on longer interval spreads and on white pack spreads, less so respectively on red and green pack spreads.

Volatility increases with wider spread intervals

Chart 3.2 shows how a longer interval within the spread increases volatility by showing the declining correlation of the sequential futures to the front month (Z5). It is clear how a spread between the front month and the next delivery month has a much lower *net* correlation (the difference between the two correlations) than one between the same front month and say, a delivery month one year later such as Z6. This widening net correlation, as the interval between the delivery months widens, is reflected by the increasing standard deviations. This means as the interval between Z5 and the next series widens, the volatility and risk also increases.

Chart 3.2: Chart showing the correlations of sequential series against the front month (Z5) plotted against the standard deviations of the spreads against Z5

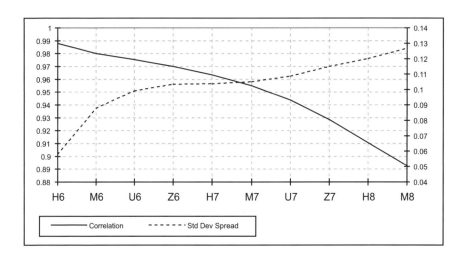

Spreads of any interval will be more volatile in the front white pack than spreads in the red pack, which in turn will be more volatile than spreads in the green pack. By using the same data set for 2005 as used before, but rolling over each delivery month at expiry to make a continuous series, a notional front white spread, front red spread and front green spread can be constructed and their relative price sensitivities compared.

Table 3.5: Average and standard deviations between notional Euribor 3 month spreads in the white pack, red pack and green pack (3 Jan 2005 to 25 Nov 2005)

	White spread	Red spread	Green spread
Average Deviation	0.057	0.025	0.018
Standard Deviation	0.076	0.031	0.024

Or as shown graphically as in Chart 3.3

Chart 3.3: Price movement for notional Euribor 3 month spreads: The white pack, red pack and green pack (3 Jan 2005 to 25 Nov 2005)

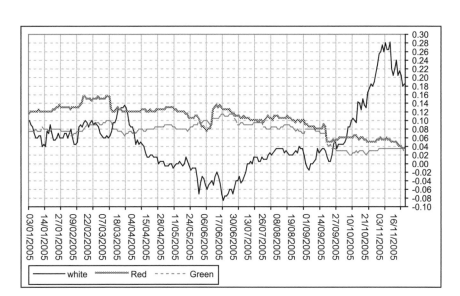

It is apparent how the front white spread moves more than the red and green spreads. This can be due to a number of factors driving the STIR futures prices, including liquidity, the economic outlook and incidence of interest rate expectations. Most of these factors tend to be concentrated into the first year of the STIR futures price curve simply because forecasting is an imperfect science and making longer dated forecasts is unreliable. This is often why the majority of curvature in the STIR futures price curve is present in the first four, and then the following four delivery months, representing the white and red packs or two years of the yield curve.

Calendar spreads are effectively yield curve capture trades, and the amount of curve being captured is dependent on the spread interval. Put another way, they are a price representation of a yield curve shape at a given time and the changing shape of the yield curve will drive their prices.

Yield curve effect on calendar spreads

Previous sections have shown how yield curves are usually positive but they can be flat or even negative in times of impending recession. Table 3.6 shows how calendar spreads will respond to a changing yield curve shape on a positively shaped curve. A steepening curve refers to a widening of the difference between a longer-term yield and a shorter-term yield and will cause calendar spreads to widen. A flattening curve refers to a narrowing of the difference between a longer-term yield and a shorter-term yield and this will cause calendar spread to narrow. The opposite effects will occur for negatively sloping yield curves.

Table 3.6: Yield curve effects on calendar spreads for a positive yield curve

	Calendar spreads price
Yield curve steepening	↑
Yield curve flattening	↓

It should be remembered from previous sections (Liquidity considerations of the micro curve) that segments of the yield curve, and hence the STIR futures price curve, can have both steepening and flattening effects within a section as small as two years. This can lead to the interesting situation of some spreads moving up and others moving down, making the butterfly spreads of particular relevance.

Trading example

Another way of trading the Eurozone interest rate rise expectations of December 2005 (instead of taking a macro view and trading the outrights, as shown in an earlier example), would be to trade the steepening shape of the yield curve by using calendar spreads.

Chart 3.4 shows the Euribor H6M6 spread over the same time period. An anticipation of higher interest rates could prompt a purchase of the calendar spread, in expectation that the yield curve would steepen as the markets looked for further rate rises. This would cause the calendar spread to rise in value as the further dated contract (M6) declined more quickly than the nearer H6.

Chart 3.4: Euribor H6M6 calendar spread – July 2005 to January 2006

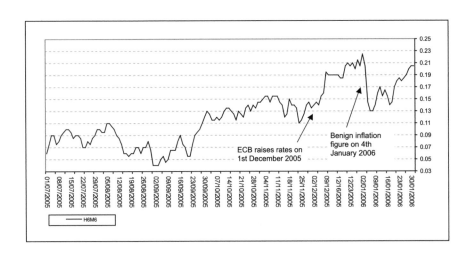

The spread could have been purchased at around 0.13 when rates were increased on 1 December 2005. The spread then mirrored the steepening yield curve and increased to 0.21, until being sharply corrected by the benign inflation figure on 4 January 2006.

Although the calendar spread is directional and will be influenced by the movements in the outright futures, it has a much lower risk profile than the outright future. The Z6 contract (in the earlier example) moved approximately 20 ticks whereas the H6M6 spread moved just 6 ticks.

Calendar spread matrix

A useful way of presenting calendar spreads is via a matrix. Most ISVs incorporate them into their trading software and they have the advantage that all spreads, of all permutations and intervals, can be observed in a single space.

Table 3.7 shows a typical matrix, with prices taken from 25 Nov 2005. Different matrices will differ slightly, but generally all will display a sequential series of futures along the X and Y axes with the spread prices embedded accordingly. Table 3.7 shows the futures strip, with symbols and prices along the top row and the futures symbols diagonally across the matrix. The spread prices are stacked so that the offer is above the bid although some matrices will exhibit these prices side by side or allow the user to customise.

Table 3.7: Euronext.liffe Euribor spread matrix – 25 Nov 2005

	Z5	H6	M6	U6	Z6	H7	M7	U7	Z7
OFFER	97.495	97.325	97.220	97.170	97.115	97.080	97.030	96.985	96.930
BID	97.490	97.320	97.215	97.165	97.110	97.075	97.025	96.980	96.925
	Z5	**H6**	**M6**	**U6**	**Z6**	**H7**	**M7**	**U7**	**Z7**
	Z5	*0.175*	*0.280*	*0.330*	*0.385*	*0.420*	*0.470*	*0.515*	*0.570*
		0.170	0.275	0.325	0.380	*0.410*	*0.460*	*0.505*	*0.560*
		H6	*0.110*	*0.160*	*0.215*	*0.250*	*0.300*	*0.345*	*0.400*
			0.105	0.155	*0.210*	0.245	*0.290*	*0.335*	*0.390*
			M6	0.055	*0.110*	*0.145*	*0.195*	*0.240*	*0.295*
				0.050	0.105	0.140	0.190	*0.230*	*0.285*
				U6	0.055	0.090	0.140	*0.190*	*0.245*
					0.050	0.085	0.135	*0.180*	*0.235*
					Z6	0.040	0.090	0.135	*0.190*
						0.035	0.085	0.130	0.185
						H7	0.050	0.095	*0.155*
							0.045	0.090	*0.145*
							M7	0.045	*0.105*
								0.040	0.100
								U7	*0.060*
									0.055
									Z7

Bidding the H6U6 at 0.155 against selling H6M6 at 0.105 will result in being long M6U6 at 0.05.

Selling M6M7 at 0.195 against buying U6M7 at 0.140 would result in being short M6U6 at 0.055.

By following one symbol from the diagonal row to underneath another symbol on the top row, the market spread price for that combination can be found. For example, following the M6 on the diagonal row to where it is underneath Z6 on the top row will give the six month M6Z6 spread as 0.105 bid, 0.110 offered. The diagonal row is always quoted first. It can be seen that the 0.110 offer is in italics and this is because it is an implied price. However, these can contain a quantity of market participants' orders, making a combination of implied and outright orders and different ISV have different ways of showing this order information. It can be noted that in the depths of the matrix, towards the top right hand corner, prices are generally all implied with the bid/offer spread defaulting to the spread implied by the bid/offer prices of the outright futures. This is because spreads of such a large interval are not popular and so traded volumes are low and hence liquidity can be poor.

Conversely, prices towards the diagonal symbols tend to be tighter and more liquid since these are the three-month spreads. The diagonal row above these is the six-month spreads and the one above those are the nine-month spreads and so on. Generally, as mentioned earlier, spread liquidity will decline as the spread interval grows larger or, as displayed by the matrix, as one moves upwards from the diagonal symbols towards the apex of the matrix.

A spread matrix is not just a useful visual aid, allowing the trader to view all spreads in one space. It can also be used as an alternative trading mechanism.

The trader is faced with two simple choices when trading a spread. They can enter their order in the spread order book, and, if trying to join the bid or offer, join the queue of other orders all trying to do the same thing. Spreads tend to be highly liquid, particularly the low interval ones, with thousands or even tens of thousands of contracts on the bid and offer. Exchange trading computerised algorithms will usually ensure a pro-rata trade allocation but can be geared towards preferential treatment for certain kinds of order. The reality is that the order is usually completed only when the entire spread price has traded out. That's fine if the trader really wants to buy or sell that price, if perhaps they have an absolute view on the curve, but if their motive is being able to buy the bid before everyone else or sell the offer whilst it's still offered, it's not much use. The second choice is to leg the trade via the individual component futures. It's a very effective method when done successfully but it is subject to outright or leg risk.

Creating spreads from spreads

There is a third way however. It is possible to create spreads from spreads. A 12 month spread like the Z5Z6 must be the same as the four 3-months spreads within its interval period, in this case Z5H6 + H6M6 + M6U6 + U6Z6. It must also be the same as:

- two 6-month spreads (Z5M6 +M6Z6), or
- 9-month + 3-month spread (Z5U6 + U6Z6), or
- 3-month + 9-month (Z5H6+H6Z6).

The wider the spread interval, the more trade permutations and ways of establishing other spreads there will be. Most traders will use this approach to either convert an existing spread into another that is perhaps more liquid, or has a shorter interval, or even to convert a long position in a spread into a short position if their views on the shape of the curve had changed.

An easier way to look at this and the trading possibilities is to reduce the matrix to show only the spread intervals.

Table 3.8: Data from Table 3.7 but only showing the spread intervals

1. *Columns* – The "18" spread minus the "15" will be the "3" spread

Z5	H6	M6	U6	Z6	H7	M7	U7	Z7
Z5	3	6	9	12	15	18	21	24
	H6	3	6	9	12	15	18	21
		M6	3	6	9	12	15	18
			U6	3	6	9	12	15
				Z6	3	6	9	12
					H7	3	6	9
						M7	3	6
							U7	3
								Z7

Flipping the spread can be done by converted a long 3-month spread into a short 3-month spread via the 6 month spread

2. *Rows* - The "9" spread minus the "6" will also equal the "3"

As with the matrix shown in Table 3.7, the sequence of 3-month spreads lie above the diagonal symbols followed by the 6-month spreads above, then the 9 month spreads and so on, in a geometric pattern.

Converting longer interval spreads to 3-month spreads

A trader can convert almost any spread into another. Taking an 18-month spread and subtracting a 15-month spread will leave a position in a 3-month spread. Two "3" spreads will equal a "6" spread. Usually though, most traders will want to convert other spreads into a 3-month spread. The 3-month spreads have liquidity barriers that make it unappealing to merely place a bid or offer in the order book in the first place – but those liquidity barriers also make it attractive for the trader to be long on the bid or short on the offer.

There are two easy patterns to look for in the matrix to find longer dated spreads for conversion into 3-month spreads.

1. Columns

First, select the target 3-month spread, for example the H7M7 spread, and find the corresponding box with a "3" in it. Follow the *column* up to the top row with "18" in it underneath the M7 symbol. Going one cell left will be "15" for the Z5H7 spread. By subtracting this from the "18" spread will result in the "3" spread of H7M7 (see textbox). Netting out the symbols can substantiate this: a Z5M7 "18" spread minus a Z5H7 "15" spread will net out to H7M7

Table 3.9: Converting to a 3-month spread

	"18"	"15"	NET
Z5	*	*	
H6			
M6			
U6			
Z6			
H7		*	*
M7	*		*

This process can be continued down the matrix column so that going a step down will give the "15"spread (H6M7) and going one cell left will be the "12" (H6H7). Again this will net out to the H7M7 spread. This procedure can be followed down the matrix column to do the same for "12" against "9", "9" against "6" and "6" against "3". That's five ways to establish a position in the 3-month H7M7 spread. The same process can be used on any other 3-month spread, the only constraint being the depth of the matrix limiting the number of permutations.

2. Rows

Again, a 3-month spread is chosen and the H7M7 spread is used as an example. This time, instead of following the column upwards from the "3", the *row* is followed to the right to the end of the matrix where the cell is "9" for the H7Z7 spread. Going one cell down to the "6" gives the M7Z7 spread. Netting these two spreads will result in the H7M7 spread. This is the same process as *columns* but using the rows instead of the columns (see textbox).

Both these methods complement each other in that they can offer increased trading permutations for 3-month spreads. If one method is limited by the depth or width of the matrix limiting the number of permutations, then the other can be used. Note that in both cases, the second spread is of a lower interval than the first and geometrically, there will always be a downward progression towards the diagonal symbols. If a higher interval were chosen for the second spread than the first, it would just relate to an adjacent spread. Furthermore, these examples have used only one step left or down within the matrix. It is perfectly possible to use more steps but the resulting spread will be longer dated than the 3-month spreads used. The resulting spread will always be the difference between the two initiating spreads.

Reversing spread positions

Spreads can also be flipped or reversed in position. If a trader is long of a spread, for example H6M6, and the yield curve starts flattening, meaning the value of the spread is likely to decrease, the position can be shunted along to the next sequential spread and made short by use of the 6-month spread. By being long of H6M6 and selling the 6-month H6U6, a short position is made in M6U6. Netting out the positions illustrates the process.

Table 3.10: Reversing spread positions

	H6M6	M6Z6	NET
Z5			
H6	+	−	
M6	−		−
U6		+	+
Z6			
H7			
M7			

The process of using the intervals to convert longer dated spreads into shorter dated spreads can be easily transferred to the real matrix in Table 3.7. By using the *columns* method it is possible to find an alternative way to buy M6U6. It's an attractive spread to buy on the bid and sell on the offer since the actual market quote on that day (25 November) for the 3-month spread is 0.050 bid on 26450 lots and offered at 0.055 in 11,423 lots (the bid and offer sizes have not been included on the matrix for space considerations). The large size bid and offered on both sides of the spread means that a pro rata trade allocation by placing an order into the order book is going to be poor. But it would be a very attractive and well-protected trade if it could be purchased on the bid before the majority of others have traded the 3-month. One way would be to bid the H6U6 at 0.155 that was only bid for 426 lots and if filled, sell the H6M6 against it at 0.105 (bid for 203 lots) resulting in a long position in the target M6U6 at 0.050 (see textbox). The same spread might then be sold at 0.055 by using the *rows* approach, also shown as a textbox in Table 3.7. By selling M6M7 at 0.195 (831 lots on offer) against buying U6M7 at 0.140 (104 lots on offer), the 3-month M6U6 can be effectively sold at 0.055 giving a profit of half a tick. Nice work if you can get it!

Traders' notes

1. Be aware of the impact of exchange fees and commissions on the potential profit of a matrix trade. The above example of buying and selling the M6U6 spread would have involved 8 lots being traded compared to just 4 lots if the spread were bought and sold as a strategy. However, fee rebates are often available for high volumes of trade, particularly in further dated contracts. Many 'matrix traders' live off the exchange rebates.

2. Beware of trading one spread against the price of another that is purely implied. The examples above all had 'paper' bids and offers in the quotes used as well as a component of implied pricing. Implied prices have a nasty habit of disappearing just when you need them!

3. The trade allocation algorithm of each exchange is different and can be changed by the exchanges. The trader needs to be aware of how favourable the allocation would be for a longer dated spread compared to a shorter dated one, particularly when generated by a trade implied from a trade in the outright futures.

4. The implied pricing algorithms frequently generate trades in longer dated spreads from price activity in the futures strip. It is therefore more favourable, and more probable of being filled to bid when the offer is implied and vice versa, therefore 'leaning' against the implieds.

5. Remember that longer dated spreads are more volatile than shorter dated ones and can have poor liquidity. Often the prices can be purely implied and missing a leg deep within the matrix can be expensive! Look for opportunities closer to the target spread first before going deeper into the matrix.

6. Always 'net out' a matrix trade on paper first before entering the order to ensure that the result is what was envisaged.

7. Use the matrix as an escape route when prices are moving against the spread. Look for alternative ways to close an open spread by columns or rows or flip it into another spread.

International spread correlations

Comparing international calendar spreads

The relatively high correlations between international STIR futures contracts were presented earlier (*The drivers of stir futures prices*). By association, it should be expected that the spreads will be highly correlated to each other as well. However, spreads are effectively a snapshot of a segment of a country's yield curve, which in turn is influenced by its stage in its economic and interest rate cycle. Consequently, correlations of spreads can be very positive in times of similar economic outlook but they can break down when divergence occurs.

Table 3.11: Correlations between Eurodollar, Euribor and Sterling spreads (3 Jan 2005 to 25 Nov 2005)

Z5H6	Eurodollar	Euribor	Sterling
Eurodollar	1	0.866	0.443
Euribor		1	0.666
Sterling			1
H6M6	**Eurodollar**	**Euribor**	**Sterling**
Eurodollar	1	0.841	0.264
Euribor		1	0.339
Sterling			1

Table 3.11 shows the correlations between the Z5H6 and H6M6 spreads for the three main economic areas of the United States, Europe and the United Kingdom. It is quite apparent that there are strong consistent correlations for both spreads between the Eurodollar spread and the Euribor spread but both deteriorate relative to Sterling. This is possibly due to the fact that the United Kingdom was the only country to cut interest rates during 2005. International spreads can be useful predicators for other spreads but it is important to ensure that the correlations are supported by economic fundamentals.

Butterfly spread

Calendar spreads have been defined as the difference between two delivery months in the same futures contact and expressed as $P_1 - P_2$. Butterflies are an extension of the same logic but instead are the difference between two sequential spreads in the same futures contact. They are expressed as:

$$(P_1 - P_2) - (P_2 - P_3)$$

Or:

$$P_1 + P_3 - (2*P_2)$$

where P1 is the price of the nearest delivery month in the strategy and P2 is the next delivery month, and P3 the next delivery month.

Chart 3.5 shows the Euribor M6U6 and U6Z6 spreads. The difference between them is the M6U6Z6 butterfly.

Chart 3.5: Euribor Calendar, butterfly and condor spreads (3 Jan 2005 to 25 Nov 2005)

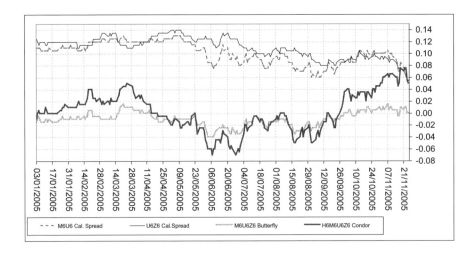

Again, as with calendar spreads, the pricing convention is of dealing the nearest month first. Buying the butterfly would involve buying the nearest dated series, and selling it would be selling the nearest dated series. Butterflies (also known as *flies* or *the fly*) don't just have to be two 3-month spreads back to back. They can be 6-month sequential spreads or even wider, provided the centre leg (P2, also known as *the body*) is the same for both spreads and the first P1 and third legs P3 (also known as *the wings*) are equidistant from the body.

Butterfly spreads also have a market bid/offer spread just like any single future or calendar spread and these can be determined by the same process as shown before for calendar spreads. The bid/offer prices can be calculated for the M6U6Z6 butterfly using the prices from 25 Nov 2005 displayed in the spread matrix in Table 3.7:

```
M6U6Z6 bid  = (M6(bid) - U6(offer)) - (U6(offer) - Z6(bid))

            = (97.215 - 97.170) - (97.170 - 97.110) = -0.015


M6U6Z6 offer= (M6(offer) - U6(bid)) - (U6(bid) - Z6(offer))

            = (97.220 - 97.165) - (97.165 - 97.115) = 0.005
```

The bid/offer spread is two-ticks wide because it is the sum of the bid/offer spreads in the four legs of the butterfly (4 x 0.005). This is similar to calendar spreads, whose bid/offer spreads were determined by the bid/offer spreads of the component futures (which were also the implied prices). However, their bid/offer spreads were often improved upon by market participants, reducing it to the minimum permitted increment. This much reduced bid/offer spread in calendar spreads can be used to improve the pricing of butterflies. Since butterflies are the difference between two sequential spreads they can also be priced as:

$$S_1 - S_2$$

where S_1 is the price of the nearest spread (M6U6) and S_2 is the next spread (U6Z6).

So again using prices from the matrix in Table 3.7:

```
M6U6Z6 bid = S₁(bid) - S₂(offer) = 0.050 - 0.055 = -0.005

M6U6Z6 offer = S₁(offer) - S₂(bid) = 0.055 - 0.050 = 0.005
```

The same butterfly now has a reduced bid/offer of just one-tick, but is frequently improved upon by market participants to the minimum permitted increment. In the example using Euribor, this is half a tick or 0.005 basis point. If the butterfly is determined to be -0.005 bid and 0.005 offered by the component spreads, it would not be unusual to find the market price was actually 0.000 bid and 0.005 offered or perhaps -0.005 bid and 0.000 offered. The price level of 0.000 is likely to be the aggregate of the last traded prices of the component futures. This is where the butterfly should trade since any deviance from this trade level will present opportunities to the trader to trade the fly against either the outright futures or component spreads.

The most popular butterflies spreads are the sequential 3-month and the sequential one-year strategies. They are usually lower risk than their component spreads; the example above, the Euribor M6U6Z6 butterfly has a standard deviation of 0.012 compared to 0.018 for the M6U6 and U6Z6 spreads.

Butterflies will still be a directional trade against the steepening and flattening of the yield curve but less so than a calendar spread since the butterfly comprises both a long and short spread. However, some directional influence remains since in times of uniform steepening or flattening the nearer dated spread component of the butterfly will be more sensitive than the further dated one.

Butterflies are a useful tool for the spread trader:

1. They provide a trading mechanism for the relationship between the sequential calendar spreads, good for trading small distortions on the micro-curve.

2. Similar to using the spread matrix, they offer more avenues to enter or exit a trade. For example, the holder of a long position of a calendar spread that is beginning to suffer from the effects of a flattening yield curve has several choices. It could be liquidated or flipped into another spread by the matrix or be converted into a short butterfly by taking an additional short position in the preceding sequential spread.

3. Butterflies are a corner of the triangular price relationship between futures, calendar spreads and butterflies. The outright prices dictate the arbitrage boundaries via the implied in prices and the calendar spreads improve this further. The level at which trade is going through the individual futures and the calendar spreads should harmonise with the price quotes in the butterfly. If these get slightly out of line, say by a large calendar spread trade or butterfly spread stressing this relationship, then the potential to price improve can exist.

Traders' notes

1. As with matrix trading, be aware of the impact of trading expenses on the potential profit of trading a butterfly. There are four component legs in a butterfly and expenses can represent a very sizable proportion of an expected profit.

2. Remember that butterflies can be priced as both a ratio of sequential futures and a combination of sequential calendar spreads. Deriving the prices from bids and offers gives plenty of scope for error. Work things through on paper first or better still, use a spreadsheet.

3. The price of the butterfly should equal the last trade of the component futures and the two calendar spreads, provided all are liquid.

4. Butterflies are still directional trades. Beware of micro curve influences such as pivot points, liquidity factors and spread activity having an undue effect on the fly.

Condor spread

Calendar spreads are known to be the difference between two delivery months in the same futures contact, and butterflies are the difference between two sequential spreads in the same futures contact. It follows that condor spreads are the difference between two butterflies? Well, almost but not quite; they are actually the sum of two butterflies.

Looking at condors in terms of the component futures price, they are expressed as:

```
(P₁-P₂) - (P₃-P₄)
```

```
where P₁ is the price of the nearest delivery month in the spread
and Pn is the next dated delivery month (Pn = P₁…P₂….P₃….P₄…).
Note that the difference between P₂ and P₃ must be the same time
period as that between P₁ and P₂, and P₃ and P₄
```

An example could be Z5H6M6U6 and in terms of the prices in use for the previous examples;

```
H6M6U6Z6 bid =
H6(bid) - M6(offer)) - (U6(offer) - Z6(bid)) =
(97.320 - 97.220) - (97.170 - 97.110) = 0.040


H6M6U6Z6 offer =
(H6(offer) - M6(bid)) - (U6(bid) - Z6(offer)) =
(97.325 - 97.215) - (97.165 - 97.115) = 0.060
```

Or, expressed as the sum of the two butterflies:

```
B₁ + B₂ = H6M6U6 + M6U6Z6 = 0.050 + 0.000 = 0.050


where Bn are the sequential component butterflies.
```

Or even as the constituent spreads

```
S₁ - S₃ = H6M6 - U6Z6 = 0.1050 - 0.055 = 0.050.
```

Condor spreads are more volatile than the butterfly and the calendar spread. The example given above has a standard deviation of 0.329 and this is obvious when viewed graphically in Chart 3.5. There is little correlation to any other strategy since condors are different from calendar spreads and butterfly spreads. They represent disparate views; opposite opinions on different sections of the yield curve which are more pronounced and volatile when used with larger intervals of six or twelve months For example, a trader thinking that the yield curve might steepen at the front part of the curve but not continue this effect much beyond one year, might purchase the one year condor, hence being long the white 1 year calendar spread and short the green 1 year calendar spread (+Z5–Z6–Z7+Z8). However, it requires a very particular opinion and due to the multiple transaction fees involved, a similar objective might be achieved by use of a calendar spread only.

> **Traders' notes**
>
> It's worth keeping an eye on condor quotes. A tight "paper" price might make it possible to trade the two butterflies, or two component spreads against it but will require a decent payoff to justify the multiple fees incurred.

Introduction to strips, packs, bundles and stacks

Strips, packs, bundles and stacks are not strictly spreads since their overall position totals do not net out to zero. Instead, they are the sum of their totals and all legs have the same signage, meaning that all legs are long or all legs are short. They have been included in this section on intra-contract spreads because, although they are usually used to spread against other instruments and not intra-contract, all the component legs of the strategy are part of the same STIR future and quoted as a strategy. Consequently, this section will provide a description of them and the next will detail their common uses.

Strips

Strips are a generic term for any number of sequential STIR futures contracts. A strip might contain, for example, three sequential delivery months such as Z5,H6 & M6 or it can contain twenty or more contracts. A strip can be the same as a Pack or Bundle but differ in that they can start or finish at any point on the range of STIR futures available, provided all contained within are sequential. Strips are often used as terminology when talking about the futures price curve. They are not traded as strategies in their own right except when they are presented as packs or bundles.

Packs and Bundles can be considered as defined strips since they cover a given number of contracts at a given point on the price curve. Strips are ill-defined since they can refer to any sequence of futures contract such as either the four quarterly months in the first year or the entire sequence of futures from year one to year ten (in the case of the CME Eurodollar). Packs and bundles provide definition in that they cover a limited number of contracts, over a specific part of the strip and can be traded as separate strategies. They can also benefit from exchange fee concessions from being traded as a single strategy.

Stacks

Stacks are multiples of a single month. They are usually used as a proxy for a pack or bundle when those are not easily available. A stack as a proxy for a pack comprising four contracts would simply be four times the individual contract.

Packs

Packs are the simultaneous purchase or sale of four quarterly contracts, equally weighted, within the yearly colour banding system.

Reminder: This colour banding system defines the first four quarterly delivery months as being white, the next four as red, then green, blue, gold, orange, pink, silver and copper. Only CME Eurodollar goes as far as copper. The Euronext.liffe Euribor stops at gold and Sterling at blue. Generally, liquidity can become poor after the blue packs.

An example of a white pack would be

```
P1+P2+P3+P4
```

```
where P1 is the first quarterly delivery month and Pn are the
consecutive quarterly delivery months.
```

A red pack would be

```
P5+P6+P7+P8
```

Packs are priced and quoted on the net change between the current trading price and the previous day's settlement price.

- **Euronext.liffe** uses a quote convention of the *totals* of the net change, and

- **CME** uses the *simple average* of the net change.

By using the following fictitious net change data for a white pack, the effects of these different conventions can be observed.

Z5	H6	M6	U6
-0.03	-0.03	-0.03	-0.02

On Euronext.liffe, the pack would be priced as of the totals of the net change

```
-0.03 + -0.03 + -0.03 + -0.02 = - 0.110
```

The CME pack would be priced as the simple average of the net change

$$\frac{-0.03 + -0.03 + -0.03 + -0.02}{4} = -0.0275$$

- The **Euronext.liffe** methodology is known as the *total change convention* and is priced in increments of half tick or 0.005.

- The **CME** is priced in quarter ticks or 0.0025 and is termed the *annualised convention* since it more accurately reflects price movements of bonds and swaps, which are popular products for inter-contract spreading.

Problem of half-tick prices

Although the CME method is more intuitive and easier to compare with other products, it does conceal a problem. Since the Eurodollar futures are priced in half ticks (the front month is even priced in quarter ticks), this presents an averaging problem for pack and bundles that are priced in quarter ticks. For example, all the net changes shown in the example above are tick integers (whole numbers) but if a fraction of a half tick is introduced for any contract, in this case the U6 delivery month, its effect becomes apparent.

$$\frac{-0.03 + -0.03 + -0.03 + -0.025}{4} = -0.02875$$

The price of -0.02875 is part way between the CME recognised quotes in quarter tick increments of -0.0275 and -0.0300. Consequently, this price of -0.02875 is not tradable, even though the individual prices might infer it. In practice, the pack would be quoted as having traded at either -0.0275 or -0.0300 and the actual futures prices traded would be generated by the CME pack and bundle trading algorithm. This is achieved by dealing with the integer portions first. Each component future would be initially assigned a net price of -0.025 and then each contract, starting with the furthest dated contract, would be adjusted downwards until the trade price is achieved. In this case, if the pack had traded –0.0300, then all futures would simply be trade at –0.0300 net price change from the previous day's settlement price. If the pack had traded –0.0275, then the algorithm would adjust the prices of the individual futures in the pack. All futures would initially be assigned a –0.020 net change and then revised downwards until the traded price of –0.0275 was achieved. This would be done by assigning –0.0300 for the last three contracts.

Euronext.liffe does not have the same issue since it does not use averaging for pricing packs and bundles and its algorithm for assigning prices is slightly different. If the pack price trades at a level reflecting the current market price then those will be used as the individual strategy legs. However, if the pack trades at a price that is not easily matched by current market prices, then the algorithm will assign generated net change prices to each individual leg in equal amounts if the difference warrants it or by a process of adjusting the most deferred leg first until the pack trade price is achieved. The benefit of this is that it keeps the individual prices of the nearer dated, more liquid months assigned to the pack closer to the current prices trading in the market.

Since the main market for Eurodollars is on the CME and the market for Euribor is on Euronext.liffe, the differences between the two quote and allocation methodologies for packs (and bundles) are irrelevant in that each has to be used with its corresponding product. However, these differences are interesting to observe for the trading ramifications.

1. The CME offers tighter pack and bundle quotations for the Eurodollar than Euronext.liffe does for the Euribor.

2. Euronext.liffe offers an allocation algorithm that will generate prices closer to those actually trading in the markets. The algorithm used by CME will generate prices to reflect the pack price but its use of integers only, and a deferred first approach, means that nearer prices might diverge a little from current market prices. In reality, these differences are quite negligible. It's the price that the pack was traded at that is important, not necessarily the price levels of individual futures used.

3. Euronext.liffe's total change quote will appear larger and more volatile than the average used by CME since it is more sensitive to prices changes. For example, on Euronext.liffe, a half tick change in each of the four individual futures of the pack will cause a two-tick change in the price quote of the pack (the sum of four half ticks). On CME, the same futures price change would only change the pack price by a matching half tick. Movements of less than a half tick for each contract, such as only one contract being bid up half a tick would be insufficient to move the price quote, but would be shown in the Euronext.liffe pack.

Bundles

Bundles are a variation on packs. Bundles are the simultaneous purchase or sale of a series of consecutive futures contracts starting with the first quarterly delivery month in the strip but classified by year. They are usually a minimum of two years since a one year bundle would consist of the first four quarterly delivery months and so is effectively a white pack. A two year bundle is the first eight quarterly delivery months (the same as a white plus the red pack), a three year bundle is the first twelve quarterly delivery months (the same as a white and red and green pack added together) and so on until the ten year bundle on CME Eurodollar. Euronext.liffe currently trades bundles to five years that would cover the first twenty quarterly delivery months.

Table 3.12: Bundles

Bundle	Delivery months	Pack Equivalent
2 Year	First 8 quarterly delivery months	White + Red
3 Year	First 12 quarterly delivery months	White + Red + Green
4 Year	First 16 quarterly delivery months	White + Red + Green+ Blue
5 Year	First 20 quarterly delivery months	White + Red + Green+ Blue + Gold

Bundles are priced the same as packs; simple averaging on the CME and totals on Euronext.liffe. The allocation algorithms are the same as for packs for each exchange.

Intra-contract spreading with packs and bundles

There are two intra-contract trades that can be done with packs and bundles.

Bundles versus packs

Since combinations of packs are effectively bundles, the two can be spread against each other, either for arbitrage or price improvement. The tendency is for the bundles to be priced tighter than the sum of the packs and so the trade requires a liquid market which allows the spread trader to buy or sell most or all of the legs on the bid and offer. It's a trade worth watching and any pack or bundle trader should be aware of price action in one or the other. Fees will make a big impact on the profit and loss payoff and due to the number of legs involved is best left to those exchanges with single fee strategy pricing.

Pack or bundle versus a stack

The second spread is the pack or bundle versus a stack. Here, one of the constituent futures of the pack or bundle is traded against the strategy itself. For example, if the red pack were to consist of Z6,H7,M7and U7, any of these futures but preferably one towards the middle such as H7 could be purchased or sold in a 4:1 ratio. The H7 is suitable since the resulting net position would be both long and short calendar spreads, giving a better risk profile against yield curve changes, and it would tend to be more liquid than the more deferred months.

Table 3.13: Pack versus a stack

	Z6	H7	M7	U7
Sell 1 Red pack	-1	-1	-1	-1
Buy 4 H7		+4		
Net	**-1**	**+3**	**-1**	**-1**

The table shows an example of buying 4 H7 against selling the red pack. The net position can be regarded as two 3-month spreads (one short, one long) and a six-month spread (long). Alternatively, it could be viewed as short one Z6H7M7 butterfly and long a six-month spread. There would be plenty of permutations to exit the spread but really it is all about price improvement; buying a constituent future cheap to the pack or selling it dear to the pack. It's not easily done and is really only achievable when the net changes of the futures in the pack are slightly different to each other or a market participant buys or sells a pack dearly or cheaply.

Summary – when to use strategies

- **Calendar spreads**

  These can be regarded as the bread and butter of strategy trading. Judicious buying and selling by trading yield curve movements can return small but high frequency profits for little risk.

- **Butterflies and condors**

  Similar to calendars but the additional costs make them a strategy to be watched or used sparingly to convert or exit existing positions. Paper bids and offers can tighten prices beyond those implied by the outright futures or spreads and can present opportunities to the watchful.

- **Packs and bundles**

  More applicable to inter-contract spreading, but a useful way of buying and selling futures on or near the bids and offers if there is buying and selling in the strategy order book. Can be traded against stacks.

Spread Trading: Inter-Contract Spreads

Inter-contract spreads are the spreading of STIR futures against other interest rate products, such as bonds, with similar price sensitivities and term structures, or international STIR futures, which introduce currency implications.

Price sensitivity

So far, the intra-contract spreads detailed in the previous sections that consist of one future spread against another, or others within the same contract, have been quite simple to construct. Apart from gauging the risk associated with the spread and directional influences, the ratios of these spreads has always been 1:1 since the price sensitivities for each component future have always been the same, as have the currencies. The *price sensitivity* is defined as how the prices of all the component instruments move in relation to a change in yield or underlying interest rate. It is important to equalise this price sensitivity between products as well as ensure that the terms of the products are similar and that currency influences are negated.

By their very nature of being different products, inter-contract spreads are bound to be more volatile and complex than intra-contract spreads. They also require multi-exchange connectivity and involve increased leg risk and higher margin requirements than intra-contract spreads. Furthermore, a degree of numerical process is required in order to work out the hedge ratios. This is the proportion in which the two contracts are spread against each other. However, in return, inter-contract spreads can offer a multitude of trading opportunities, not least being the lack of obvious competition relative to intra-contract spreads.

There are three main types of inter-contract spread:

1. bond futures against STIR futures

2. swap futures against STIR futures

3. STIR futures against STIR futures

The first two involves the spreading of bond and swap futures against strips of STIR futures and involves some calculation of hedge ratios and understanding of the risk factors. The third, whilst easier to construct, introduces the elements of currency and economic risk.

Spreading bond futures against STIR futures first requires an understanding of the characteristics of bonds and notes. This is because bond futures are not cash settled but settled by delivery of cash bonds. Consequently, bond futures are priced and gain their sensitivities from the underlying cash bonds.

Introduction to bonds

Bonds and notes are different products compared to STIR futures. They are interest-paying products typically issued by a government as a process of public sector borrowing. Notes usually refer to maturities around two years to ten years and bonds for maturities beyond that.

The most popular bonds and notes to be spread against STIR futures are:

- **US treasury notes and bond futures** spread against Eurodollar bundles and packs. They are issued by the United States Treasury Department in different maturities, ranging from 3 months to 30 years. The most popular ones for inter-contract spreading are the 2-year and 5-year notes. The treasury note futures traded on CBOT are popular products to spread against Eurodollar.

- **German bonds** are considered as European benchmarks, given Germany's status as the largest European economy. The German Federal Treasury issues notes (Bundesschatzanweisungen) for maturities to two years, obligations (Bundesobligationen) to five years and Bunds to ten and thirty years (Bundesanleihen). The Schatz and Bobl futures traded on Eurex are popular products to spread against Euribor.

Bond pricing

A bond or note may look a bit like this in a newspaper:

```
€100 5% 2010
```

The €100 is the *par value* (also known as the *nominal value*). It is the amount that the investor will receive when the bond matures, in this case in 2010. The amount that the investor paid for the bond in the first place might amount to more or less than the par value – this is dependent on the amount of interest the bond pays, otherwise known as the coupon rate. The coupon in this example is 5% and it is the amount of interest that the investor will receive expressed as a percentage of the par value. For example, if a bond has a par value of €100 and a coupon rate of 5%, the investor holding the bond will receive €5 a year and this interest will be paid either quarterly, semi-annually, or annually, depending on the terms of the bond. If interest rates were around 5% at the time of purchase, then an investor might expect to pay around €100 for €100 of bond paying 5% of interest a year. The yield on the bond would be similar to that available elsewhere and so a payment of €100 paying €5 per annum and returning the capital in five years is fair value. However, if interest rates were 6% instead of 5%, the investor would not want to pay so much for €100 of bond if that only returned 5%. Given that the coupon rate of the bond is fixed at 5% for its maturity, they would instead purchase €100 for less than the par value and exchange a lower income for a capital gain from the difference between the price paid and the par value redeemed at maturity. The price paid for the bond would be set so that the yield of the bond matched the interest rate of 6%.

The price of a bond[19] is determined by the net present value of the bond's cash flows (its interest payments) and can be expressed as:

$$P = \frac{C}{(1+r)} + \frac{C}{(1+r)^2} + \ldots + \frac{C}{(1+r)^n} + \frac{M}{(1+r)^n}$$

where,

P = Bond Price
C = coupon payment
n = number of payments
r = interest rate or required yield
M = Par value

Bond calculations

Fortunately, this does not need to be calculated manually since computer spreadsheets such as Excel[20] contain a bond pricing formula that assumes regular periods between cash flows. Bond calculators are also available online (see www.investopedia.com/calculator). In Excel the formula is contained within **Function** found under the **Insert** tab (the formula is shown in the **help** button). Within **Function,** select **Financial** and then **PRICE.** This is the bond pricing function and will require certain variables.

Using the variables of:

- start (settlement) date: 7 Dec 2005
- maturity date 5 years later: 11 Nov 2010
- coupon: 5%
- required yield: 6%
- coupons paid annually
- day count: actual/360

results in a bond price of 95.83[21].

---

[19] Coupon paid annually

[20] Excel 2002 onwards

[21] =PRICE(date - settlement, date - maturity, 5%,6%,100,1,2) where date - settlement is expressed as DATE(2005,12,7) and date - maturity is expressed as DATE(2010,11,11)

This price of €95.83 is what the investor would be willing to pay for a bond returning €100 in five year's time paying a coupon of 5% (or €5 per €100 per annum) when interest rates were 6%. The gain on maturity of €4.17 is compensation for accepting a lower interest payment than is otherwise available in the markets.

Bond prices are quoted on a *clean basis* – that is without including interest due from the date of the previous coupon. Once this accrued interest is added to the clean price, the price is then termed *dirty*.

Price sensitivity to interest rate movements

It will be intuitive that, in the same way as STIR futures prices, a bond's price will fall as interest rates or yields rise, and conversely its price will rise as interest rates fall. They will both react the same way to movements in the underlying interest rates.

The next question is: by how much?

If interest rates were to move 1% (100 basis points), how much would both bonds and STIR futures move? With STIR futures, it's easy. One tick equals one basis point and so a movement of 100 basis points or 1% (0.01) in the underlying interest rates will move the STIR futures by 100 ticks. This can be given a monetary value by:

```
Notional value x no of basis points x 90/360
```

Or in the case of Euribor:

```
1,000,000 x 0.01 x 90/360 = €2,500
```

Reducing this movement to 1 basis point (0.0001) would give:

```
1,000,000 x 0.0001 x 90/360 = €25
```

which is known as the *basis point value* (BPV) or, in the United States, as the *dollar value of an 01* (DV01).

Modified duration

Bonds use a price sensitivity measure called *modified duration* to calculate the price sensitivity to a 1% movement in underlying yield. It is literally a modified version of the measure of *Macaulay duration* (named after its creator, Frederick Macaulay).

Macaulay duration expresses, in years, how long it takes for the price of a bond to be repaid by its internal cash flows and as such is a reflection of the bond's volatility. Generally, a bond with a higher duration figure will be more volatile, and a higher duration is caused by the lower the coupon rate, the lower the yield and the longer to maturity. Macaulay duration is derived from the weighted average term to maturity of the cash flows from a bond and this term figure doesn't easily compare as a risk measurement against other instruments. A measure of a bond's price sensitivity expressed in years cannot be directly compared with the price sensitivity of a STIR future. However, by modification, it can be adjusted to express the change in price with respect to a change in interest rates.

Modified duration is the modified version of Macaulay duration. It is expressed as:

$$\text{Modified duration} = \left(\frac{\text{Macaulay duration}}{1 + \left(\frac{\text{Bond yield}}{\text{number of coupons per annum}} \right)} \right)$$

Modified duration can be found within Excel's **Function** as **MDURATION**. It takes the same variables as before and returns a modified duration figure of 4.20 for the bond example above. This figure of 4.20 reflects the projected price change given a 1% movement in interest rates either up or down, It is used to adjust modified duration figures when large interest rate moves are considered. However, for small incremental moves of a basis point or so (0.01 of 1%), it is not really necessary. Instead, the modified duration figure can be again modified to reflect the effect of a basis point move on the bond price. This is the *basis point value* (BPV) of the bond and is expressed as:

$$\text{BPV} = \text{modified duration x dirty price x } 0.0001$$

Where the dirty price is the clean price quoted in the market with interest accrued from the last coupon date. Accrued interest can be calculated in Excel using **ACCRINT**.

The BPV of the bond example, with rates at 6% is 0.0405, meaning that if rates were to increase to 6.01%, the €100 of bond could be expected to drop by €0.0405, and if it fell to 5.99%, the €100 of bond would rise by €0.0405.

This can be verified by re-pricing the bond with the formula used earlier with an interest rate difference of 10 basis points. This change of 10 basis points is a more suitable reflection of a typical yield move on a spread between a bond and STIR futures. With the BPV of 0.0405, it would be expected that the bond should fall by €0.405 (10 x 0.0405). By changing the rate to 6.10%, the bond price falls to 95.42 from 95.83; a change of €0.41 and decreasing the rate to 5.90% increases the bond price to 96.23; a change of €0.41.

Convexity

The small difference of €0.005 between the actual change and the change predicted by the BPV is due to convexity. *Convexity* is due to the relationship between a bond's price and yield and the way duration uses it. As shown in Chart 3.6, the price/yield relationship is curved in a convex shape, caused by the effects of compounding cash flows within the bond pricing methodology.

Chart 3.6: Bond convexity at a given price and yield point

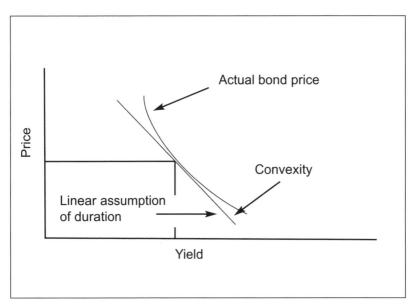

In contrast, the duration calculation presumes a linear relationship as shown in the chart and the difference between this and the curvature is the convexity. Using modified duration for large changes in yield changes will tend to underestimate the price of the bond and it is common practice to adjust it by the convexity value.

Determining the hedge ratio

The calculation of BPV provides a comparable measure of price sensitivity for bonds and it is now possible to determine by how much both a bond and a STIR future will change in relation to a change in interest rates. A hedge ratio can be determined from the BPV of the STIR futures and the bond.

Earlier, the BPV of a Euribor future was shown to be €25, and the BPV of the bond described above is €0.04 per €100. If €1,000,000 of the bond were purchased, the BPV of the position would be

$$\frac{€1,000,000}{€100} \times 0.04 = €400$$

In order to determine how many Euribor futures would be need to purchased, the BPV of the bond position is divided by the BPV of the Euribor making:

$$\frac{€400}{€25} = 16$$

Sixteen Euribor futures would be required to hedge €1,000,000 of the bond used in the examples. However, this is a hedge for a cash bond and since the majority of inter-contract spreads are between futures contracts, it is necessary to look at bond futures.

Introduction to bond futures

Bond futures are different to cash bonds in that they are a derivative based on notional characteristics.

For example, the 2-year Treasury note future is traded electronically by the Chicago Board of Trade (CBOT) and is deliverable and based on a notional 2-year note with a 6% coupon. It is 'deliverable' meaning a bond needs to be delivered against an expired future, and it is 'notional' because it is unlikely that any issued cash bond used for delivery will match the futures characteristics. The coupons are likely to be different and the maturities unlikely to match. Instead, the future is based upon a deliverable basket of cash bonds, determined by the exchange. These bonds will fulfil certain criteria; in the case of the deliverable bonds for the 2-year Treasury note futures, these must have an

original maturity of not more than 5 years and 3 months and a remaining maturity of not less than 1 year and 9 months from the first day of the delivery month but not more than 2 years

Source: CBOT

Eurex quotes a remaining lifespan on its deliverable bonds. In the case of the 2 year Schatz, this would be 1.75 to 2.25 years and 4.5 to 5.5 years for the Bobl. The exchange equates the coupon of the future with those of the deliverable basket of cash bonds by use of a conversion factor, again determined by the exchange.

On expiry of the futures contract, which are traded on a three-month March, June, September and December cycle (but the front month is usually the most liquid), the deliverer is faced with a choice of bonds to deliver. These deliverable bonds have been determined in advance by the futures exchange and any will be suitable as a proxy for the future. However, in most cases, one bond within the deliverable basket will have a combination of factors, such as maturity date, coupon, coupon payment date, and price, that will make it cheaper to deliver than any of the others. That bond is called the *Cheapest to Deliver* (CTD) and it is from this bond that the future's price sensitivities are calculated in order to determine the hedge ratios for use against other futures.

There are two processes for calculating which bond is the CTD[22].

1. Basis

There are two types of basis. The *gross basis* of a deliverable bond is the cash price of the bond minus the futures price, equated to the bond by the conversion factor. It is expressed as:

```
gross basis = bond price - (futures price x conversion factor)
```

The gross basis is used by Hull[23] to determine the cheapest to deliver bond. The bond with the lowest gross basis will be the cheapest to deliver. However, this method is basic and does not take into account the effect of accrued interest or the cost of carry.

---

[22] See *The Treasury Bond Basis* by Galen Burghardt et al or *The Futures Bond Basis* by Moorad Choudray, for more information.

[23] *Options Futures and other Derivatives*, John C Hull, Prentice Hall.

Bonds are quoted clean without interest added from the date of the last coupon and this has to be added to the bonds price to provide an overall purchase price. This price is called the dirty price. The cost of carry is the difference between financing a bond position and the coupon earned whilst holding it. When the gross basis is adjusted for these variables, it is called the *net basis* and the bond with the lowest net basis will be the CTD.

2. Implied repo rate

The implied repurchase rate is a measure of return from the net basis. It is the rate of return from financing the bond in return for its cash flows over a given period and this period is equated to that of the delivery for the bond future. It will be the opposite of net basis so that the bond with the highest IRR will be the CTD.

Although both methods are satisfactory for determining the CTD, the IRR is popular amongst financial software vendors. Subscribers to these services will find the IRR easy to compute but it is not difficult to calculate it oneself in Excel. Several of the parameters are supplied by the exchanges and price information can be found on the web.

The IRR is calculated by:

$$IRR = \left(\left(\frac{(\text{Futures price x CF}) + \text{accrued interest from last coupon date to delivery}}{\text{Price of bond} + \text{accrued interest from last coupon until settlement date}} \right) - 1 \right) \times \frac{360}{n}$$

```
where n is the difference between the settlement date and the
delivery date and CF is the conversion factor
```

First the following parameters need to found:

The list of deliverable bonds and their respective conversion factors:

These are published publicly by the exchanges and can be found on their websites. In the case of US Treasuries this will be the CBOT (www.cbot.com) and for German bonds, EUREX (www.eurexchange.com). The list of deliverable bonds and their conversion factors will be related to a futures contract, such as the 2-year or 5-year, and its delivery cycle.

Delivery dates

Again, these can be found from the exchange websites, usually under the futures contract specifications. Generally, German bonds deliver on the tenth day of the delivery month (so that would be 10 Mar 2006 for the H6 contract) and US bond deliver on the last day of the delivery month.

Coupon rates and last coupon dates

These can be determined from the bond information in the list of deliverable bonds. The coupon should be obvious and the clue to the last coupon date lies in the bond's maturity. A deliverable bond for the CBOT 2-year Treasury note will appear like this:

```
4 % 30/9/2007 0.9672
```

The coupon is 4% and the conversion factor is 0.9672. The bond matures on 30 Sep 2007 and since it is a US bond, it pays its coupons semi annually. One coupon will be on 30 September each year and the other will be six months away, on 30 March. German bonds are even easier in that they only pay one coupon per annum and that will be paid on the maturity day of each year.

Bond and future prices

The futures prices are usually easily found on an exchanges website but the cash bonds are a little trickier to find on the web. For the IRR calculations in table 3.14, the US bond price information was found at Yahoo Finance[24] and the German bond prices were found on the website of Xetra, the electronic platform of Deutsche Börse[25].

---

[24] http://screen.yahoo.com/bonds.html

[25] http://deutsche-boerse.com > trading and clearing > xetra > tradable instruments > classify by instrument groups > BOND. Find the issue and put its code into the quote function.

Using the above sources we can find the parameters for the for the 2-year Treasury note; 4% 30/9/2007, which is a deliverable bond for the CBOT 2-year Treasury note Future (Z5).

Coupon	4%
Bond price (decimalised)	99.375
Futures price (decimalised)	102.71875
Conversion factor	0.9672
Date of last coupon	30/9/05
Delivery date	30/12/05
Settlement date	15/12/05

Substituting these values into the IRR calculation gives:

$$IRR= \left(\left(\frac{(102.71875 \times 0.9672) + 1.00}{99.375 + 0.8333} \right) -1 \right) \times \frac{360}{15} = 3.38\%$$

The accrued interest is calculated using Excel's ACCRINT function. (The parameters are the same except 'issue' is made the same as First_interest (last coupon date)).

However, until the IRR for all the eligible deliverable bonds are calculated, it is not known whether this bond has the highest IRR, and so CTD status. Table 3.14 shows the IRRs for all bonds within the 2-year deliverable baskets for both US and German markets. The bonds with the highest IRR are the CTD.

Table 3.14: IRR for deliverable bonds for US and German 2-year bonds as at 15/12/05

US Treasury 2 year deliverable basket (Z5)						
Bond	Last coupon	Conversion factor	Bond price	Futures price (CBOT T-note Z5)	IRR (%)	Gross Basis
3% 15/11/07	15/11/05	0.9464	97.531	102.71875	-4.73	0.3179
4% 30/9/07	30/9/05	0.9672	99.375		3.383	0.0254
4.25% 31/10/07	31/10/05	0.9700	99.777		0.892	0.1398
4.25% 30/11/07	30/11/05	0.9687	99.801		-2.877	0.2973
German Schatz 2 year deliverable basket (H6)						
Bond	Last coupon	Conversion factor	Bond price	Futures price (Eurex Schatz H6)	IRR (%)	
3% 11/4/08	11/4/05	0.942660	100.65	105.475	-2.122	1.2293
5.25% 4/1/08	4/1/05	0.987187	104.98		1.4758	0.8564
4.25% 15/2/08	15/2/05	0.968798	103.15		0.1486	0.9660
2.75% 14/12/07	14/12/05	0.946935	99.97		2.360	0.0920

It is apparent that the 2.75% 14/12/07 German 2-year bond is clearly the CTD for the Eurex H6 Schatz future, whereas the US 4% 30/9/07 2-year Treasury note is the CTD for the CBOT Z5 Treasury note future.

Both bonds also have the lowest gross basis as well as the highest IRR to reinforce their status as CTD. It can be observed that the US bonds for Z5 delivery have a much lower gross basis than the German bonds for H6 delivery reflecting the differences in time to delivery.

CTD status does not change frequently

Once calculated, the IRR does not need to be recalculated too often since although the CTD status of a bond can change, it is fairly infrequent. However, traders need to be aware of auction schedules[26] since a thinly populated basket of deliverable bonds might be augmented by new stock and hence the possibility of a new CTD. It is also important when two bonds have similar IRRs and so might switch status as CTD. Even so, the price sensitivities of two bonds with similar IRRs are likely to be

---

[26] Auction schedules: For US bonds see www.ustreas.gov and for German bonds: www.bundesbank.de

highly similar. It's not picking the absolute correct bond for delivery that is the objective but rather to establish the price sensitivities to spread against STIR futures.

The hedge ratio for the cash bond against a STIR future was established earlier. Now a proxy for the bond future has been found in the form of the CTD cash bond, it's relatively straightforward to calculate the ratio, but there are two main differences.

1. Bond futures are standardised contracts and so are quoted in standardised quantities. These quantities are quoted as part of the futures contract specifications. They are usually in denominations of 100,000, except for the US 2-year Treasury note futures, which is $200,000.

2, In order to equate the CTD bond with the future, its BPV, once calculated, must be divided by its conversion factor.

To calculate the hedge ratio between the CBOT 2-year Treasury note future and the CME Eurodollar requires the BPV of the CTD bond: 4% 30/9/07. Using the methodology above, this would be calculated as:

BPV = modified duration x dirty price x 0.0001

```
1.70 x (99.375+0.8333) x 0.0001 = 0.017/100 = 0.000170
```

(Note that the BPV figure of 0.017 is per $100 nominal and so needs to be divided by 100 to represent a value per $1)

This is calculated to be 0.000170. For a 2-year Treasury note future with a quantity of $200,000 the overall BPV would be:

```
200,000 x (0.000170/0.9672) = $35.14
```

This is divided by the BPV of a Eurodollar contract, which is $25.to give the hedge ratio of:

```
35.14 = 1.40
-----
  25
```

This figure of 1.40 is the ratio of how many Eurodollar contracts would be needed to offset a 2-year Treasury note future position. 140 Eurodollar futures would hedge a position of 100 2-year Treasury note futures.

The ratio for the Eurex Schatz future would be calculated in the same way but only using a nominal quantity of €100,000. The CTD is 2.75% 14/12/07 and the BPV is calculated to be 0.000192:

and the BPV of the futures is calculated as:

```
100,000 x (0.000192/0.946935) = €20.27
```

This is divided by the BPV of a Euribor contract, which is €25 to give the hedge ratio of:

$$\frac{20.27}{25} = 0.810$$

This figure of 0.810 is the ratio of how many Euribor contracts would be needed to offset a Eurex Schatz future position. 81 Euribor futures would hedge a position of 100 Eurex Schatz futures.

Spreading STIR futures strips against bond futures

Term spreads

The quarterly delivery cycles of STIR futures have long been used as building blocks to hedge the cash flows of bonds. Bonds of certain duration could be matched by a corresponding STIR futures strip of a similar term, giving rise to the generic name, the *term spread*. Term spreads originated from the TED spread, popular in the 1980s. This was a trade between the Treasury bill market and Eurodollar futures strip and was a finely engineered trade matching the cash flows between a treasury bill and a fully articulated STIR future strip. (The "T" came from the Treasury bill and "ED" is the symbol for the Eurodollar.) However, the short-term Treasury note market and the CBOT Treasury note futures have largely surpassed the use of Treasury bills, and although this trade still exists in a pure form, the spread is now commonly traded by using exchange traded bundles, packs and stacks.

Popular versions of the spread are the two-year term spread. This is between a 2-year bond future and 2-year STIR future bundle and the 5-year term spread between 5-year bonds and 5-year STIR future bundles. The bundles can be replaced by variations of packs or stacks in return for an acceptance of higher (curve) risk.

Bond future	Bundle	Pack	Stacks
CBOT 2-Year Treasury note	CME Eurodollar 2-year bundle	CME Eurodollar packs	CME Eurodollar futures
CBOT 5-Year Treasury note	CME Eurodollar 5-year bundle	CME Eurodollar packs	CME Eurodollar futures
EUREX 2-Year Schatz	LIFFE Euribor 2-year bundle	LIFFE Euribor packs	LIFFE Euribor futures
EUREX 5-Year Bobl	LIFFE Euribor 5-year bundle	LIFFE Euribor packs	LIFFE Euribor futures

Term spreads are multi faceted and have many moving parts. They are riskier trades than intra-contract spreads and the combinations of the different kinds of inherent risk can add up to amounts that would be unpalatable to an intra-contract trader. However, in return there can be more short-term opportunities, but it is important to understand the mechanics of these spreads and where the movement in the spread is originating.

The mechanics and risks of spreading bonds futures against STIR futures can be categorised into four areas.

1. credit spread,

2. yield curve risk,

3. interest rate volatility component, and

4. stub risk.

Credit spread

It is important to understand that term spreads are essentially credit spreads, since they are spreads between assets of different credit class. Government bonds such as the US Treasurys or German Schatz and Bobls have the highest credit rating and lowest credit risk of any class of security. This is because they are issued and guaranteed by the treasuries of national governments. In contrast, STIR futures, such as Eurodollars and Euribor, are based on the inter-bank market. Whilst this market still commands a high credit rating, the deposits are backed by commercial organisations and subject to the possibility of failure and default. The failure of a major financial organisation is relatively uncommon, but it is not unknown. The Continental Illinois National Bank and Trust crisis of 1984 is cited as a prime example and consequently set new standards for global banking supervision and regulation. Shocks to the banking system can also be indirect. The failure of the over-leveraged hedge fund LTCM in 1998 threatened the banking system, not as direct participant but as a counterparty to trades held by the banks. Although the chance of bank failure is low, it is always a statistical possibility and so is reflected in the spread between treasury instruments and STIR futures. This spread is also subject to event risk such as September 11, or systemic risk factors such as the Asian financial crisis (1997). In fact, it is vulnerable to anything that might cause a flight to quality, as investors find the safest home for their money, notably the debt of large economic nations such as the United States of America or Europe.

This credit spread that exists within the term spread between the bond and STIR futures is derived from the primary market measure of credit risk; namely the spread between the benchmark treasury bond and the swaps market. The bond markets are supplied by new issuance from the treasury and the amount and frequency of issuance is governed by treasury funding requirements driven by government policy. Typically, an auction schedule is published in advance of issuance, and an ongoing process of bond auction to primary dealers creates a turnover of bonds where one issue is replaced by a more recent issue of the same maturity. The new issue becomes the *on-the-run* benchmark issue whilst the previous becomes an *off-the-run*. Since the new benchmark is usually the most liquid tradable bond within its maturity, its yield is taken as being the representative for that segment of the market. By comparison, the off-the-run has usually been purchased and now held as part of the portfolio of institutional investors and its yield will generally be slightly higher than the benchmark reflecting the difference in liquidity. The other side of the credit spread is the interest rate swap rate and this is the market representation of inter-bank risk. It is a liquid over the counter market with maturities between two and fifty years.

Chart 3.7 shows the relationship between the yields on the European 2 year swap rate and the 2-year benchmark bond during 2005. Their yields are shown on the left axis and it can be seen that the two track each other very closely, having a correlation of 0.995. The difference in between is effectively the credit spread between the two asset classes, and is shown by the swap/benchmark bond spread on the right axis.

Chart 3.7: European 2 year interest rate swap and benchmark yields and their spread

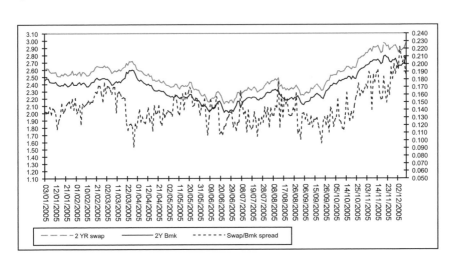

Source: Reuters 3000 xtra

It is this spread, between the interest rate swap and the benchmark, that the term spread between the bond and STIR futures will replicate. The chart shows the 2-year instruments and resulting spread, but there will be a similar relationship for the 5 year and 10-year term spreads. These will be more volatile since their durations will be higher.

The term spread can also be displayed in a similar way and its relationship to the swap/benchmark spread compared. Finding the yield for the cheapest to deliver bond to represent the future is straightforward, but finding the equivalent yield for the futures is a bit more complex. Initially, an equal term needs to be found. This can be either finely articulated by using an appropriate number of futures contracts or, if using bundles, the 2-year Euribor bundle will compare to 2-year Schatz bond future. A 5-year bond future would be matched by a 5-year bundle. The 2-year bundle consists of eight futures displayed in price format each one indicating a forward yield for their respective period. Then the entire sequence of futures needs to be converted into one yield in order to display its characteristics relative to the bond future. There are several ways of doing this, some considerably more technical than others. A simple method to calculate the futures strip yield can be expressed as:

$$\left(\left(\begin{array}{l}(1+((r \times t/360) \times (1+((f_1 \times t/360) \times \\ (1+((f_2 \times t/360)... \times (1+((f_n \times t/360)\end{array}\right) -1\right) \frac{360}{\sum t}$$

where,

t is the time to the next futures expiry
f is the sequential futures expressed as a rate (100 - futures price)
r is money market rate for the stub period to the expiry of the first future

The strip yield for the Euribor 2-year bundle can be calculated with prices taken from 20 Dec 2005. A period of 83 days and a 3-month Euribor rate of 2.47% need to be used to cover the period from 20 Dec 2005 to the expiry of the first futures contract on 13 Mar 2006. This is called the *stub period*.

Table 3.15: Futures prices used to calculate their rates and the day count methodology and calculation steps

STIR	Price(P)	Rate (100-P)	Days (t)	(1+((r x t /360)	(1+((f$_1$ x t /360)
STUB		0.02470	83	1.005695	
H6	97.290	0.02710	91		1.006850
M6	97.100	0.02900	91		1.007331
U6	97.005	0.02995	91		1.007571
Z6	96.945	0.03055	91		1.007722
H7	96.925	0.03075	91		1.007773
M7	96.895	0.03105	91		1.007849
U7	96.875	0.03125	91		1.007899
Z7	96.840	0.03160	91		1.007988
			360/ $\sum$t	**0.44389**	**x**	**0.0686856**
				=	**Strip Yield**	**0.03049**

Populating the equation results in a strip yield of 0.03049 or 3.049%:

```
(( (1+((0.02470 x 83/360)  x  (1+((0.02710 x 91/360)  x         )  )
   (1+((0.02900 x 91/360)  x  (1+((0.02955 x 91/360)  x         )  )          360
   (1+((0.03055 x 91/360)  x  (1+((0.03075 x 91/360)  x    )-1   )      _____
   (1+((0.03105 x 91/360)  x  (1+((0.03125 x 91/360)  x         )  )    (83+91+91+91+
   (1+((0.03160 x 91/360)                                        )  )    91+91+91+91+91)
```

```
= 0.03049 or 3.049%
```

Calculating the term spread

The futures strip yield can be used to find the term spread value. Using the following data from 20 Dec 2005:

Euribor 2 yr bundle yield	3.049%
CTD yield	2.832%
2 yr swap	2.993%
Benchmark yield	2.813%

Source: Reuters

The 2-year term spread can be calculated as:

```
2 yr Euribor term spread = 3.049 - 2.832 = 21.7 basis points
```

This can be directly compared to the swap benchmark spread

```
2 year interest rate swap/ benchmark spread = 2.993 - 2.813 =
18.0 basis points
```

This method of calculating the strip has three disadvantages when used to compare with the yield on the CTD bond:

1. It is the yield on a futures strip, in this case a 2-year bundle. This does not necessarily match the maturity of the CTD bond, making a true comparison and calculation of the term spread difficult. The bundle has a maturity of 15 Mar 2008 (the Z7 contract is a 3-month forward rate starting on the December expiry) compared to 14 Dec 2007, and this difference of approximately three months will cause the bundle yield to be higher than the CTD bond yield, making it a source of curve risk.

2. The futures strip is calculated in an annualised money market convention. This is not so much of a problem for European products, where bonds are also quoted on a annualised yield (they pay only one coupon per annum) but US strip yield will need to be converted to a semi-annual bond equivalent (US bonds pay coupons semi-annually) for a true comparison.

3. The strip yield method applies an equal weighting to each quarterly rate, implied by the futures price. In comparison, bond future cash flows are effectively weighted since the nearer dated cash flows benefit from the effects of reinvestment. This means that the nearer dated coupon payments of bonds are more important than further dated ones and, in order to truly compare a strip yield to the a bond yield, a method of weighting the cash flows of the futures strip is necessary.

Yield curve risk

The strip yield method of calculating the strip yield has the inherent disadvantages of having maturity mismatches and using equally weighted cash flows. It might be tempting to adjust the maturity of the strip by changing the amount of futures in the strip. For example, using just seven futures by ignoring the Z7 contract would almost match maturities (the futures strip then being 21 Dec 2007 and the CTD bond being 14 Dec 2007). However, although this would return a yield of 3.011% and a more accurate term spread of 18 basis points, it would mean that using a bundle in the term spread would not be possible.

Also, it would still be applying an equal weighting to each quarterly rate and cash flow of the strip/bundle, in contrast to the cash flows produced by the CTD bond, which effectively weight the nearer dated cash flows more than the further dated ones since these can benefit from the effects of reinvestment. This difference in cash flow weighting means that curve steepening or flattening might have little effect on the STIR future strip yield, but will have an effect on the yield of the coupon paying CTD. This could create a situation where, if the yield curve were changing shape but the average rate remained the same, the STIR future strip yield could remain unchanged whilst the CTD yield changed, resulting in a net change to the spread not necessarily mirrored by the swap/benchmark spread. By applying a weighting effect to the cash flows of the futures strip yield, this curve risk effect can be almost eliminated, leaving the term spread a better reflection of the credit spread.

There are several methods that weight the strip yield and effectively remove the curve risk. Two of these were devised by Galen Burghardt[27], whose book is regarded as the seminal text for term spreads and should be considered required reading for aspiring term spread traders.

---

[27] The Eurodollar Futures and Options Handbook by Galen Burghardt – McGraw Hill

Calculating the strip yield – Method 1

The first method calculates the strip yield by constructing a notional coupon-paying bond with the same characteristics as the CTD bond, but using the rates from the STIR futures strip to generate its price. This will effectively price an identical bond to the CTD, but based on the credit rating of the futures strip. The difference in yield between this notional bond and the actual CTD will be the term spread, and by expressing the futures strip as a coupon-paying instrument, it is more likely to respond to movements in the yield curve in a similar fashion to the CTD. Consequently, the spread between them is more representative of the credit spread and not unduly influenced by the changing shape of the curve. The weighted version of the above example returns a strip yield of 3.016 %, as calculated in table 3.16.

Table 3.16: Weighted yield of a synthetic bond priced from the Euribor futures strip to match the CTD, 2.75% 14/12/07

A	B	C	D	E	F	G
Days (t)	$1+(r \times t /360)$	Coupon dates	$1+(f_1 \times t /360)$	Value of €1 $(D \times D_n)$	Cashflow (coupon 2.75%)	Discounted cash flows (F/E)
83	1.005695		*1.005695*	1.005695		
91			1.006850	1.012584		
91			1.007331	1.020007		
91			1.007571	1.027729		
3		**14/12/06**	**?**	**1.0279906**	**2.75**	**2.675**
91			1.007722	1.035665		
91			1.007773	1.043716		
91			1.007849	1.051907		
91			1.007899	1.060217		
1		**14/12/07**	**?**	**1.0605890**	**102.75**	**96.88**
91			1.007988	1.068686		
					Bond price (ΣG)	**99.555**
					Accrued Int.	**0.0611**
					Clean Price	**99.494**
					Bond Yield	**0.03016**

Notes on the table:

- t is the time to the next period

  f is the sequential futures expressed as a rate (100 - futures price)

  r is money market rate for the stub period to the expiry of the first future.

- **Column A**

  The day count from the settlement date of 20 Dec 2005. The first period of 83 days covers the period from the settlement date to the expiry of the first future, which will be the front month H6 contract. Since there is no future to cover that period (the Z5 having expired the day before), this *stub* period is covered by a 3-month Euribor money market rate.

- **Column B**

  Shows the value of €1 after 83 days using the stub rate of 2.47%. The following periods of 91 days are the intervals between each successive futures contract. However, the coupon payable on 14 Dec 2006, as shown in column C, falls just beyond one of these intervals by 3 days and this is the day for which further computations need to be made. The same process continues for the following year to the expiry of the bond on 14 Dec 2007.

- **Column D**

  Is the value of €1, invested on 20 Dec 2005, at its respective day count. The first value is simply the stub rate value from column B. The stub rate is already expressed in rate form and so its calculation differs from that of the futures since they need to be converted to an interest rate by subtracting from 100.

- **Column E**

  Is the compounded effect of all these cash flows, since moneys received after each period will be reinvested at a new rate implied by the STIR futures quarterly delivery cycle. The missing values in columns D and E representing the coupon dates can be found by linear interpolation or simple averaging. More sophisticated methods of interpolation can be employed but generally, the above method will suffice.

- **Column F**

  From these values, the bonds cash flows shown in column F can be discounted to their net present values in G. The sum of these values will be the price of the notional bond but it will be its dirty price, including accrued interest. Since yields are calculated from clean prices, the accrued interest (calculated by the ACCRINT function) needs to be deducted and from this price the yield can be found using the YIELD function in Excel. The yield of 3.016% will be the implied Euribor strip yield and subtracting the CTD yield of 2.832% will return a term spread of 18.4 basis points.

Calculating the strip yield – Method 2

The second method is a variation on the first by using a fixed spread method. It adjusts the rates implied by the STIR futures by a uniform fixed amount until the clean price of the bond is equal to that of the CTD and the fixed spread will be the term spread value. In practice, this would involve adapting the f value in column D to incorporate this incremental increase so that the calculation would be:

```
(1+(((f₁ - s) x t/360)
```

```
where s is the uniform fixed rate.
```

A process of iteration or trial and error is used to find the fixed amount that creates a bond price that most closely matches that of the CTD. A value of $s = 18.3$ is returned for the above example and this value will be the term spread.

Both these methods will be a more accurate representation of the pure credit qualities of the term spread but in order to truly capture the credit spread, the term spread will require the amounts of STIR futures in the strip to be weighted in quantity to truly reflect the cash flows of the notional bond, which effectively rules out the use of bundles and packs. Accordingly, some degree of curve risk must be accepted when using these strategies to trade term spreads.

Interest rate volatility risk

It can be seen that the term spread is higher than the swap/benchmark spread and that the STIR futures strip yield is higher than the swap rate, despite them being of equal credit stature. This is due to convexity bias, which is the source of interest rate volatility risk within term spread. The concept of the convexity adjustment to STIR futures prices was introduced earlier, and it is a consequence of the different settlement procedures between STIR futures and forward rates. Futures are settled daily and their profit or loss added or subtracted to or from the margin account, whereas the forward rates are not settled until maturity. This allows the futures to benefit from the compounding effect of reinvestment of the daily cash flows and so the rates implied by the STIR futures will be higher than the underlying forward rates. The effects of convexity are small for term spreads with maturities of 2 years but increase exponentially as the term increases. The convexity bias is sensitive to interest rate volatility meaning that an increase in rates can cause a widening of the term spread whilst a decrease can have the opposite effect.

Stub risk

The weighted term spread uses a money market rate for the stub period between the date of inception and the expiry of the first futures contract. This stub rate can have an influence on the term spread, especially if the period is near to its maximum of three months. It is unlikely that the futures trader will have access to the money markets on professional terms and so they face the choice of using a proxy for the rate or leaving it unhedged. However, unless an accurate proxy is used, an element of outright risk will be introduced into the term spread.

The use of a proxy for the stub period might include a range of futures products available to cover very short-term interest rate exposures. Serial futures months within the STIR futures can be used but are based on forward rates and not deposit rates. Very short term rate futures such as EONIA futures on Euronext.liffe and EUREX and LIBOR futures on CME or 30-day Fed funds futures on CBOT provide the best hedges for stub periods, but liquidity can be a factor.

Special factors that can affect the spread

Change of CTD status

The bond future interest rate sensitivities and the consequent hedge ratios are derived from the CTD bond, which itself is derived from the basket of deliverable bonds. It is advisable to ensure that this deliverable basket is fully populated and that the bond auction schedule will not introduce more eligible bonds of deliverable grade into the delivery basket. If this happens, then it is possible that the CTD status can suddenly change suddenly, creating new hedge ratio characteristics. There is a higher possibility of this happening when a greater period of time to the bonds delivery exists and the trader will need to estimate the possible consequences. It might be that a new CTD bond might not significantly change the hedge characteristics but it can be advisable to model the characteristics of this yet to be auctioned bond and compare its sensitivities to the existing CTD bond. Details of forthcoming bonds are available on government auction schedules and it is realistic to price them in advance using the yields from similar issues. Generally though, as a rule of thumb, if interest rates are below the notional coupon on the future, then the bond with the lowest duration will be the cheapest to deliver. Where bonds have similar durations, the bond with the highest yield will be the CTD.

CTD bond liquidity squeeze

There is also the serious market risk of squeezes in the CTD bond. These occur near to delivery when there might be a shortage of stock of the CTD freely available in the market for purchase to deliver against the future. Fortunately, this is a fairly rare occurrence but it is advisable to check the amount of the bond issue against similar bonds. A particularly small issue might suggest the possibility of squeezes. There is also the possibility of a squeeze due to a deliverable bond becoming 'special'. This is where it is heavily borrowed in the repurchase market thus reducing the amount of stock in the free market available for delivery. Usually, a bond starting to trade expensively against its peers can be indicative of a forthcoming squeeze

The term spread is based on the credit spread inherent in the swap/benchmark spread. This credit spread is affected by event risk, systemic risk or any influence that might cause a monetary flight to quality and security. In this situation, the credit spread will widen and by association so will the term spread. It is important to appreciate that the credit spread is asymmetrical; its upside is potentially unlimited whereas the downside is limited to around zero. It would be almost impossible to imagine a situation where bank rates are given the same credit status as those of government securities and so it would be fair to assume that the credit spread will always have a positive value. This is a consideration for trading term spreads. Going long a term spread involves buying the bond or bond future and selling the STIR future strip against it. Not only does this approach prevent the possibility of a risk scenario of potentially unlimited losses, it also insures against the possibility of squeezes by nature of already being long the bond.

Trading term spreads with packs, bundles and stacks

Using bundles, packs or stacks to trade term spreads against bond futures requires an acceptance of the numerous risks involved in return for easy execution and management. The credit and curve risk elements will be the main drivers of the spread but interest rate volatility risk and stub risk can add to the volatility of the spread. Furthermore, there are the special factors discussed above to watch out for. The cumulative effects of all this risk should not be underestimated, but on the other hand this potential volatility can lead to good trading opportunities.

The choice of bundle, pack or stack

Bundles, packs or stacks can be traded against bond futures as a proxy for the STIR futures strip. All three can be easily executed, the first two as exchange traded strategies, and stacks as outright trades.

Intuitively, bundles should make the best hedge since they will most closely replicate the cash flows and duration of the bond future. However, the correlations in table 3.17 show that the red pack and any stack from Z6 onwards make an equally good proxy. However, note that using shorter term strategies such as packs and stacks involve an acceptance of increased curve risk.

Table 3.17: Correlations between Eurex Schatz Z5 and Euronext.liffe Euribor (21 Sep 2005 to 8 Dec 2005)

Z5	H6	M6	U6	Z6	H7	M7	U7	2-yr bundle	White pack	Red pack
0.9327	0.9704	0.9795	0.9884	0.9937	0.9943	0.9937	0.9930	0.9920	0.9759	0.9944

Indeed, it is only the white contracts and white pack that provide a lesser hedge, but, at approximately 0.97, this is still a good proxy. The only contract to be avoided as a spread against the bond future is the front month since that will tend to lock into cash.

Correlations for the 5-year bond future, the Bobl future, show a similar picture except the white strip, traded as either stacks or as a pack makes a very poor hedge for the Bobl. This effect influences the 2-year bundle, but the Reds, either as stacks or packs, improve to a correlation of approximately 0.93. Any Red pack stack or the 5-year bundle makes the best hedge, but all correlations are lower than for the Schatz as the duration has increased leading to more curve risk and convexity bias.

Table 3.18: Correlations between Eurex Bobl Z5 and Euronext.liffe Euribor (21 Sep 2005 to 8 Dec 2005)

Average white	Average red	Average green	Average blue	5-yr bundle	2-yr bundle	White pack	Red pack	Green pack	Blue pack
0.399	0.930	0.960	0.958	0.953	0.832	0.459	0.932	0.961	0.958

The choice between bundle, pack or stack will be mainly due to preference and acceptance of the different amounts of curve risk. Stacks are easily transacted and have the advantage that their number can be adjusted to provide an easy hedge ratio. However, they are a single point on the yield curve and so will have the highest curve risk. Packs and bundles have less curve risk respectively but can be less easy to transact, hedge and monitor.

Displaying the spread

Buying the spread involves buying the bond future and selling the futures strip.

Selling the spread involves selling the bond futures and buying the futures strip.

Displaying a term spread as the difference between the strip yield and the yield of the CTD bond is useful to compare relatively with the swap/benchmark spread, but rather meaningless when trading the spread between two instruments whose markets prices are presented quite differently. There are several ways to display term spreads, but it is important that the contract price, trade ratio and tick values are incorporated in order for the spread to represent all the variables involved. One method is to present the spread in price format. This incorporates the prices of the relevant instruments, their quantities as determined by the hedge ratio and the respective tick values per basis point.

This is expressed as:

```
(P_bf x T x Q_bf ) - (P_s x T x Q_s)

where,

P_bf  is the price of the bond future
T     is the tick value per basis point
Q_bf  is the number of contracts used
P_s   is the price of the futures strip. This is a simple average
      of the prices used, whether for a bundle, pack or stack.
Q_s   is the quantity of contracts used
```

The quantities are determined by dividing the total BPV of the futures strip by the BPV of the bond future. Given that the BPV of a single Euribor future will always be €25, the BPV of a bundle is simply the number of contracts within that strip multiplied by €25. There are eight contracts within a bundle, so the BPV will be €200 (8 x €25). This figure is divided by the BPV of the Schatz future, say €20, giving a figure of 10. Therefore, one bundle, comprising eight contracts, should be traded against ten Schatz futures.

The same methodology can be used for using packs instead of bundles. A pack will have a BPV of €100 (4 contracts x €25); dividing this by the BPV of the Schatz future (€20) gives a ratio of one pack to five Schatz futures.

Stacks are slightly more flexible in that they can comprise any number of contracts, but the same methodology is used. A stack of, say, 10 Euribor Z6 futures will have a BPV of €250 (10 x €25) and dividing that by the BPV of the Schatz (€20) will result in a hedge of 12.5 Schatz futures.

> ### US bond futures pricing
>
> Note that US bond futures are quoted in fractions, not decimals like European bond futures. It is advantageous to convert the US bond future, such as the Treasury note, into a decimal format to allow direct comparison with a decimalised Eurodollar bundle, pack or stack. This can be done in Excel by using the integer (INT) function as shown by the following formula:
>
> ```
> ((Tnote price-INT(Tnote price))/0.32)+INT(Tnote price)
> ```
>
> The tick value has to be changed accordingly, at present it being $15.625 for a minimum increment of ¼ of 1/32, making a total of $2,000 for a full point movement (4 x $15.625 x 32). Dividing the full point movement of $2,000 by 100 returns a revised tick value based on 1 basis point (0.01) which in this case is $20 ($2,000/100). The decimalised price and revised tick value can then be used in the price display formula as shown above for price spreads using Treasury notes against Eurodollars

Rounding

This raises the issue of rounding. Should the trader use 12 or 13 contracts? It's not a problem for stacks, since the number of contracts within the stack can easily be changed to eliminate the fraction, but bundles and packs with fixed numbers of contracts will require a rounding decision. This is potentially a source of slippage in the hedge ratio and will add to the overall risk profile of the spread.

A pricing example

Given the following prices as at 28 Oct 2005, the average of the eight contracts of the 2-year bundle is 97.2281.

Euribor	Z5	H6	M6	U6	Z6	H7	M7	U7	Average
	97.630	97.460	97.320	97.220	97.125	97.075	97.020	96.975	97.2281

The Schatz Z5 future is 105.70 and the hedge ratio is calculated as 10 Schatz futures per bundle (8 contracts). The spread is then calculated as:

```
(105.70 x 10 x 10) - (97.2281 x 25 x 8) = -8,875.625
```

Although the value of the spread is large, it has the benefit of behaving like an intra-contract spread An increase in the value of the spread will lead to a profit for a long spread position – that is a long position in the bond and a short position in the strip, and vice versa. Furthermore, the difference between the purchase and sale price of the spread will indicate the overall profit of loss on the trade.

Trading example 1

28 Oct 2005

Chart 3.8 (this is a shorter time period version of Chart 3.7 shows the rising trend of the swap benchmark spread and the correlated price spread (0.74), driven by increasing swap and bond prices against an economic outlook suggesting higher interest rate rises. However, movements in one spread are not exactly mirrored in the other. There are the known risks of credit, curve, stub and convexity to consider, as well as vagaries in the data between the four instruments involved in the graphical display. Different settlement times, use of bids, offer or mid prices and data errors can all affect the display properties of these spreads.

Chart 3.8: Euribor term spread (2 year bundle) compared to swap benchmark spread

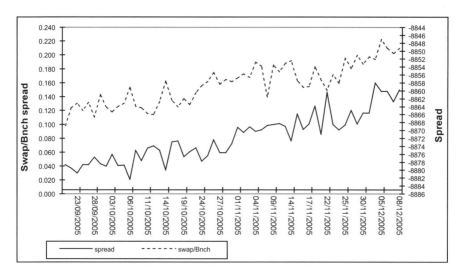

A sharp rally in the swap/benchmark spread from 24 October was partially reversed on 28 October, but with the price spread falling more sharply. This presented an opportunity to buy the spread cheaply, looking for a continuing upward trend.

The following market prices were available. The Schatz was trading down 2.5 ticks on the day and the 2-year Euribor bundle was trading down 10 ticks (remember that Euronext.liffe bundles and packs are quoted as the cumulative net change).

The weighted term spread was calculated to be 16.89 compared with a value of 16.48 for the swap/benchmark spread.

Eurex Schatz Z5	105.70

Euribor	Z5	H6	M6	U6	Z6	H7	M7	U7	Average
	97.630	97.460	97.320	97.220	97.125	97.075	97.020	96.975	97.2281

The CTD bond was the 2.25% 14/9/07 and its BPV for the Schatz Z5 future was calculated to be €19.99. The Euronext.liffe 2 year bundle had a BPV of €200 (8 x €25) and the ratio determined to be 10 Schatz futures per bundle. Ten Schatz futures were purchased and one bundle sold, effectively buying the term spread. The price was calculated to be:

```
(105.70 x 10 x 10) - (97.2281 x 25 x 8) = - 8,875.625
```

3 Nov 2005

Both spreads have bounced back by 3 November and the following prices were observed.

Eurex Schatz Z5	105.64

Euribor	Z5	H6	M6	U6	Z6	H7	M7	U7	Average
	97.610	97.400	97.250	97.150	97.060	97.005	96.950	96.900	97.1656

Making a price spread of

```
(105.64 x 10 x 10) - (97.1656 x 25 x 8) = -8,869.125
```

The spread was purchased on 28 October for –8875.625 and sold on 3 November for –8869.125, a difference of 6.5. Multiplying 6.5 by 100 gives a profit of €650 verified by the individual profit and losses below.

	28 Oct	3Nov	P/L (€)
Schatz	105.70	105.64	-600
Z5	97.630	97.610	+50
H6	97.460	97.400	+150
M6	97.320	97.250	+175
U6	97.220	97.150	+175
Z6	97.125	97.060	+162.50
H7	97.075	97.005	+175
M7	97.020	96.950	+175
U7	96.975	96.900	+187.50
		Σt	650.00

The swap/benchmark spread had widened from 16.48 to 16.77, a change of 1.76%, and the term spread had moved from 16.89 to 17.19, a change of 1.77%. By comparing the movement in the swap/benchmark spread to the movement in the term spread it is possible to detect what might be the driving factor. In this case, where both spreads have moved equally and a weighted strip yield has been used, it suggests that the upward price spread movement was probably driven by credit spread widening rather than curve risk or interest rate volatility.

Trading example 2

22 Nov 2005

On 22 November, a sharp spike in the price spread was noticed with no observable equal reaction in the benchmark spread. The price of the Schatz had risen sharply from 105.465 on 21 November to 105.565 on 22 November, a rise of 10 ticks, whereas the average price of the 2-year bundle had actually fallen 0.04 ticks. It was decided that the Schatz was too expensive relative to the futures strip, especially since there had been no major increase in the credit spread; the swap/benchmark spread.

A decision was taken to sell the spread, but unfortunately no suitable prices were available in the bundles and packs (imaginary scenario!). It was decided to use a stack instead, concentrating on Euribor H7, which displayed a correlation of 0.9943 against the Schatz future. 20 contracts were bought at a price of 96.955 and the total BPV calculated to be 500 (20 x €25). The Schatz future had a BPV of 19.99 and so 25 (500 divided by 19.99 and rounded) contracts were sold at 105.565.

The spread was calculated to be:

```
(105.565 x 10 x 25) - (96.955 x 25 x 20) = -22,086.25
```

23 Nov 2005

One day later, the spread had corrected. The Schatz had fallen to 105.52 and the Euribor H7 had risen to 96.980. The spread was bought back to close and it was calculated to have fallen to -22,110.00, a change of 23.75, which multiplied by 100, returned a profit of €2,375. This was verified by calculating the profit on the Schatz as €1,125 (105.565-105.520 x 25 x €10) and the profit on the Euribor H7 as €1,250 (96.980-96.955 x 20 x €25).

Trading conclusions

Both these examples are based upon real data and prices that were available for trading. Although both conveniently return a profit, it is hopefully clear that by referencing the price spread against the credit spread, trading opportunities can be found and an easy methodology employed to calculate the hedge ratios and monitoring of the price spread. The measurement of the term spread and its comparison to the price spread and swap/benchmark spread gives an indication of what might be driving the movement.

> **Trader's notes**
>
> In a situation like this, where the bond future has rallied and the STIR futures strip has not, it is advisable to check that the CTD bond is not being squeezed or going special. A quick call to a cash bond desk is the best option. Alternatively, observe the bond future carefully and see whether movements in the swap/benchmark spread explain its movement. Wait until it shows signs of reversing its trend before selling the spread.

An alternative method – regression analysis

The previous sections have shown how the interest rate sensitivities for bond futures and STIR futures, both individually or for bundles and packs, have been calculated and used to determine the hedge ratios. These are industry standard methods and so it might be intuitive to think that these hedge ratios might be inherent in the time series data between two instruments. After all, if a Euribor future has a BPV of 25 and the Schatz has a BPV of 20, then it might be expected that a ratio of 1.25 (25/20) Schatz trading to 1 Euribor would be reflected by the rate of change of the Schatz futures measured against the rate of change of the Euribor future.

In fact, this is the case. By using regression techniques, the time series data will indicate a ratio that will most reduce the difference in standard deviation between the two instruments. This ratio can be determined by using regression statistic *Beta*. This will measure the amount of fluctuation of one variable against another and this can be found within Excel as the function SLOPE.

The measurement of Beta needs to be verified as being statistically significant by the use of the R-squared value, found within Excels RSQ function. This R-squared value is the proportion of the variance in one instrument that is attributable to the variance in another. The higher the R-squared number is, the greater the relationship between the performances of the instruments.

Using the previous data set from 21 Sep 2005 until 8 Dec 2005, the Beta of the rate of change of the cash flows[28] of the 2-year Euribor bundle (using an average price) is 1.12 with an R-squared of 0.76. This means that the time series data is suggesting that a hedge ratio of 1.12 Schatz to 1 Euribor (implying a Schatz future BPV of 22.32 (€25/1.12)) most reduced the amount of fluctuation in returns between the two contracts. However, the RSQ figure of 0.76 states that only 76% of the variance of returns to the Euribor was due to the variance of returns of the Schatz. The rest was noise.

Using the Euribor H7 contract instead of the bundle returns a beta ratio of 1.32 and a R-squared of 0.76. This suggests that a higher proportion of Schatz to Euribor would have been a preferable based on that data set, but the 24% noise (100-0.76) inherent in the Betas for both the bundle and the H7, makes their use arbitrary.

Regression is a useful way of verifying a hedge ratio or fine tuning a ratio that does not appear to be performing as expected, perhaps due to unexpected volatility. But it should be treated as an accessory rather than the main tool for evaluating hedge ratios. Regression statistics are highly susceptible to the data sets being used. Time periods, vagaries or errors will seriously affect the Beta and R-squared values, and the resulting hedge ratios.

Trader's notes

- When calculating the BPV of a CTD bond, it can be useful to recalculate it forward at the delivery date of the bond against the bond future. This will generate a forward BPV to compare with the spot version. The difference between the spot and forward BPV might not be much, but could help the decision making process when rounding hedge ratios.

- Compare the swap/benchmark spread to the term spread, calculated from weighted strip yields to minimise yield curve effects on the spread value, to determine what is driving the spread.

- Short sellers of term spread should always be aware of the asymmetrical nature of the spread and the potential effects of bond squeezes and specials.

- When trading term spreads, go to the point of least liquidity first. Strategies such as bundles and packs will be less liquid than the bond futures. Plan to get filled on that part of the trade first, to minimise execution risk.

---

[28] It is necessary to use the rate of change of the cash flows to fully represent the proportional differences between the two contracts, taking account of the different tick values. The cash flows are calculated as the contract price multiplied by the tick value per basis point. The regressions are run on the rate of change of these cash flows.

Spreading STIR futures against swap futures

The swaps market is a highly liquid over-the-counter market with maturities ranging from 2 years to 50 years. They are one of the most widely used over-the-counter[29] (OTC) derivatives in terms of notional value. Futures on swap products were introduced by the exchanges shortly after the millennium, to try to capture a share of the hugely liquid swaps market by constructing standardised contracts to replicate the OTC market.

Three exchanges, CME, CBOT and Euronext.liffe, launched swap futures in different forms, but all have remained fledgling. It is not clear whether this is due to reluctance by swap traders to embrace these products as a hedging tool, or apathy and lack of understanding amongst the general trading community. However, swap futures provide an ideal spread partner for STIR futures since their yield curve is almost identical to the STIR futures yield curve and so have little of the credit risk associated with spreading against bond futures.

The three types of swap contract offer a variation on the same theme. Table 3.19 summarises the key points for each product.

---

[29] Non-Exchange traded transactions directly between two parties, usually Banks, Institutions or Corporations.

Table 3.19: Main swap futures summaries

Exchange	CME	CBOT	Euronext.liffe
Product	Swap futures	Interest Rate swap	Swapnote
Currencies	$	$	€ [30]
Trading Unit	A notional amount of ISDA USD benchmark term swap rate	Notional price of swap with fixed rate of 6%, semi annual payments and notional 100,000 principal versus floating side based on 3-month Libor.	A bond future, with 100,000 notional principal and 6% coupon referenced to the swap market.
Term, Size & tick value	2 year $500,000 (€25) 5 year $200,000 (€25) 10 year $100,000(€25)	5 year $100,000 ($15.625) 10 year $100,000 ($31.25)	2 year €100,000 (€5) 5 year €100,000 (€10) 10 year €100,000 (€10)
Settlement	Settles to ISDA[31] benchmark mid-market par swap rates for that specific maturity. The swap rate assumes fixed semi-annual coupon (per 30/360 basis) vs. 3-month LIBOR (per actual/360 basis).	The notional price of the Trading Unit on the last day of trading, based upon the ISDA Benchmark Rate for that specific maturity U.S. dollar interest rate swap on the last day of trading	The EDSP is the present value, as of the delivery day, of the notional principal amount and the notional coupons of the note. The discounting of the cash flows is performed using a swap curve which is constructed, on the last trading day, from the ISDA Benchmark Euribor Swap Rate fixings

An introduction to swaps

A swap is an agreement to exchange one set of interest flows for another, with no exchange of principal.

A standard or vanilla interest rate swap is an agreement between two counterparties, where a set of cash flows from a fixed rate are exchanged for a set of floating rate cash flows. The holder of the fixed leg of the swap makes regular uniform payments to the holder of the floating leg. This party, in return, makes regular payments to the fixed leg party, but the amounts of these vary according to prevailing interest rates. The coupon dates of the fixed leg can coincide with the interest rate dates of the floating-rate side, but it is common for swaps to incorporate other conventions such as the fixed side paying annual coupons against the floating side paying semi-annually.

Swaps are initially set by calculating the present values of their cash flows. At the inception of the swap, the difference between the present values of both cash flows

[30] Euronext.liffe also offer a US dollar denominated swapnote, omitted here for the sake of expediency. There is also a Yen Swapnote listed on Tokyo Financial Exchange (TFX).

[31] ISDA – International Swaps and Derivatives Association. They are a global trade association for over the counter derivatives, and maintainers of the industry-standard ISDA documentation.

is set to zero so that fixed side pays a rate that values the total of the fixed cash flow at the same present value as the variable rate cash flow total. Consequently, when the swap contract commences, there will be no advantage to either the fixed or floating side of the swap and therefore no upfront payment. During the lifetime of the swap contract, the present values of the variable side of the swap, based on changing rates, will deviate from the fixed rate side, which do not change, crediting one side at the expense of the other.

Table 3.20 demonstrates the process of determining the cash flows of a notional 2-year swap starting on 1 Feb 2006. The fixed rate payments are based on a 6% rate and both cashflows are paid semi-annually and the principal amount is 1,000,000.

Table 3.20: Interest rate swap cash flows

1,000,000	FIXED 6%	FLOATING	RATES	AF	DF
1st Feb 2006					
1st Aug 2006	29966.20	13334.96	0.0267	0.50278	0.993355
1st Feb 2007	30233.98	14109.19	0.0280	0.51111	0.985891
1st Aug 2006	29523.11	14171.09	0.0288	0.50277	0.978667
1st Feb 2008	29762.40	14633.18	0.0295	0.51111	0.970513
PV	119485.70	56248.42	2.8245%		

- **AF Accruals factor**
  The fractional part of the year expressed as a decimal based on a 360 day year convention. Since the cash flow are semi annual, it is to be expected that this value will be approximately 0.50 (180/360). However, small differences in day counts and non-business days affect the figure accordingly.

- **DF Discount factor**
  Coefficients derived from zero coupon bonds, used to find the present value of the cash flow. The one-year factor is expressed as:

$$\frac{1}{1+ AF \times r}$$

where r is the rate and a process of bootstrapping, basing the next period rate on the previous ones, extends the factors to longer time horizons. The discount factors used above are approximations.

It can be seen that the present values of the fixed coupon cash flows change little, only when there is a slight difference in day count between periods. They are the product of the principal, coupon rate, accrual and discount factors and calculated as

```
principal x coupon rate x AF x DF
```

The cash flows for the floating side are calculated in the same way, except floating rates are used each period. These cash flows will vary according to the rate levels and shape of the yield curve.

The totals of the fixed and floating cash flows columns are the present value of the cumulative income streams, as at the start date of 1 Feb 2006. The fixed leg amounts to 119,485.70 and floating side is 56,248.42. The difference is nearly double, since the fixed side pays a 6% rate compared to approximately 3% for the floating leg. This difference between the totals must be set to zero at the inception of the swap, so that there is no advantage to either counterparty. This is achieved by changing the fixed rate on the fixed leg to another rate that will equalise the present value totals of both the floating and fixed legs and reduce the difference between the present values of the fixed and floating cash flows to zero. This rate is known as the *swap rate* and in this case, it is 2.8245%, calculated by using solver[32] in Excel.

Swap calculators, either in information vendor systems or spreadsheets, usually set the fixed rate automatically to the one that zeros the difference between cash flow totals. The present values of the cash flows are calculated by using discount factors. These are calculated from zero coupon yield curves, which convert the yields of different financial instruments into standardised zero coupon bond yields. Usually, deposits are used to around nine months, then STIR futures to approximately two years, and then swap rates for further periods.

CME swap futures

CME swap futures are uniquely designed to compare and trade directly with the Eurodollar futures in an easily understood format.

There are three swap futures; a two year, five year and ten year contract based on notional values of $500,000, $200,000 and $100,000 respectively. They are all based on a fixed leg semi-annual rate (30/360 basis) versus 3 month LIBOR (actual/360) with quarterly reset and settlement in arrears. CME swap futures are unique in that each contract has the same Basis Point Value (BPV) calculated by:

---

[32] Solver is an optimisation program in Excel. The parameters are set so that difference between the two cash flow totals equals zero by changing the 6% rate.

```
Notional Value x 0.0001 x term (years)

2-year: $500,000 x 0.0001 x 2 = $100
5-year: $200,000 x 0.0001 x 5 = $100
10-year: $100,000 x 0.0001 x 10 = $100
```

Each swap future has a BPV of $100 with the minimum price movement (tick) being one quarter of one basis point ($25), which matches the BPV of a Eurodollar contract. CME swap futures are priced to appear like Eurodollar futures by the Index Points convention of subtracting the swap rate from 100. If the swap rate were 4.50%, then the swap future would trade approximately 95.50: 'Approximately', because the swap rate of 4.50% is a rate for a swap starting today. The CME swap futures are based on a swap starting on the contract expiry which is the second London business day preceding the third Wednesday of the delivery month. This can amount to a difference of up to three months between the actual swap rate and the swap rate starting on the contract expiry. Calculating the swap as a forward start swap[33], commencing on the contract expiry day, can compensate for this.

The 2-year CME swap future is currently traded at 95.20, on 20 Jan 2006, implying a forward swap rate of 4.80%. The spot 2-year swap rate is 4.77% (mid), a difference of 3 basis points. Calculating the swap as a forward start swap on 13 Mar 2006 returns 4.80%, which implies a fair price of 95.20 (100 – 4.80) for the future, which matches its market price exactly. The 5-year swap has a market price of 95.21, a spot swap rate of 4.78% and a forward start value of 4.79%, again matching the market price.

Trading with CME swap futures

The design of the CME swaps futures makes spreading Eurodollars against them very easy.

Since the BPV of all the swap futures is always $100, and the BPV of the Eurodollar futures will always be $25, then the ratio is simply 4 Eurodollar futures to 1 swap future. This ratio lends itself conveniently to the trading of packs and bundles against the swaps future. A pack will have a total BPV of $100 (4 x $25) and will be matched by 1 swap future. A 2-year bundle will have a total BPV of $200 (8 x $25) and so would be hedged by 2 swap futures (2 x $100 = $200). The use of a two-year bundle against a 2-year swap future should be expected to provide a good hedge, but remember that using a pack or stack instead, will leave curve risk.

---

[33] A commercial swaps calculator should be used for determining forward start swap rates. The complexities of constructing a zero coupon yield curve, the correct choice of component instruments and valuation conventions do not lend themselves easily to spreadsheet construction. These forward start swap rates were calculated in Reuters 3000xtra. However, knowing the fair value for any future is useful, but not essential for trading.

CBOT interest rate swap futures

The 5-year and 10-year CBOT interest rate swap futures are designed to appear similar to the CBOT 5-year and 10-year Treasury note futures. They all have a notional value of $100,000, a notional 6% coupon, and are denominated in 32nds (1/32), each having a value of $31.25 per 1/32. All but the 10-year swap future are traded in minimum increments of one half of a 32nd, with a value of $15.625. The 10-year swap is traded in 32nds only.

The interest rate swap futures are based on the notional price of the fixed rate side of a swap with notional $100,000 principal and semi annual payments of 6% per annum, exchanged for floating 3-month LIBOR. They trade in price terms of points ($1,000) and 32nds ($31.25) of the notional value ($100,000) and can be priced according to the following bond pricing formulae:

```
5-year: $100,000 x [ 6/r+(1-6/r) x (1+0.01 x r/2)⁻¹⁰] = futures
price
```

```
10-year: $100,000 x [ 6/r+(1-6/r) x (1+0.01 x r/2)⁻²⁰] = futures
price
```

```
where r is the forward start swap rate
```

Substituting a forward start swap rate of 4.80%, based on a 5-year swap starting on 13 Mar 2006 into the above equation returns a theoretical price of 105.28. The 5-year interest rate swap future is currently trading at 105.09 (105 9/32), which, decimalised, is 105.28, the same as the theoretical value.

For the 10-year interest rate swap future, a forward start swap rate of 4.872%, based on a 10-year swap starting on 13 Mar 2006, returns a theoretical price of 108.846. The 10-year interest rate swap future is currently trading at 108.27 (108 27/32), which, decimalised, is 108.844, virtually the same as the theoretical value.

Note: The Interest Rate Swap future prices can also be calculated by using the PRICE function in Excel and substituting the yield for the forward swap rate. An approximation for the forward swap rate can be found by using the price of CME swap futures (100 - CME swap future price).

Hedge ratios for the interest rate swap futures can be calculated by determining their BPV. This can be defined as the price difference that occurs when a ½ basis point is added or subtracted from the forward swap rate and inputted into the formula. The BPV will be the difference between the changes in prices multiplied by the tick value.

For the 5-year interest rate swap future, reducing the forward start swap rate by ½ basis point from 4.80% to 4.795% will change the price to 105.3012. Increasing the swap rate by ½ basis point to 4.805% will change the price to 105.2558. The difference between the two prices is 0.0454, and dividing this by the decimalised value of 1/32 (0.03125) result in 1.4528, which multiplied by the value of 1/32 ($31.25) gives a BPV of $45.40.

Trading CBOT interest rate swap futures

Once the BPV of the interest rate swap future has been calculated, spreads against Eurodollar packs, stacks and bundles can be calculated in the usual way. It should be noted that the BPV of the interest rate swap futures will vary as the forward start swap rate moves, whereas the Eurodollar BPV will remain static at $25.

Since interest rate swap futures are priced in 32nds and the Eurodollars are decimalised, the pricing difference can make the visual monitoring of the spread between the two instruments a little difficult. The best approach is to monitor the cash flows of the trade in a spreadsheet, where both sides of the spread reflect the price, ratio and tick value in a similar way to what was demonstrated for trading term spreads. Note that the CBOT interest rate swap future should be decimalised for comparison with the Eurodollar (the methodology is shown in *Trading term spreads with packs and bundles > displaying the spread*). The decimalised tick value will be $10 (($31.25 x 32)/100).

Apart from trading against Eurodollars, these interest rate swap futures are very suitable for trading against the CBOT Treasury note futures. The combination of the these two allow term spread trading without the convexity bias inherent in the Eurodollar forward rates, or the complexities and liquidity issues when trading bundles for 5 years or 10 year (if available or liquid).

Euronext.liffe € Swapnote

Swapnote is a unique product, patented by UK money broker ICAP and licensed to Euronext.liffe. Swapnote is not a future on a swap but rather a bond future priced from the swap curve (instead of the benchmark curve used for bond futures based on Government issued debt). Consequently, Swapnote is more like a corporate bond having the same credit rating as the swaps market than a swap rate. It is available in two, five and ten year maturities and is based upon a notional €100,000 6% coupon bond, and is priced by the total of the net present values of the cash flows derived from a zero coupon yield curve comprised of a range of industry standard financial instruments that represent the swaps curve. This makes Swapnote representative of the term structure and credit pricing of the swap market.

Swapnote is settled to ISDAFIX, which is an International Swaps and Derivatives Association (ISDA) fixing. This is considered to be the leading benchmark for rates on interest rate swaps worldwide. ISDAFIX are calculated daily; on its expiry day Swapnote will settle to the sum of the present value of its cash flows derived from the ISDAFIX fixing rate, using a basis convention of an annual 30/360 fixed side versus 6 month Euribor. The fixing is calculated from a range of rates collected from a sample of swaps dealers These swaps dealers will be pricing their rates from a broadly similar zero coupon yield curve. This tends to be made up of deposits to around nine months, STIR futures to two years and market swap rates thereafter.

Swapnote can be priced by any bond or asset swap calculator that can incorporate a zero curve derived from deposit, futures and swap rates and permits forward starts. Euronext.liffe provides two Swapnote calculators on their website. One is based on cash rates, including deposits to 9 months and swap rates thereafter, and the other uses the Euribor futures strip. This second calculator can only really be used for the 2-year Swapnote since liquidity becomes thin in the futures strip after about three years.

Pricing a 6% annual coupon bond on a 30/360 convention versus a 6-month Euribor floating leg for a forward start on the 2-year Swapnote H6 delivery day (15 Mar 2006) using a zero yield curve from 23 Jan 2006 produces the following cash flows:

Dates	Rate	DF	Cashflow	NPV
15 Mar 2007	6%	0.9713	6000	5827.80
15 Mar 2008	6%	0.9408	106000	99724.80
			Total NPV	**105552.60**
			Adjusted	**105.555**

The Swapnote is quoted in units of €1000 and so the sum of the cash flows is divided by 1000 and rounded to the nearest half- tick to return an adjusted theoretical value of 105.555. The market price on the morning of 23 January was a similar 105.550. The yield will be the single rate at which all the bonds cash flows are discounted. The Euronext.liffe Swapnote calculator can supply the yield; in this case 3.09%, or an approximate measure of yield can be substituted by using the YIELD function in Excel. This returned a value of 3.09%.

The BPV from the Euronext.liffe calculator can be used or it can be calculated manually either from the modified duration or by toggling the yield by a half basis point and observing the effect on the price. No interest is accrued prior to the expiry date and the first coupon is valued in full in the futures settlement procedure, meaning that the BPV calculation does not need to add accrued interest to the Swapnote price. Both methods return a BPV of €20 per Swapnote future.

Trading Euronext.liffe € Swapnote

Swapnote is designed as a bond future – but without the disadvantages. It is cash settled, so there is no delivery option and hence no possibility of price squeezes.

Swapnote can be traded as a term spread trade against the EUREX bond futures, with credit risk; the 2-year Swapnote would be traded against Schatz, the 5-year against the Bobl and the 10-year versus the Bund. Swapnote can also be traded easily against Euribor stacks, packs or bundles without the credit risk associated with term spreads. Both Swapnote and Euribor occupy almost the same position on the swap curve and so movement in the spread between them will be due to curve risk only.

Table 3.21 shows how closely correlated the Euribor futures are to the Swapnote. The 2-year bundle shows an almost perfect correlation to the H6 Swapnote future with an equally impressive R-squared value, which explains the proportion of variance in Euribor that is due to the variance in Swapnote.

Table 3.21: Correlation (C) and R^2 for 2-year € Swapnote Z5 versus Euribor (14/6/05 to 19/12/05) where R^2 is the proportion of the variance in Euribor attributable to the variance in Swapnote

	Z5	H6	M6	U6	Z6	H7	M7	U7	White pack	Red pack	2-yr bundle
C	0.975	0.992	0.996	0.998	0.998	0.996	0.992	0.985	0.995	0.995	0.999
R^2	0.950	0.984	0.993	0.996	0.996	0.992	0.984	0.971	0.989	0.990	0.998

The White and Red Packs also return very high correlations, as do the individual futures contracts, perhaps with the exception of the front month, making them excellent spreading instruments against Swapnote.

Chart 3.9 displays the history for 2-year Swapnote Z5 contract versus the Euribor 2-year bundle and U6 stack displayed as a price spread. This is expressed in the same way as was shown for term spread price spreads:

```
(Price of Swapnote x tick value x hedge ratio) - (Price of
Euribor x tick value)
```

The price of Euribor can be either the average price of the bundle or single outright price of the U6 Stack. The hedge ratio is the product of the BPV of the two contracts (€25/€20 = 1.25), meaning 1.25 Swapnote are bought for every Euribor sold.

Chart 3.9: Price spreads between Swapnote H6 and Euribor 2-year bundle, Euribor U6 stack using a hedge ratio of 1.25 (22 Sep 2005 to 19 Dec 2005)

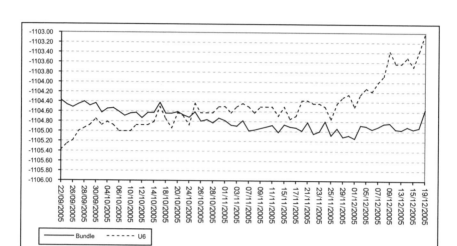

The chart shows how closely the Bundle tracks the Swapnote over a three-month period. Since the spread is displayed in a price-spread format, the spread range will be the change in value of the spread for whatever quantities are selected. The bundle has a relatively narrow range, exhibiting close mapping to the swapnote future. The U6 Stack would have provided a more volatile spread, reflecting the curve risk inherent in trading a single spot on the yield curve against a term instrument.

Spreads between international STIR futures

Trading the spreads between international STIR futures is a popular trade, based upon the interest rate differential. The positive correlations between the major STIR futures were introduced earlier in the text ['Correlated markets']. Correlations of 0.81 were found between Eurodollar and Euribor and 0.91 between Euribor and Euroswiss, making the spreads attractive to the trader willing to assume the economic and currency risk.

Calculating the hedge ratios for the spreads between international STIR futures is easy to do but can be tricky to get right. They are simply the currency-adjusted ratio of their relative BPVs. The BPV of STIR futures are always fixed. Most of the contracts of interest have a BPV of 25 based on a nominal contract value of

1,000,000. (1,000,000 x 0.0001 x 90/360 = 25), but Euronext.liffe Short Sterling is different in that it has a smaller contract size of £500,000 and a tick size (and BPV) of £12.50 (500,000 x 0.0001 x 90/360 =12.50).

The trickiness in calculating hedge ratios between two international STIR futures is due to reciprocal currencies. A currency pair such as the Euro against the Dollar can be quoted as either:

```
€/$ 1.206, meaning that €1 is equivalent to $1.206
```

or

```
$/€ 0.831, meaning that $1 is equivalent to €0.83
```

One is the reciprocal of the other (divide 1 by the currency to calculate the other).

Mistakes are easy to make when using currency pairs to calculate hedge ratios for STIR pairs. The best approach is to use one methodology only and always reason the answer with common sense. One approach is to decide which contract is to be bought and which is to be sold and apply the currency pair that starts with the currency symbol of the contract being purchased to give the hedge ratio:

$$BPV_{buy} \Bigg/ \frac{BPV_{Sell}}{Currency\ rate}$$

For example: 1 Euribor is purchased, and Eurodollars sold

$$25 \Bigg/ \frac{25}{€/\$1.206} = 1.206$$

Buy 1 Euribor, sell 1.206 Eurodollars.

It can be useful to derive a spreadsheet matrix, either linked to a currency feed or with the currencies being manually updated regularly.

Table 3.22 shows the hedge ratios for four different STIR futures in four different currencies. The contract being purchased is selected from the left hand side and the hedge ratio of the contract being sold found by moving right through the matrix. As a rule of thumb, the amount to sell of a contract will be the same as the currency rate provided the BPVs are equal and the currency symbol starts with the same denomination as the purchased contract.

Table 3.22: Hedge ratios (bold) for international STIR futures

		SELL		SELL		SELL		SELL	
			BPV		*BPV*		*BPV*		*BPV*
		Euribor	**€25**	Euro-dollar	**$25**	Sterling	**£12.50**	Swiss	**Chf25**
BUY 1	Euribor	**1**	€	**1.206**	€/$ 1.206	**1.364**	€/£ 0.682	**1.540**	€/Chf 1.54
BUY 1	Euro$	**0.831**	$/€ 0.831	**1**	$	**1.136**	$/£ 0.568	**1.280**	$/Chf 1.28
BUY 1	Sterling	**0.730**	£/€ 1.46	**0.880**	£/$ 1.760	**1**	£	**1.130**	£/Chf 2.26
BUY 1	Swiss	**0.649**	Chf/€ 0.649	**0.780**	Chf/$ 0.78	**0.882**	Chf/£ 0.441	**1**	Chf 1

Trading international STIR futures

Trading international STIR futures carries two risks:

1. specific risk reflecting economic differences between the two countries, and

2. risk of currency rate changes altering the hedge ratio.

When looking for two international STIR futures to trade against each other, a good positive correlation needs to be matched by currency stability. Chart 3.10 shows the hedge ratios for Euribor traded against Eurodollar, Euroswiss and Short Sterling during 2005.

Chart 3.10: Historic hedge ratio between Euribor versus Eurodollar, Euroswiss, Short Sterling during 2005 (H6)

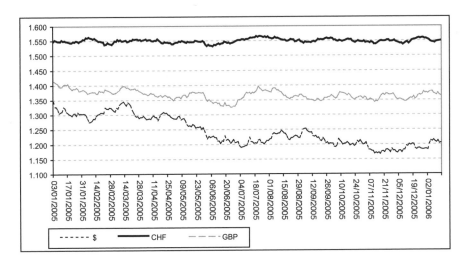

Although both Eurodollar and Euroswiss have good positive correlations to Euribor, it is apparent that the Euribor versus Euroswiss hedge ratio appears very stable when compared to Eurodollar or Short Sterling. Its hedge ratio (which is also the currency rate) has a standard deviation of 0.006 compared to 0.049 for the Eurodollar. The Swiss franc clearly tracks the Euro closely, and so a trade between Euribor and Euroswiss futures looks attractive, benefiting from both a strong correlation and currency stability.

Although the correlations between a certain pair might appear enticing, the dangers of de-correlation should not be under estimated. This can be caused by a specific risk factor such as an unexpected change in policy in one country or by a sudden currency shift and can quickly de-couple the relationship that might have existed between the two contracts for some time. It is important not to rely on statistical analysis too heavily and always be aware what is driving each component STIR future.

Summary – when to use the strategies

- **Term spread**

  Trading the term spread by using bundles packs or stacks is a popular trade for both short term and long horizons. Term spreads can be position traded by using the best match between the STIR futures and bond futures, which will tend to be bundles. Packs and stacks can be used for short-term high frequency trading, bidding and offering them against the liquidity of the bond futures. Remember that this will be a volatile spread compared to others described in this book.

- **Swap futures**

  A great substitute for bond futures, virtually eliminating the credit spread risk against STIR futures, but compromised by the current lack of business in swap future products. High frequency short-term traders should look to trade the Swap first and then hedge where available, with stacks being the easiest option.

- **International STIR futures**

  A tricky spread to trade long term due to the complexities of currencies and country economics but a good short term trade. Look for price action between established pairs, such as Euribor/Euroswiss or Euribor/Eurodollar. What is happening in one STIR future can often portend what is going to happen in the other.

4

Trading Considerations For STIR Futures

Zero Sum Game – Know The Players

Futures trading is a zero sum game, which is where one participant's financial gain or loss is exactly balanced by the financial losses or gains of other participants. Put another way, one trader's gain is another trader's loss. During each trading day, a very considerable sum of money changes hands as price movements translate into changing profits and losses. This monetary swing is based upon both traders' existing positions and on new money coming into the market. For each existing position in the market or for each new position taken out in the market, there has be to a trader on the other side of the deal. For buyers there has to be a seller and for sellers there has to be a buyer, but only one of them can be the winner. The aim of the trader, whose success depends on their profit and loss account, is to consistently be that winner, on-balance being a net taker from the market. Surprisingly, not all market participants have the same objective and so it is important to know your fellow players.

Players

'Players' is a collective term for all market participants. Not all have the same objectives and they all have different sensitivities to market price movements. Some players are not overly concerned about giving away the edge to complete a transaction, but for others it is critical. Some participants might expect to give away money in order to build a position in the market. For example, a large seller selling into a rising market in order to build a larger position that would otherwise have been unachievable in a falling market. Since all trading is anonymous, it is not possible to be sure who is on the other side of a trade or what their motive is. However, being aware of the different player categories and being familiar with their characteristics can be beneficial in trying to decipher price action. These different kinds of player can be broadly classified as being a:

- *price taker*: someone who buys the offer or sells the bid price, since filling the transaction is of prime importance, or

- *price maker*: a player who works the bid and offer in order to achieve the best possible fill level.

Hedge funds

Hedge funds are a relatively new market participant of note. They have been around since the 1950s when Alfred Jones developed leveraged market neutral trading, where a long position is offset with a short position - effectively *hedging* the trade from broad market risk. Hedge funds became a generic term for all types of alternative asset management, from the huge macro players such as Soros, Robertson and Steinhardt, to the sophisticated niche players in esoteric areas such as convertible bond arbitrage. By the new millennium the number of hedge funds had increased exponentially as investors diversified away from the languishing post dotcom long only stock markets, and talented managers were enticed by the performance-based remuneration potential to set up new funds. Unsurprisingly, this large increase in the number of hedge funds all seeking to trade alternative markets, coupled to a fall in market volatility, led to reduced trading opportunities. Many hedge funds have therefore entered the futures markets (among others), exploiting the leverage on leverage, in the search for new opportunities.

Since hedge funds have large amounts of leveraged capital upon which they need to make meaningful returns, they are normally confined to directional trades in outrights, rather than spreads or strategies. They are commonly present in STIR futures markets when building a position based on their expectations for futures interest rates. They can be generally characterised by their persistent buying or selling around certain moveable levels, and sometimes into resistance in order to facilitate the business. Although they can establish positions of tens of thousands of lots, they are unlikely to spook the markets by trading abnormally large clips, but rather rely on market ebbs and flows to work multiple orders around market demand. Hedge funds are not over concerned about small costs or slippage, preferring to get the business done. Consequently, they are more price takers than price makers.

Banks

Banks are normally the highest volume players and this can cover both proprietary and agency trading. Their proprietary business can appear much in the same manner as hedge funds and it can be virtually impossible to distinguish between them, although this is ultimately of little consequence since their motives will be similar. Their agency business comprises telephone brokerage and electronic order routing business. Trade quantities will be variable from medium to large orders, but with high frequency. Very large orders might be transacted wholesale via block trades, where larger trades are pre-negotiated by the bank representing both counterparties. Block trades have minimum quantity criteria defined by the exchanges and are permitted a delay in reporting the transaction to market. They are characterised by a label attached to the reported trade.

Agency business is characterised by high frequency institutional sized business and is the backbone of the markets order flow. Sometimes it appears more noticeable after events, such as economic releases, where traders immediately drive market movements, but larger institutional orders enter the market minutes later when the number has been disseminated by the banks to their clients. Banks are primarily concerned with transaction flow but price is important to them since they will often be acting on price orders or routing electronic limit orders. They are usually price makers and will often work the bids and offers. Their business is often termed *paper*.

Hedgers

Hedgers are usually corporate bank customers who are either using the STIR futures markets directly to hedge an interest rate exposure, or using a tailored over-the-counter bank product to achieve the same effect, in which case the bank will be hedging the exposure directly. Hedgers' business can be classified under bank or broker agency since they use them as an intermediary. Their business can be both price taking and making but might be more inclined towards the former because the fill can be of prime importance.

Brokers

Brokers are similar to a bank's agency business but smaller in size, perhaps specialising in retail business instead of institutional business. Their business might be based on electronic order routing, characterised by small but frequent volume flow with a mixture of price taking and making.

Independent traders

Independent traders include both individual traders and proprietary groups. They are primarily price makers; actively working the bids and offers of outrights or spreads to gain a profit, although they will easily switch to price taking in volatile conditions. They are the main cause of noise in the STIR futures markets by their sheer numbers and low propensity for risk. A lot of their business is scratched (bought and sold at the same price for zero profit or loss) and reimbursed by exchange rebate schemes or Clearing Member volume discounts, but their collective influence on the markets should not be underestimated. They can be principal causes of congestion in markets and often position themselves in the same direction, adding to the noise surrounding that particular trade.

Flippers

A generic term for market bullies. Flippers are a variation on the independent trader or scalper, being large, high frequency traders who try to exploit the activities of smaller traders. They are both price makers and takers but their main aim is to 'shake the tree' of smaller traders with much lower risk profiles. They act very much like market bullies, trying to identify what other traders are trying to do and then trying to loosen their position on a trade.

Algorithmic trading – the rise of the machines

Algorithmic trading (also known as black box or program trading), is the computerisation of futures trading taken to its ultimate level, where software programs replace the trader in the decision making process. Algorithmic trading has seen explosive growth in the last few years, fuelled mainly by hedge funds and proprietary trading groups. Some market participants put its involvement at up to 60% of all speculative business, although this figure is very subjective and probably includes ISV trading products such as auto-spreaders (which by their very construction and operation are a form of algorithmic trading).

Most algorithmic programs are written directly to an exchange or ISV API by software developers Whilst algorithmic trading is portrayed as being highly sophisticated, in the absence of reliable artificial intelligence most of their trading rules are very black and white, qualified by a lot of "what if" statements. The algorithms tend to be based on four trading premises: technical, mean reversion, event and copycat.

1. **Technical analysis**

   Algorithmic trading programs will try to emulate the technically-inclined trader and identity buying and selling opportunities using conventional technical analysis. More advanced mathematical refinements might be added, such as economic noise reduction filters (e.g. Kalman filters), which aims to smooth trends by stripping away confusing extraneous activity.

2. **Mean reversion**

   Mean reversion (or mean regression) works on the basis that prices will return to a historic mean price after deviating away due to trading factors. Price history is used to calculate trading bands around a mean, and these are used as the base for trade initiation. Mean reversion is commonly used for spreads and spreading strategy-type trades.

3. **Event trading**

    This is the automated response and trading of events, primarily economic indicators. Economic figures and indicators can move markets substantially and it is relatively easy to link trading applications with information sources, even through simple Excel-based dynamic data exchange (DDE) links. Such programs tend to be refined beyond the simple "bad figure – sell" or "good figure – buy" methodology by using "if" and "but" parameters.

4. **Copycat**

    Why concern yourself with the complexities of technical and mean reversion models? Why not let someone else do the development and just copy their moves? This is the basis of copycat trading, where the activities of market participants are closely monitored and those who are deemed to be successful are emulated. Algorithmic trading tends to be very rule bound to the point where a buy or sell signal is executed in a default size reflecting the trade potential. Analysis of intra day price history can often identify these trades and several programs are designed to piggy back them.

Algorithmic trading is highly fashionable at present, but it is debatable as to whether its popularity is based on true potential or the desire to remove the inefficient and costly human element from the trade process. Whilst algorithmic trading remains strictly black and white, and rule bound, its true success will lie in its extension of technical and model-based market behaviour. The ability to understand how the algorithms are driving the markets will extend the trading life of the human trader a little longer!

Supporting cast

There's a supporting cast of players surrounding the markets. Some are essential, providing infrastructure, such as software providers or clearing services, but some are purely peripheral and should carry a wealth warning.

Snake oil salesmen

These are the peddlers of trading systems, offering to cure all ills and make money in the futures/stock/commodities markets. They are not to be confused with information or charting packages, which provide the data and analytics upon which the trader can base their own decisions. They are normally internet-marketed systems, using a form of technical analysis to generate buy and sell signals. The methodology might be sound and some might work for some traders, but a healthy dose of scepticism and common sense is required. Systems can work in some markets for a time, but there's no one-size-fits-all solution to futures trading. Trading systems can be economical with the truth regarding drawdowns - which is the amount of loss a position might suffer before it becomes profitable. And their studies might be based upon lagging indicators, which always look better in hindsight. If a system is so great, why is it being marketed? If it sounds too good to be true, it probably is.

The pundits

The pundits are the television and newspaper commentators, analysts and economists who provide the markets with their opinions. Most are highly qualified and well regarded in their fields, but talk is cheap and, again, a measure of scepticism is required. Very few pundits are mavericks, preferring the comfort of consensus, and they are usually content gradually shifting or spinning their opinions as the consensus changes over time. Also it's important to gauge their motive. Most pundits will not publicly air their opinions until their paying clients have been briefed, which means that if their opinion is highly regarded, then it's probably already discounted in the markets. Often, a market opinion might just serve as a public reinforcement of their company's position or outlook.

Collective market consensus is a useful tool. Polls or surveys indicting futures expectations of interest rate movements of many pundits can accurately portray the market in relation to that viewpoint; however, the lone voice should be treated with caution.

How to play

Specialisation

Most successful traders find a niche within the markets where they become completely familiar with the contract characteristics, market drivers and the other types of participant. Niches can be a particular STIR futures contract, or a specialisation within a group of contracts, such as trading packs and bundles. The benefit of a niche speciality is that it usually provides the bread and butter daily earnings of trading, and can finance the more occasional macro trade. Very few traders specialise in more than one or two contracts, even with electronic trading opening up the world markets onto a desktop, since there is a limit to how much information can be closely monitored by one person.

The choice of niche will differ between traders according to their propensity for risk. Some will prefer the action of the outrights, willing to accept losses in exchange for greater gains, whereas others will seek the stability of spread trading, looking to make steady if unspectacular returns but with little downside. Finding a niche takes time and usually money in the search process, but it is important to find it since it is this specialisation and intimate knowledge that becomes the trader's edge or advantage over other market participants.

Traders should be prepared to change specialisations according to market conditions, as some strategies might become busier than others, or a period of low volatility might push traders into the outrights in search of profits. However, being a specialist in a particular area will always be key to successful STIR futures trading.

Key characteristics and considerations

There's no such thing as a blue print for the perfect trader, but successful traders often share common traits and responses to market situations. Certain desirable characteristics should be obvious, such as expertise, common sense, a sense of proportion, emotional stability and the ability to concentrate; but other characteristics are more important by how they are applied to the markets.

Conviction versus dogma

There's a world of difference between these two, but it's not always easy to see it. Confidence and conviction are useful characteristics to have in futures markets, provided the trader doesn't allow them to become dogma, usually through intransigence. Having an opinion on a market or a trade is a reflection of confidence and conviction, but deciding what the market will do is dogma.

Sometimes, this distinction becomes blurred when the conviction necessary to support a trade verges on dogma, reflecting a trader's confidence in that position. Great traders, such as George Soros, walked a very fine line between the two, but by doing so were able to build the large positions that made their reputations. Traders of any repute should always frequently question their position, outlook or trade. What has changed within the last five minutes that might change the traders view? Has there been, or will there be, any new information coming to market that might change the trader's view? Once the questioning of the validity of an open position stops, intransigence sets in and conviction turns to dogma.

Conviction can be a very useful trading tool. Whereas specialisation will normally yield the daily profit or loss, having the conviction to trade the occasional large position when it is right to do so can make the difference between traders. It is by no means necessary to make large directional trades to be a successful trader, especially if the trader is content with their lot, but specialisation can occasionally highlight opportunities where, for example, something is far oversold, overbought or out of kilter against something else. Having the conviction to recognise this and the confidence to establish and responsibly manage a position can make the difference between an average monthly performance and a spectacular one.

Variant perception

Variant perception was the phrase coined by hedge fund manager, Michael Steinhardt, to describe differences between his viewpoint on a market and that of the consensus. He considered a complete understanding of market expectations to be a vital part of his success and benefited enormously when the gap between his disparate perception and the market consensus closed. Variant perception is not merely taking a contrarian view to that of the market, but using the high level of understanding that comes from fully knowing a market to support a conviction.

Variant perception can be adapted for use in STIR futures markets to highlight differences between the market consensus and market prices. This exists when the market consensus might indicate one possible interest rate outcome, but the STIR futures prices are predicting another. For example, in February 2006, market consensus expectations were for the next movement in UK interest rates to be a cut from the present level of 4.5%. A Reuters poll of forty economists showed that thirty three of them expect the next move in UK interest rates to be down, based on a poor outlook for economic growth and a fragile consumer sector. However, the Short Sterling M6 contract was trading as low as 95.40 in early February, implying higher rates of 4.6%, and assigning virtually zero chance of a rate cut.

This gap between the perception of the market consensus and that indicated by the STIR futures prices has significant potential to narrow, should a catalyst change the STIR futures prices perception. The Short Sterling M6 will be very susceptible to upward corrections from benign data or central bank rhetoric because it has already stretched the variant perception. Of course, the market perception might change to that of the price perception over time, but whilst the variance remains, traders can exploit the asymmetrical potential.

Respect

A good trader will always be respectful of other market participants and considerate of their actions. This has nothing to do with social niceties and more to do with the trader's instinct for survival. There should always be respect for the person on the other side of a trade and the trader should always be asking why are they selling or buying. What can they know that I don't?

The fourth dimension

The fourth dimension is commonly defined as time, and logic dictates that because of the passage of time nothing is ever the same or can be repeated. In this respect, markets are always changing over time and the successful trader needs to adapt to these changes. Although markets can repeatedly trade a price range, it is unlikely that the drivers behind the market will remain exactly the same. The variant perception might have shifted or new information becomes available. The markets might have attracted new types of player, adding noise or volatility or a cross-market influence might be having an effect.

Traders, too, are subject to the fourth dimension. Even though they might continually trade the same market and the same niche, their attitude to the market will change over time. Confidence ebbs and flows with success and failure and attitudes to risk can change with personal circumstances. Even the trappings of success over time can change a trader's perspective as their hunger diminishes.

A successful trader should always be aware of the changing effects of time on both the markets and themselves. Being able to recognise how the trader is personally responding to the markets and how the markets are responding to new drivers is a key psychology of trading.

Deep play

Deep play was a concept developed by Jeremy Bentham, the father of Utilitarianism, where the stakes in an endeavour become so high, that it is irrational for anyone to engage in it at all since the marginal utility of what stands to be won is grossly outweighed by the disutility what stands to be lost.

Deep play was not specifically targeted at financial markets, but its message is clear. At times of extreme volatility or uncertainty, the risk between what might be made against what could be lost can become so disproportional that it is futile to be involved. Fortunately, these situations are quite infrequent, but they do happen and often outside market trading hours which can be harmful to holders of overnight positions.

Perfect storms, such as the UK Exchange Rate Mechanism (ERM) debacle of the early nineties, are a prime example of deep play. The UK's entry to the ERM was announced just after the market close in October 1990, causing a discrete price spike the next day, but the real deep play was reserved for when the UK left the ERM on 16 Sep 1992. During that trading day, interest rates were increased from 10% to 12% and UK officials then threatened to increase them further to 15%. This caused unprecedented movements in Short Sterling futures markets, which were almost paralysed by the volatility and extreme reluctance of any traders to establish new positions. The swinging prices, although offering the possibility of abnormal profit, also carried the very likely risk of catastrophe, and those traders with an instinct for self survival kept their hands firmly in their pockets.

Traders nemesis

The trader's nemesis is the source of harm or ruin that can come from hubris. Success can easily breed the presumption that the markets owe a living and can be dipped into at will to provide for the good things in life. It is uncanny how a trader can appear to lose their touch just as they've taken on a large mortgage for a new house, or the markets to trough a new low in volatility just as performance is needed. The futures markets will always remain a speculative pursuit and should always be regarded as such. Markets and trading careers should never be taken for granted.

Game Play

Game play is about strategy and tactics. There are no clear answers and those that do exist are subjective to individual perspective. Ideally, every trader should have a defined strategy for their trading and tactics for their methodology, but in practice these need to be moveable and adaptable. Game play tends to stem from a trader's own personality. Are they a team player, usually following the consensus, latching onto trends or a contrarian, the devil's advocate deliberately taking the other side, What is their attitude to loss? Some traders just can't tolerate them; others view them as arbitrarily as they look upon profits. The answers usually come with experience and traders need to learn to adjust accordingly.

Those traders with a low risk tolerance will be more suited to lower risk activities such as spread and strategy trading. Contrarians might find success in moderation by fading yield curve moves, which tend to be limited in their range and quite elastic and trend followers might be more suited to outright trading, looking for the macro trades. Ultimately it's about finding out what works and what doesn't for a particular trader.

The discovery process

The discovery process is the selection procedure for what kind of trading works and what doesn't. It is dependent on the trader profile, but also on the variables of market conditions, incentives and aptitude.

The criterion of trader profile is concerned with the type of trader and how suited they are to a class of trading. It will include the desirable characteristics and key considerations mentioned earlier and these will influence the trader's choice between outright trading and the relative value of intra and inter-contract spread and strategy trading.

Market conditions can vary substantially from month to month and what worked earlier might not work so well later on. Intra-contract spread trading needs a certain amount of yield curve movement in order to provide trading opportunities; in quieter times, or times of parallel yield curve shifts, it is likely that the spreads will be characterised by little movement and congestion. The trader then needs to be asking whether their time is better spent elsewhere, perhaps inter-contract spreading. Conversely, in times of volatility, the intra-contract spreads might prove a safe harbour.

The concept of incentive is the deliberate use of exchange rebate schemes as a profit centre. Exchange rebate schemes are targeted at traders specialising in back month

STIR futures trading and those traders deciding to specialise in intra-contract spreads might be directed towards these far months, in order to maximise their revenue by judicious use of the incentives available.

The final criteria of aptitude are simply to stick at what you are good at. Some traders will have a natural affinity towards more complex reasoned types of trading whilst others will prefer the simple black and white trading of the outrights. Experience is really the only way of finding out for sure what fits and where a traders talent is best deployed.

Trigger point

Every trade needs a trigger, which is causation at the point of trade. There are broadly three categories of trigger that might be ascribed to the decision to buy or sell.

The first is a reactive response to price action, possibly driven by news or events.

The second is proactive, which should be the majority of a trader's activity. This is where trades are implemented after due consideration to open a position that has a good chance of returning a profit. A proactive trade might be the deliberate legging of a spread on the bid or offer, resulting in a risk free position, by trading one side in full expectation of a higher than average chance of receiving the fill on the other side. Proactive trading is considered and thought out, maximising the balance of probability in favour of the trader.

The third trigger is signals. These are actions based on buy and sell signals, which invariably tend to be technical in nature. Technical signals are the consequence of technical analysis, which is the abstract study of price movements in order to attempt to predict future movements. Technical analysis is the antipathy of fundamental analysis, which includes the basic drivers of STIR futures markets, and it is primarily concerned with price action rather than what might be behind market movements. Technical analysis is based on the three premises that market prices discount everything (that all available information is already included in the futures price), prices move in trends and history repeats itself.

There are a wide range of indicators based on technical analysis that try to predict future price movements by generating buy and sell signals based upon identifying price trends or overbought or oversold market conditions. Traders tend to either be big fans of technical indicators or have a very capricious attitude towards them. However, their use is widespread within the trading community and some familiarity is useful, even if it is solely to be aware of how other traders are using it.

Guide to technical indicators

Technical analysis is a vast field and it is beyond the scope of this book to cover every indicator in existence and provide empirical research to validate each one. However, many indicators are variations on existing ones and they stem from four main categories.

Trend indicators

Trend indicators are some of the simplest types of technical indicators. They try to give an objective measure of price direction by separating the trend from the surrounding noise. Noise can be defined as the excess price fluctuation or variation from the trend and is very common in futures markets.

Moving Averages

Moving averages are one of the most popular and easily understood indicators. In their simplest form, they are a rolling average price over a period of time; for example, a ten-day moving average would be the average of the last ten days' prices. For each subsequent day, the latest closing price replaces the oldest value, which maintains a population of ten days at all times. Periods of five, ten, twenty, fifty and one hundred day moving averages are popular choices. The shorter periods will be most responsive to short-term price fluctuations whereas the longer period moving averages will smooth out more of the noise.

This kind of moving average is known as a simple moving average and they are very easy to interpret since the technique smoothes price series and makes trends easier to identify. Moving averages are commonly used in multiples for technical analysis, either as a double or triple moving average. A double moving average will use two different observation periods such as a 10-day and 20-day period and the triple moving average plots three moving averages of different observation periods such as a 10-day, 20-day and 50-day periods. The use of double or triple moving average plots allows the identification of crossovers. A double crossover is where the shortest moving average crosses through the longer one and is commonly considered to be a buying signal, as the longer average is viewed as price support level. A triple crossover provides stronger evidence of the buy signal when the shortest moving average passes through the two higher ones. The opposite can also be used to identify sell signals.

Moving averages are, by nature, laggard indicators because they change only after the price has already begun to follow that trend. They are most effective when the market is trending and are useful for identifying trends but will not predict them. It should be noted that any form of moving average analysis using a longer averaging period will generate fewer signals and will require a larger price move before responding. This might be considered as sacrificing potential profits in order to confirm the signal. A shorter averaging period will generate a larger number of signals as it requires less of a price move before responding; however, the risk that the signal is false will increase.

There are further variations of moving average, which incorporate a weighting component in their structure. The weighted moving average also smoothes the price data by removing the noise over the period but is more sensitive to recent price changes since it assigns a greater weight to the most recent prices, whereas the simple moving average gives all prices equal emphasis. There are several further versions of weighted moving average.

The exponential moving average analysis is a variation on the weighted version in that they both assign greater weight to the most recent data. However, they differ in that instead of dropping off the oldest data point in the selected period of the moving average, the exponential moving average continues to maintain all the data. For example, a 10-day exponential moving average will contain more than 10 prices. Each observation becomes progressively less significant but still includes in its calculation all the price data in the life of the instrument. The exponential moving average can be considered as another method of weighting a moving average.

The other weighted moving average type is the volume-adjusted moving average. These are weighted moving averages that use volume as a weighting mechanism. Volume-adjusted moving averages assign the majority of weight to the days with the most volume.

Average Directional Movement Index (ADX)

The Directional Movement Index (DMI) was developed by J. Welles Wilder.[34] It is a technical indicator that measures the directionality of price movement over time to identify trending and non-trending periods. The DMI actually comprises two directional indicators, which are then averaged to produce the ADX. This is plotted on a scale of 0 to 100, with values below 20 indicating a trendless market and a value above 30 indicating a trending market. Crossovers can be applicable to this indicator

It should be noted that ADX is a laggard indicator and so will not perform well as a trading signal generator. It is usually used in combination with other indicators.

---

[34] New Concepts in Technical Trading Systems by J. Welles Wilder, Jr, Trend Research, 1978

Vertical Horizontal Filter (VHF)

The Vertical Horizontal Filter is similar to the ADX in that it is also an indicator of trends within markets. It is calculated by analysing the difference between the highest and lowest values versus the daily fluctuations and rising values indicate trending prices whilst falling values can be indicative of level or congested prices. As with the ADX, the VHF is commonly used with other indicators to provide additional verification of a price movement but can be used to determine the amount that prices are trending. A higher VHF value will indicate a higher degree of trending and points to the use of trend-following indicators. The VHF can also be used as a contrarian indicator, where congestion periods might follow high VHF values and trends could follow low VHF values.

Example – moving averages, ADX and VHF

Chart 4.1 illustrates the M6 Short Sterling price history with a 30-day and a 10–day simple moving average. The sub chart contains the VHF and ADX indicators for the same time and price sample.

Chart 4.1: Short Sterling M6 (3/1/05 to 28/2/06) with 30/10 day double Simple Moving Average (SMA) and sub chart featuring Vertical Horizontal Filter (VHF) on left axis and Average Directional Movement Index (ADX) on the right axis

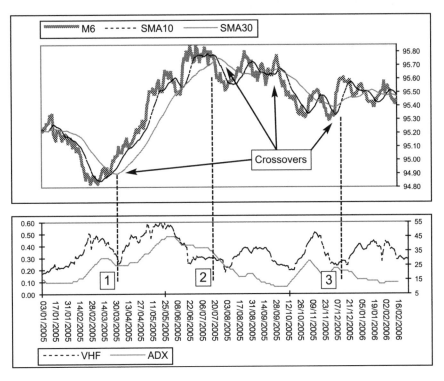

Analysis

The use of crossovers on the moving averages seems to provide indications of major trends with mixed assistance from the trend indicators.

1. The first crossover in March 2005 (1) is shown on the left hand side of the chart, where the 10-day moving average crosses the 30-day moving average, and appears to predict the major uptrend that continues into July 2005. The VHF indicator confirms the rising trend more quickly than the ADX.

2. By July 2005 (2), the falling ADX appears to catch the end of the trend more accurately than the VHF, which faltered earlier even when there continued to be good upward price momentum.

3. The last crossover in December 2005 (3) lags the rally to an extent that might have resulted in buying near the top of the move. In this case, both the VHF and ADX indicated a trend less market and so might have served as sufficient warning.

Traders' notes

Moving averages are a useful indicative tool for major trends, but need to be qualified because of their laggard characteristics. This tends to make their charts look better in hindsight than predicting forward. The VHF and ADX indicators appear useful indicators of the validity of a trend, but need to be used cautiously.

In conclusion, trend indicators are useful for removing noise and can provide confirmation of major trends, but should not be exclusively relied upon.

Oscillator and volatility indicators

Oscillator and volatility indicators measure the periodic variation of price. They are useful in non-trending markets where prices fluctuate in horizontal bands of support and resistance.They are commonly used to predict over-bought and over sold conditions.

Price oscillators

Oscillators are generally the difference between two moving averages, usually in either absolute and percentage terms. Common forms are the Price Oscillator (PO) with variations including volume, momentum and stochastic; they normally fluctuate around a zero line or a band, indicating overbought or oversold conditions. This is where prices have risen or fallen too far and the oscillator is commonly used as a predictor in the expectation that the prices might retrace this move. If the oscillator reaches a very high value above the zero line, the market is considered overbought, whereas if a very low value below the zero line is reached, the market is termed oversold. Overbought and oversold signals are considered most reliable in a non-trending market where prices are making a series of equal highs and lows.

Oscillators can be also be used to generate buy and sell signals when the oscillator values move above and below zero. A buy signal is given when the Oscillator moves from below zero to above zero, and a sell signal is generated when the Oscillator moves from above zero to below zero

Bollinger bands

Bollinger bands are volatility indicators that visually portray the relationship between price and volatility changes. They are based upon an exponential moving average price with two bands created a specified number of standard deviations above and below this moving average. These bands expand and contract as price action becomes volatile or quietens into a tighter trading pattern.

Like oscillators, Bollinger bands are commonly used to identify overbought and oversold markets. An overbought or oversold market is one where the prices have risen or fallen too far and are therefore likely to retrace. Prices near the lower band signal an oversold market and prices near the upper band signal an overbought market. These signals are most reliable in non-trending markets but, if the market is trending, then signals in the direction of the trend are likely to be more reliable. For example, if prices are in an uptrend, a trader might prefer to wait until a temporary price pullback gives an oversold signal before entering a trade.

Bollinger bands can also be used to warn of an impending price move. The bands can often narrow just before a sharp price move. This is based upon the concept that a period of low volatility often precedes a sharp move in prices and low volatility will be reflected in narrow bands.

Average true range

This is another J Welles Wilder indicator. The Average True Range (ATR) is a volatility indicator based upon the exponential moving average of the true range, which is the largest of:

1. current high less current low,

2. the range between current high and previous close, and

3. the range between current low and previous close.

This true range captures the volatility created by an overnight gap and positive values are required so absolute numbers are used.

Wilder found that high ATR values often occurred at market bottoms, following a sharp sell-off; low ATR values are often found during extended sideways periods, such as those found at tops and after consolidation periods.

Example – Bollinger bands, ATR, price oscillator

The same Short Sterling data used in Chart 4.1 is used in Chart 4.2 with a price oscillator, Bollinger bands, and Average True Range (ATR).

Chart 4.2: Short Sterling M6 (3/1/05 to 28/2/06) with 20-day period 2.0 Standard deviation Bollinger Bands, 14-day period Average True Range and Price Oscillator

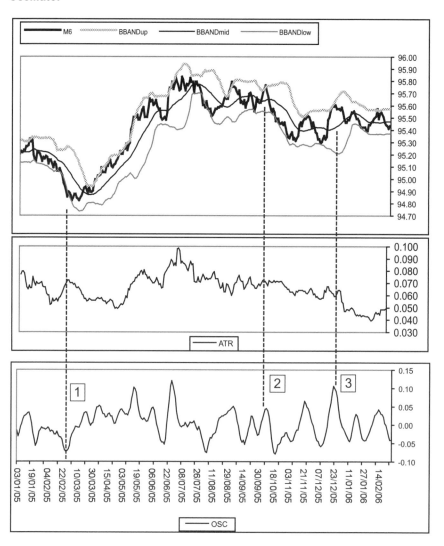

Analysis

1. The first study in February 2005 (1) shows the market hitting a downside trough in sequence with a low, below zero oscillator and a relatively high ATR, all correctly indicating an oversold condition.

2. The next study in October 2005 (2) shows the futures price touching the upper Bollinger band, a moderately high oscillator and a constant ATR giving a weak overbought signal.

3. A third signal is shown in late December 2005 (3) given by a very high value oscillator, price almost touching the upper Bollinger band and an indifferent ATR, reflecting the sideways movement previously in the market.

The Bollinger bands and the oscillator support all three examples. The ATR appears to work well in a directional market but offers little insight beyond this. It should be remembered that Bollinger bands and oscillators are, essentially, moving averages and so will share their laggard qualities. It is highly likely, therefore, that these indicators will perform better in hindsight.

> Traders' notes
>
> The Bollinger bands and oscillator are similar, but refined versions of moving averages and suffer from the same disadvantages and advantages. Overbought and oversold indicators can give the same signal for quite extended periods of time.
>
> The ATR appears a more sporadic tool, reflecting volatility but not necessarily direction.

Momentum and strength indicators

These types of indicator differ from the previous ones in that they can be considered leading indicators. Leading indicators are supposed to change before the actual price begins a new pattern or trend.

Relative Strength Index

The Relative Strength Index (RSI) is a momentum indicator that measures price relative to past prices. It operates in a range between 0 and 100 that reflects the internal strength of a price move. Zero is the most oversold situation and 100 the most overbought one. Generally, anything over 70 is considered overbought and anything below 30 is considered oversold. It is time-period dependent, meaning that a choice of a shorter period will return more volatile results.

Overbought and oversold signals are usually most reliable in non-trending markets. In trending markets, the most reliable signal is the direction of the trend and the RSI can be used for confirmation of a signal by, for example, in an upwardly trending market, only trading buy signals after the RSI has moved back above 30 after dropping below.

The RSI is also a popular indicator for looking for failure swings. These are where the futures price might be making a new high but the RSI is failing to surpass its previous highs. This divergence is an indication of an impending reversal. Divergence between the RSI and the price can also indicate that an up or down move is weakening. However, it should be noted that although divergences indicate a weakening trend they do not in themselves indicate that the trend has reversed.

Accumulation/distribution line (ADL)

The Accumulation/Distribution line measures the buying and selling pressure into and out of a futures price from the difference between accumulation (buying pressure) and distribution (selling pressure). Accumulation is when the current closing price is higher than the previous close and distribution occurs when the close is lower than the previous close

The strongest signals on ADL are when it diverges from the futures price. A buy signal is generated when there is an upward divergence and a sell signal when there is a downward divergence.

Rate of change (ROC)

Rate of change is an oscillator type of indicator that measures market momentum by comparing later prices with earlier prices. It is presented in bands around an equilibrium level, based upon the historic characteristics of the futures price. It is commonly used in ranging markets, to detect trend strengths and weaknesses, and in this respect is similar to the RSI. As with the RSI, a low value means an oversold condition and a high value means an overbought one.

Example – RSI, ADL and ROC

These indicators, particularly the RSI and ROC, should lead price movements within the same sample of Short Sterling M6 as used earlier. Chart 4.3 shows the three studies of RSI, ADL and ROC against the M6 price chart.

Chart 4.3: Short Sterling M6(3/1/05 to 28/2/06), with 14 day RSI, 14 day ROC and ADL

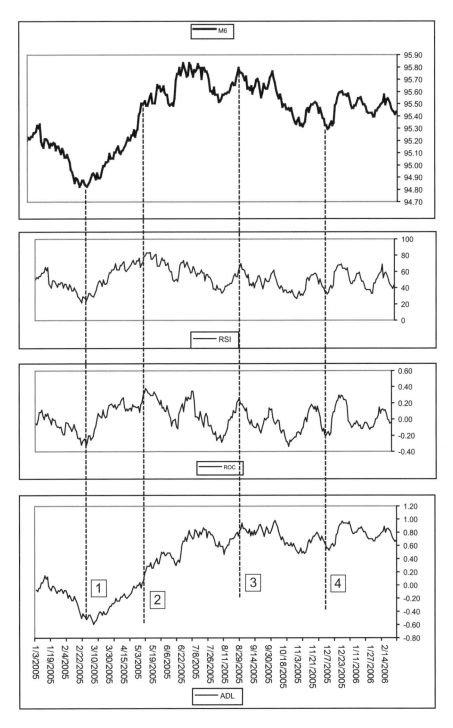

Analysis

1. The RSI has several points at which it has breached or touched the 70/30 boundaries. The M6 price low reached in February 2005 (1) is matched by an RSI below 30, indicating an oversold state. The ROC is also towards its lower trading range and the ADL shows clear distribution but is insufficiently leading to suggest that this might be slowing. In this case, the RSI and ROC seem to correctly forecast an oversold signal and a purchase at this point would have been a profitable trade.

2. An equally clear but unprofitable signal is given by both the RSI and ROC in May 2005 (2), indicating an overbought state. In this case the futures price only temporarily slows its upward trend and the ADL was still rising, which might have raised concerns that buying pressure was still present.

3. The third study in September 2005 (3) shows an RSI at 70 and a peaking ROC and ADL, indicating that momentum and buying pressure had reached a top. This nicely captures the top in M6 and would have been a good trade.

4. This is mirrored in study four in December 2005 (4), where troughs in RSI, ROC and ADL predict a low price point.

> ### Traders' notes
>
> These leading indicators, particularly RSI and ROC, appear to be useful predictive tools, having identified three out of four overbought and oversold situations. They are most successful in non-trending markets, as illustrated by the failure of (2). The ADL could be considered more of a supporting indicator, providing verification for the others.

Line indicators

Line indicators include the simplest studies and also some of the most complicated. They are characterised by their use of straight lines to identify support and resistance levels.

Trend lines

A trend line is a straight line that connects two or more price points and then extends into the future to provide support and resistance levels. Trend lines can be horizontal or sloping: upwards for an uptrend and downwards for a downtrend. A trend line is considered more valid the more price points that are used.

Chart 4.4: Short Sterling M6 (3/1/05 to 28/2/06)

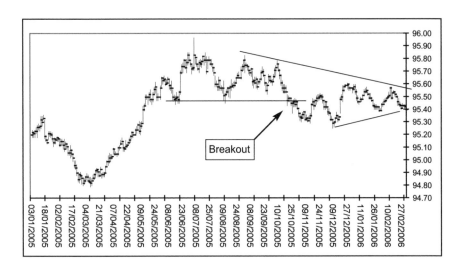

Chart 4.4 illustrates some trend lines. The horizontal line starting in June 2005 and extending to October 2005 is based upon two low price points, providing support at approximately 95.48. In October, this support is breached and the price trends lower.

The upper and lower sloping lines show a narrowing trading range from December 2005 onwards (reflecting lower volatility, that is shown in the falling ATR indicator used earlier). The futures price is currently touching the lower support at 95.40 and a breach of this could lead to a lower trading range, or alternatively it might find support there and move upwards, thereby creating another price point and further validating the trend line.

The effectiveness of trend lines varies from market to market but they remain one of the most popular studies since they easily illustrate trading price points. Generally, horizontal trend lines seem to provide better support and resistance levels than sloping lines.

Gann

W.D. Gann (born 1878) developed a variety of technical analysis methods based around the premises of price, time and range being the only factors to consider. He also considered markets to be cyclical in nature and geometric in design, believing that the ideal balance between time and price exists when prices rise or fall at a 45-degree angle relative to the time axis. This lead to the *Gann Angle*, where a one-unit price rise matches a one-unit time increment makes a 1 x 1 angle. Gann then developed these further angles

Ratio	Angle (degrees)
1 x 8	82.5
1 x 4	75
1 x 3	71.25
1 x 2	63.75
1 x 1	45
2 x 1	26.25
3 x 1	18.75
4 x 1	15
8 x 1	7.5

Gann observed that each of the angles could provide support and resistance depending on the trend. During an up-trend, the 1x1 angle could provide major support, and a reversal would only be signalled when prices fell below this angle. If this happened, prices could then be expected to fall to the next trend line, which would be the 2x1 angle. In summary, as one angle is breached, prices can be expected to move to and consolidate at the next angle.

Gann Angles are drawn between a significant bottom and top. An example of a Gann fan (a chart illustrating all the Gann angles) is given in Chart 4.5, drawn from the significant low in March 2005 of the Short Sterling M6 sample.

Chart 4.5: Short Sterling M6 (3/1/05 to 28/2/06) with Gann fan study

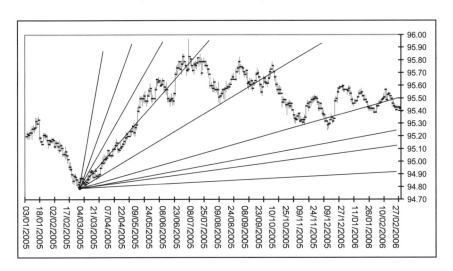

The Gann fan is based on the significant low of March 2005. The 1x1 angle provides good support twice in August 2005 and is broken in September and October. Gann would then predict that prices would gravitate downwards to the next angle, in this case the 2x1 at 26.25 degrees. In fact, prices performed almost as predicted, first touching the 2 x 1 angle in November and then continually breaching it, suggesting a future move to the 3x1 angle.

Gann has many supporters but his analyses can be subjective and very dependent on how they are used. It is a comprehensive study and although being relatively simple to use, it can be difficult to master successfully.

Fibonacci

Fibonacci was an Italian mathematician born circa 1170, renowned for the Fibonacci numbers. These are a sequence of numbers in which each successive number is the sum of the two previous numbers, for example:

```
1, 1, 2, 3, 5, 8, 13, 21, 34, 55, 89, 144, 233, 377, 610, etc.
```

These numbers have several interrelationships. For example, any given number is approximately 1.618 times the preceding number, and any given number is approximately 0.618 times the following number. This relationship was called Phi. Phi is considered important since almost everything with dimensional properties complies with these ratios, and many believe this includes financial markets.

When Phi is applied to technical analysis, it is typically converted into three percentages; 38.2%, 50% and 61.8% and used several ways, two of the most popular being Fibonacci retracements and fans.

[a] **Fibonacci retracements**

These use horizontal lines to identify areas of support and resistance. They are constructed by identifying the two highs and low of a market movement with the 100% and 0% levels being placed on the highs and lows respectively. A centre line is then drawn at the 50% level and the others at the phi ratios of 38.2% and 61.8%.

• **Fibonacci Fan**

A Fibonacci Fan is displayed by drawing a trend line between two extreme points, for example, between the two highs and low of a market movement. Then an invisible vertical line is drawn through the second extreme point. Three trend lines are then drawn from the first extreme point so that they pass through the invisible vertical line at the Fibonacci levels of 38.2 percent, 50.0 percent, and 61.8 percent.

Chart 4.6: Short Sterling M6 (3/1/05 to 28/2/06) with Fibonacci retracement and fan studies

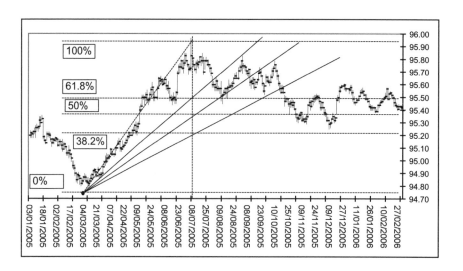

Chart 4.6 illustrates the Fibonacci retracement lines and fan on the Short Sterling M6 data sample. Retracement lines are used to predict potential levels of retracement following a market move and the horizontal lines of 0% and 100% reflect the relative low and high of the move. The Fibonacci levels of 61.8% and 38.2% are the set percentages of the move to which the market might be expected to adjust to from its extreme points.

Analysis

1. From the high of the 7 July London bombings, Short Sterling retraced to the Fibonacci level of 61.8% by August, before bouncing back upwards. The 61.8 level was breached on a subsequent down move in October and the 38.2% level providing support in December. The Fibonacci retracements appear to provide a good indicator of the extent of the retracement with an acceptable degree of accuracy.

2. The Fibonacci fan is based on the March low and the July high, with the fans intersecting the vertical line at 61.8%, 50% and 38.2%. The 61.8% phi was easily breached with the 50% showing better support in August. A breach of the 38.2% level in October leads to a continued move downwards and the level is never regained. The fan does not seem to yield usable results as well as the retracements.

> Fibonacci will always be dependent on the choice of extremities; the high and low points used and a shorter time period, instead of the annual data used, might yield different results.

Conclusion – technical analysis

None of the technical indicators described in this section can claim to be an accurate predictor of the future course of markets and neither can more complicated indicators be shown to be more reliable than simpler ones. Each trader needs to find from experience which technical indicators or combinations of indicators work best for them. The successful use of technical analysis seems to be about this process of discovering which combinations of indicators seem to work best and when. Combinations of technical indicators do not need to be confined to category. Trend line indicators might easily be used with momentum studies, which can be used with oscillators.

The use of technical analysis can play an important part of the trade decision-making process, either as a stand-alone trade generation system or by substantiating an existing opinion. Some traders will apply more weight to technical indicators than others and it will be necessary for each to find their own balance. Technical analysis will always be subjective, but can be an asset when used in a considered manner as a decision-support tool and not allowed to become a dependency.

5

Endgame

This section contains a fictional story - a day in the life of a STIR futures trader; plus an interview with a real trader. The purpose of this section is to draw everything together and to show how all the information and techniques presented in this book can be used, giving a glimpse into a possible trading future.

A Day In The Life of a STIR Futures Trader

A fictional account of a day in the life of a STIR futures trader with most of the trading techniques presented earlier playing a starring role. Many trading days can be quite slow, so a little artistic licence has been employed. Dates have shifted, events been fabricated and names changed to protect the guilty!

06:30

I switch the computer on. The screen flickers and bursts into life with prices, news, graphs and spreadsheets.

Game on.

I'm fully wired now. Nothing that really matters can happen in the world without me knowing about it. It might be on the wires or TV but the prices will break it first. The prices are everything. Fact and fiction distilled. Omniscient.

Storm clouds have been gathering overnight. The Dow is down 300 points and bonds have shed 20 ticks. The Fed's Chairman has voiced concern at the recent "elevated diachrony in asset prices", alluding to the inflationary effects of the recent oil price spike which topped $100 in New York trade overnight. The situation in the Middle East is tense. The papers have been full of the leaked US intelligence story suggesting that Iran has achieved uranium enrichment and might now have weapons grade plutonium. The UN Security Council has convened a meeting later this week to discuss extending sanctions and the US Seventh Fleet has entered the Straits of Hormuz, ostensibly on manoeuvres, but no one's buying that.

I'm fully loaded today and a little nervous. I'm short beaucoup spreads across the Euribor strip and the risk is that the yield curve might steepen. I'm hoping that the inflationary talk will bring rate rise expectations closer down the strip and that the front months will fall more relative to the backs. But we'll see. I've also got a few butterflies on. OK, they're a little off-market – the result of a few trades gone wrong, but at least they balance things out a little.

The red light on my voicemail is blinking. It's David from the Risk Department reminding me that I'm touching my net liquidating balance. I download yesterday's trading statements. I see what he means. I'm building positions but adding little to the P&L. Maybe I'll shed a little weight on the open. Bunds are called to open 30 ticks lower so Euribor will be down a few ticks. I'm hoping that might bring some spread selling as the outright sellers go for the liquidity in the fronts causing the backs to lag. I'm short the one-year calendars - they'll move the most. I enter buy orders in the spreads a tick lower than last night's close.

Ten minutes to go until the whistle and over the top we go. I have a quick root around the news service to see what's going on. The economic diary tells me that it's going to be a busy day, UK CPI at nine-thirty and US Non-Farm Payrolls at 1330, the mother of all figures. There's a couple of A-list Central Bankers due to speak after a big lunch. I'll keep an eye out for them; sometimes the Port loosens the rhetoric a little

06:58

The Euribor boys go first at seven, followed by the big guns – the Eurex Bunds, Bobls and Schatz. The Brits are still in bed, with Sterling opening at seven-thirty and Gilts just before lunch at eight. All heads are down and the trading room banter dies. Traders in London, Frankfurt, Gibraltar, some early birds in the States and a few insomniac Australians and Japanese make up the global spider web, all looking for the angle, seeking the edge.

07:00

A momentary pause and then a sea of red as prices fall. My workstation 'dings' as fills report in. Within two minutes I've covered my entire spread position for a small profit. David in Risk will be pleased. I lean back in my chair and take a sip of tepid coffee and congratulate myself on a good start to the day. Prices start to stabilise after the opening adjustment. Bunds are down 50 ticks from yesterday's close and Euribor is down 7 ticks in the whites and 6 ticks in the reds. Looking at the ticker, I can see front month opened down 5 ticks and then fell to a low of down 8 ticks, maybe as the overnight longs panicked out ahead of the short sellers before bouncing back a tick.

It's a good start but I've still got those dodgy short back month butterflies on. They're yesterday's legacy from a long outright position that felt wrong the moment I put it on. Sometimes you get a gut feeling when it's just not going to happen and so I sold out the wings of the outright to leave a short butterfly spread. They're not too offside; they should be a scratch and there'll be a back month fee rebate. It usually pays to leave such positions to work out in the spread book, especially when it's on the market, but today it's much better bid than offered and that'll take forever. They always say, 'never leg a closing spread' but it's very tempting sometimes, especially when the outright prices make it look very do-able.

'Ding', reports the computer as I sell out the body. I quickly put two bids into the market for the wings of the butterfly and now it's just a case of waiting for a bit more selling to come in. There's good quantity on the offers for both months but quite a lot of it is implied prices only. The back months are always thinner than the fronts, especially so early in the day and I begin to regret my impetuousness. There's nothing like the initial flush of success to breed a bit of hubris.

07:30

The Bund starts to pick up a little, the selling looks to be over and the bargain hunters are moving in. The Bund is at the 10-year part of the yield curve but it'll have a knock-on effect at the front end. Already the bid quantities in 2-year Schatz are increasing along with the front month Euribors. Suddenly my leg doesn't look so good. Others join my bids and the offers start melting away. It's a familiar scenario, one that I've played many times before. The choice is stark – buy now and take the loss or brazen it out? 'Ding ding'. I double click twice without further thought. 'The first cut is always the cheapest' and I'm not one for enduring pain. It's irksome though, the butterfly looks OK as a trade now but I've managed to leg out of it above the offer price – anymore trading like that and I'll be on the other side of the Starbuck's counter.

08:30

Short Sterling and Gilts are open now but there's not much going on there. Since they lag the European products in opening times, they tend to just mirror the downward trend rather than set price precedence. The volumes are OK though, meaning that there's plenty of open interest out there readjusting. I have a quick look through the Sterling spreads to see if there's anything obvious - like a spread slightly out of kilter versus the others or some butterfly action stressing the futures strip. Everything should be in equilibrium against each other but sometimes when the tree has been shaken overnight, things can get a little out of balance. I can't see much and there's little implied action, like where an implied price is pushing against a large spread bid or offer. Usually it's large bid or offer because it's a good technical level or a good trade relative to something else, reflecting the market's enthusiasm to trade at that price.

MSN messenger pops up a window. 'Breakfast?', types Tim, a friend sitting all of twenty feet away. I take another quick look around the market. There's CPI at 09.30 and so its breakfast now or go hungry. I'm flat now and with no positions and there's no point in loading up before the number, after which everything can change I type 'OK' back and grab my coat.

09:28

'Beep', the screen alarm clock with its two-minute warning. There's UK CPI at 09:30 and it's going to be choppy. Inflation has been on the rise globally and it's the number in focus these days. The markets are looking for a high number, in the region of +0.3% month-on-month and +2.2% year-on-year, well above the Bank of England's mandate to keep it below 2% on a two-year horizon. Market reaction will be swift and there's never time to fully read and digest the number. You've got to eyeball the number, have a buy or sell order already loaded and be just one click away. Since the markets are gunning for a high number, I'm going the other way and hovering over the buy button. I'm not just being contrarian, there's usually more chance of a bigger move if the market is wrong-footed. I load up a buy order in the market depth, a tick above the offer. There's rarely much available in the best bid and offer just before a number and so you've got to pay up to trade. The seconds tick towards the half hour...

"09:30 UK CPI -0.1% MM +2.0% YY (CONSENSUS +2.2%)"

I see the minus sign and click without reading the rest. That's all I need to know and...'ding' reports the computer as the fill comes back. The market spikes three ticks as offers are snapped and bids ratchet upwards. I'm sitting tight for the moment waiting for the big guns to turn up. The first movement is always the guys like me, nimble and fast, looking for the quick trade. They're in and out within a few seconds but often the biggest move comes after the market has fully digested the news - the economists brief the bank traders who telephone the fund traders. When these elephants move, the trend will be confirmed. I look at the clock willing myself to hold on for five minutes. That'll be enough time, but the profits are burning a hole in my pocket and I sell half, locking in the gain. The pressure is off now; it's easier to hold on. A few large clips go through the market as the fund boys show up. I offer out my remaining lots and trade out of the position. A great return for three minutes work!

Things quieten down now. Short Sterling has stabilised and locked into its new trading range. It'll be slow for a while now. It's easy to get sucked into over-trading after a successful figure trade, but often prices establish themselves and the extra transaction fees just dilute the profit. I move back to Euribor, which is calm. It's moved up a tick in sympathy with Short Sterling, which it shouldn't do really. After all, what's a small monthly move in UK CPI to do with European interest rates? That's just the way of electronic trading these days. Correlations are sometimes enforced by the ease by which one contract can be traded against another. I'm sure that in my trading floor days, the two never moved so much in unison.

I take a close look at the Euribor matrix; looking for longer dated spreads that I can roll down into other, move attractive spreads. The plan is to find a three-month spread that I'd like to either buy or sell on the bid or offer and see if there was an easy way in by trading a twelve-month calendar against the nine-month, or a nine-month against a six-month. It becomes quite easy with practice and a quick scan reveals nothing outstanding, but there's a reasonable trade in the back reds. I could bid the Z6Z7 twelve-month calendar spread and sell the Z6U7 spread against it, leaving me long the three-month U7Z7 spread. This spread is equally bid and offered but I think it might be OK as an overnighter. I place my bid in the Z6Z7 and kick back my chair and pick up the paper. Time for a bit of R&R.

11:00

Around the room, everyone is relaxing a bit. The business is done for the morning and it's unlikely that there will be much going on until lunchtime, when a few early birds in the US might start moving the Treasuries around. Tim is chucking paper aeroplanes at the IT guys and Tony's trying to raise a bet to drink a bottle of ketchup. I think I'll give that one a miss. Last week, he took everyone by drinking a pint of the River Thames. If only his trading record was as robust as his stomach! Everyone looks upbeat, either they've done all right or they know they'll get it back in the afternoon session. You can't beat the optimism of a futures trader in a busy market!

'Ding'. I'm partially filled on my Z6Z7 spread, but the Z6U7 bid is disappearing fast. I manage to sell a few and offer the rest. I'm not worried. There's no real movement in the market now and I'm sure I'll sell the rest out. Even if I don't and have to sell Z6U7 down half a tick, thus buying U7Z7 on the offer rather than the bid, I reckon I'll be able to sell it out for a scratch in the next few days. I'll just have to remember to not leg it like the butterfly!

Suddenly prices begin to move.

The last trade column on my screen blinks rapidly. Large clips are passing through.

"What's going on?" someone shouts. Everyone's seen it but nobody knows.

"Israeli fighter jets over Tehran," shouts a guy on the phone. "It's on TV."

The TV is hurriedly switched from MTV to CNBC where the story is breaking news.

> *"11.45 BREAKING NEWS - FIGHTERS REPORTED OVER IRAN - SOURCE"*

Bunds bounce 40 ticks and Euribor 7 ticks. The wires have it now and everyone's scrambling for cover. Buyers hack into the offers, buying at almost any price in their flight to quality. It's war!

I've missed the boat but I'm just glad I wasn't short at the time. I'm not sure what my Z6Z7 is doing but it's not going to run away and there's no time for spreading at the moment - all the action's in the outrights. I watch the price action closely. Suddenly I see a few clips selling the bid. Someone's either taking profits or knows something. More selling, something's not quite right. In the corner of my eye, I notice movement on the wires on the other screen.

"11:55 ISRAELI DEFENCE MINISTRY DENY JETS IN IRAN"

I click trade and sell small, joining the bandwagon but with half my usual size in markets like these. Prices stop and then surge again. On CNBC I hear the reporter now saying they're American jets and I'm in flames. I'm several ticks offside now and I can feel the sweat break out on my forehead. This could really run if panic sets in. I sit rigid, eyes glued to the screen, willing the prices not to go up further. It's the nightmare scenario every trader fears – *short and caught!* But wait, there's selling coming in again, and it's getting heavier. Prices start to fall back and soon they are back to where I sold. I cover my shorts, grateful to get out of jail free.

"12:05 "JETS ARE OURS" IRANIAN DEFENCE MINSTER",

says the wire. Prices plunge downwards as traders scramble to get out. Within moments the market is lower. It's just a huge flash in the pan; rumour quashed by fact.

I lean back in my chair, exhausted as the adrenalin ebbs. John wanders back in with the lunch

"You look a bit flustered, mate. Anything going on?"

13:00

My calendar spreads got filled during the maelstrom without me really noticing. The surge upward caused the fronts to outperform the backs and my order to sell Short Sterling Z6U7 is filled. In fact, it traded a full tick better but I'm in the U7Z7 on the bid and that's looking good. I sit back and eat my sandwich and look forward to Non farm payrolls. The market is looking for a good number with the TV pundits gunning for +250,000 new jobs but the wide range of expectations between +150,000 to +300,000 reflect the potential volatility. Non-farm payroll's a tricky one. You've got to watch for the revision to last month's figure. Last month's number was +240,000 and the market's looking for something not too dissimilar. You can trade anything over this number; Eurodollars, Euribor, Short Sterling even Swissy. They are all the same over this benchmark figure of the health of the world's biggest economy. I call up two tickets, one buy and one sell, both 2 ticks into the market depth and sit waiting, the mouse tip twitching from buy to sell to buy...

13:30 US NONFARM PAYROLLS +64,000 VS LAST MONTH +210,000.

'Ding'. +64,000! An unbelievably low number. The global debt markets soar as the world tries to buy and the stock markets tank on recessionary worries. The TV pundits are frantic - hastily spinning their erroneous forecasts. David in Risk breaks out in a cold sweat, while the IT guys fan the overheating servers, muttering darkly about network traffic.

It's a bad number, and it's turning the market on its head. Bonds and Bunds bounce 60 ticks without touching the sides. Euribor spikes 9 ticks before pausing and then continues upwards. I look at my fill, aghast. I only got a third of my order, the balance still being worked 10 ticks lower. I delete it and offer out my position where it's snapped up voraciously. The markets are seesawing now but it's starting to stabilise. There's a sea change going on. The rogue payrolls number and its recessionary implications are replacing the former inflationary concerns as the key driver of the market. The yield curve is steepening as rate hike expectations are scaled back in the futures strip. The yields of the front STIR futures fall more quickly relative to the back months and the spread prices are moving upwards. It's a good time to be spreading now and I keenly buy calendars in Euribor and Short Sterling, but stick to the highly liquid front three and six-month calendars, knowing that I can always turn them round quickly, if necessary. They've been falling for the last few days as inflation worries pointed to higher rates but started to look sold out on the charts, almost as if they were looking a for a catalyst to turn them around.

14:30

All the bond and STIR markets are up on the day now. Treasury officials come and go on the wires and TV, trying to explain the sudden weakness in the number. The pundits reckon it's a one-off, but the markets aren't buying that. The US economy has been holed beneath the water line and all hands are on deck.

"Have you seen that 2-year bundle seller?" calls John, his eyes not leaving his screen.

The bid/offer spread can be wide on bundles, but I see this one is being offered down just a tick above the bid. That means that a buyer would be purchasing six out of the eight contracts on the bid price and paying the offer on the other two, assuming that all are trading on a half tick bid and offer. I scroll back up to the outrights and examine the white and red strips, carefully looking at the bid/offer spreads and particularly at the implied bid amounts in the back months. Sometimes, these can make the bundle look more attractive than it actually is, and what might look like an attractive purchase doesn't look so good when the implied support is removed by trades elsewhere. This looks good though, particularly in such a firm market.

"What do you reckon?" I ask John.

"I think he's buying the credit spread on the back of all this event risk. He's selling out the bundles and buying Schatz, looking for the credit spread to widen." John replies.

I flicked over to the news service and paged their analytics. A hastily called up chart showed the spread between the 2-year European swaps over benchmark 2-year bonds and it was clearly widening, reflecting the demand for quality.

"Well, I'm not taking the other side of that on" I said, pointing that out. Buying a bundle, however cheap, was a significant trade since it involves simultaneously buying all eight months. That's a lot of futures and traders like us need to spread it off somewhere, usually against the Schatz but that would make us short the credit spread. Not a good place to be at the moment!

"I'm doing against Swapnote," he replied. "Just wait for a decent bid to come in."

Good idea, I think to myself. There's virtually no credit difference between Swapnote and Euribor so it's the perfect contract to spread off against. Thanking John, I click and trade, buying bundles and selling Swapnote. I'll unwind it when the seller is finished.

16:00

The newswire flashes:

"INCREASING PROBABILITY OF SECOND ROUND INFLATIONARY EF-
FECTS DUE TO HIGHER ENERGY PRICES" SAYS FEDERAL RESERVE
CHAIRMAN AT INSTITUTE OF BANKERS LUNCHEON ADDRESS.

Prices fall. The rally is over. I've got positions and everything is spread off. But I'm nervous. Bunds give back ten ticks and Stirs three. The fronts months sell off more heavily than the backs and my spreads are looking wobbly. I've got my finger on the sell button but there are signs that the fall in prices is slowing. I didn't see that much selling going through the market, just a readjustment of prices to reflect the news and outright traders flattening their positions. The markets are caught between a rock and a hard place. On the one hand, inflation is raising its head, putting upward pressure on interest rates but, on the other hand, the payrolls number has inflicted serious wounds. What does the market fear most, inflation or recession? The answer seems to be the latter and the added effect of event risk from the Middle East seems to swing the balance. Prices start recovering and my positions look better. Prices continue to nudge a little higher and I start trimming my long spread holdings. There's still indecision in the market but our trading day is drawing to a close but it's still early in the US where the comments are coming from. There's not much point in being over-exposed when markets can be influenced outside our trading hours, it will only lead to a sleepless night.

17:10

It's dark outside, but I don't remember it ever getting light. The markets are still twitching but I feel like I've fought my battle today. Looking around the room I can see traders packing up and logging off. Some of the guys are staying, though. They'll be here until late, chasing the futures around the world, addicted to the buzz.

I'm pleased with the day. It's been good and I'm leaving with more than I came in with. They say it's only ever borrowed from the market and I suppose the key to trading success is holding on to it and not giving it back.

I switch the screen off and head for the door. In a little over twelve hours I'll be back at the desk and it starts all over again.

Interview With A Trader

This is an edited transcript of an interview with a trader, referred to here as "AJ". AJ is not a renowned Market Wizard, like those in Jack Schwager's book[35], but an ex-swaps broker who took the decision in November 2004 to trade STIR futures for his own account.

Q: Why did you leave a decent, secure job to venture into the unknown by trading STIR futures for yourself?

AJ: Well, it wasn't quite a leap into the unknown. I'd been trading STIR futures for the company, mainly to hedge short term swaps, and I'd got to know a few brokers in the market, and through them I'd met traders trading the markets for themselves. That always appealed to me. I liked the idea that you live or die by your own sword rather than someone else's.

Q: Describe your set-up and environment.

AJ: I started off trading at home. Costs were of great importance to me at first and that set-up was the cheapest option. I opened an account with a major futures broker and connected by the internet and ISV software. I started trading Euronext.liffe Euribor and then moved to CME Eurodollars. Trading from home was great for those late trading hours, but after a year I moved to a small trading arcade near me. It was a bit too solitary being at home all the time. Sometimes, during busy times, I'd find I hadn't left the house for a few days! I like the atmosphere at the arcade and we share costs on things like information and charting packages, which I'd not be able to afford on my own. They're a good bunch of guys and it's always nice to be able to have a moan to someone when things aren't going your way!

Q: What attracted you to STIR futures as opposed to other types of futures contracts?

AJ: I already knew the product from my days broking swaps. I was attracted by the fact that they were quite slow and stable compared to other futures, like bonds or (equity) indices, but also by the fact that there are so many spreading opportunities. They're not just a directional punt, although you can play them like that. You can find a niche for yourself by trading spreads or strategies. I like to trade the spreads around the butterfly levels. I might not always trade the butterfly as a strategy, but I know their market and will trade the spreads around them, knowing that I can always use them as an exit, if necessary – albeit an expensive one because of the additional fees.

---

[35] Market Wizards, Jack Schwager, HarperBusiness, 1993.

Q: Do prefer to trade STIR futures outright or as spread/strategies, or a combination of both?

AJ: I think I've partly answered this one in the last question. I like to trade the strategies since they suit my risk profile. I think it's better to try to make a little every day rather than make loads one day and give it back the next. Having said that, I will trade outrights when there's a bit of volatility, like over a number [economic release] or sometimes to lift a leg on a spread that's difficult to shift. There's no doubt that making money trading outrights is less effort and cheaper if you can do it consistently, but I reckon you've got to be right seven times out of ten to get ahead. It's too easy to lose. My approach is not to lose money if I can help it. I'll get into spreads or butterflies, either by matrix trading, legging when it looks OK, or more recently by using my new autospreader. If I can sell a spread on its offer or buy it on its bid, I've got no downside except costs. If the spread starts to trade out at that level, I'll usually have 'butterflied off' and I'll know I've got very little downside. I'll work the parts of the butterfly and hopefully eek a tick out somewhere. It's an intensive, high cost way of trading, but with few losses. I also get a nice rebate cheque at the end of the month for my Euronext.liffe business.

Q: Do you trade spreads directionally?

AJ: Sure, I take the view that I can use my 'make a little every day' to finance position taking in spreads. I tend to make an opinion on the shape of the curve and take a position in a spread with a bit more action such as a one-year calendar spread. On those rare occasions where I'm riding a larger move, I'll pyramid the position by establishing a core position and then adding to it in decreasing amounts as the trade moves my way. It's great when it works out well, but you need to operate a tight stop loss policy.

Q. Has your trading 'learning curve' been steeper and harder than you expected, or easier?

AJ: Almost vertical! I couldn't believe how fast and tight things were when I started. There are a lot of players out there and many are very good. There's an old market phrase: 'you've got to pay to play' and it's very true if you are not careful. But it's also the quickest way to learn. You don't make the same mistakes twice.

Q What have been the most difficult and easiest parts of learning to trade STIR futures?

AJ: Learning the nuts and bolts of trading isn't hard, and the software is very easy to learn and intuitive these days. Discipline is also surprisingly easy. The markets open and close at fixed times. They don't care whether you are there or not. You're either in it or not, there's no in-between. There's none of this home workers or self employed dilemma of getting into 'work mode'. I find the markets quite addictive, and if I've got overnight positions, there's no way I'll be sleeping in!

The most difficult part of learning to trade is to find a home, a niche in the markets where you feel comfortable and not afraid of the price action. Traders talk a lot about the 'edge'. That's not the bloke from U2, it's the advantage that a trader has, whether it be due to their presence, knowledge, speed or information flow. I couldn't see any edge in the markets when I first started and I'm not sure I see much now, but if you spend enough time immersed in something, then you develop an expertise, a feel for the product. That becomes your edge. There's certainly no shooting fish in barrels in STIR futures, but if you know your business intimately and, in my case, know how the spreads should move relative to each other, you can move in and out and hopefully nick a tick in between. That's my edge. Sometimes, it doesn't seem to work, other times it does, but it's a leveraged business and we operate in the nicks and cracks of the markets. It doesn't take much movement to turn a profit, provided you avoid those losses.

Q: How do you cope with losing streaks?

AJ: I try to avoid them where I can because I'm really not very good with losing money. It can really bash your confidence, but it happens from time to time, usually when things are quiet and I get tempted to have a go. I try to operate a very low risk, disciplined trading strategy, aiming to make a little every day but if that's not possible then I'm quite willing to sit it out until things pick up. I think everyone's got a different attitude towards risk. I see some younger traders who seem willing to have a go at everything and their P&L swings are huge. I've got family commitments these days and so making money consistently is important to me and so is not losing it.

Q: How do you make your trading decision - the decision to buy or sell? Do you use fundamental and technical analysis or a systematic approach?

AJ: A combination of both. You have to know the fundamentals behind the market, what's moving it and the market expectations. These are critical – you have to know what the expectations for a figure [economic release] or interest rate announcement are, and how the market is positioned. Its not good enough just to know the forecast, you need to know the market bias. For example, if the forecasters are expecting a weak payrolls number [non-farm payrolls], and the markets have an even weaker bias but then the number comes in stronger, the reaction is going to be much larger than if the number was on the (already discounted) weak side. Technical analysis is also important to me, as well. Sometimes, it seems like the fundamentals and technicals move hand in hand, like when you might think the market looks oversold on the chart and the technicals call it a buy, and then some bullish data comes out that starts a rally. It's almost like a self-fulfilling prophecy at times, but I don't know which drives which.

I tend to use fairly simple technical analysis. I've tried more complex analyses and the odd system, but it seems like the more complicated they are, the less reliable they can be. I use standard bar charts with support and resistances flagged and it's important to know what others think technically about the market as well – where they think the levels are.

Q: Do you trade inter-contract spreads?

AJ: Not at the moment since I've got my hands full just doing the spreads and flies. Even though screen trading can give you access to many markets, it's difficult to specialise or concentrate on more than one thing at a time.

I have traded Euribor against Eurodollars for a time. The correlation is not always there, though, and it can be volatile when compared to intra-contract spreads. Euribor versus Swiss can be good. I've occasionally traded stacks and the odd pack against Schatz, but you need to know what's going on in the credit market. I'd prefer to trade more against swap futures and swapnote but volumes are not great at present.

Q: What advice would you give to a new trader?

AJ: Take your time, try a few different markets and products and try to find that niche for yourself. Don't feel pressurised to trade or do what everyone else is doing. Sometimes there can be good opportunities in some of the quieter markets but its never going to be easy. Trading can be a good career choice for some but not all. Those who don't make it shouldn't take it personally. Not everyone is cut out for it.

Q: Do you have any concerns about the markets?

AJ: I get a bit concerned when I hear about the kind of size that some traders are throwing around. Since the markets have been electronic (post 1999), we've been in a global low interest rate, low volatility environment and some of these guys have never seen real volatility before. Some of them seem to adopt the attitude that if things are quiet, then they'll just trade larger. I think the clearers and arcades are partly to blame. It's a competitive business and they want the volume commissions. Still, you have to have faith in their risk management but those perfect storms you read about seem to hit the financial markets a lot more frequently than out at sea.

Q: What new products would you like the exchanges to consider?

AJ: All the exchanges have tried listing new products or, more commonly, trying to poach each other's with mixed success. It appears that each exchange now has its own niche and product suite. Euronext.liffe and CME cover their geographical short interest rates, and Eurex and CBOT have the bonds. I thought the move into swaps futures was sound, but I've been surprised at their lack of success. I don't know whether that's due to a lack of understanding by traders or unwillingness by the establishment to embrace them. I'd like to see an extension of this though and it'd be good to get deeper into the credit markets. STIR futures are the building blocks of finance and the concept could be carried onto different credit curves, so you'd have STIRs on benchmarks, swaps and corporate rates. It'd take a lot of promotion and education though. Also, I suppose in time there's bound to be STIR futures on Chinese Yuan and Russian Roubles.

Q: Any regrets?

AJ: No, on balance, I don't think so. There are always going to be times when I wonder whether I'll still be doing this in ten years, but I get a tremendous buzz from trading the markets and especially when I get it right. Even when I'm feeling a bit low, it only takes a look at my friends' lives, working in some giant corporate machine, to remind me how flexible my lifestyle is. Also, there's no place for politics in markets, no career ladder, no boss to please. Only the pursuit of that perfect trade!

10 Rules For Trading STIR Futures

Rules

1. Understand what is driving the markets and causing the price action.

2. Be aware of the different risk reward characteristics of STIR futures. Generally, spreads and strategies will always be lower risk than trading outrights. Spreads will become more volatile the greater the time period between component expiries and inter-contract spreads will be more volatile than intra-contract spreads.

3. Remember that inter-contract spreads can be multi-dimensional, being affected by credit, curve, interest rate and stub factors.

4. Fully understand the effects of implied pricing, how they can lean against market prices and trigger trades.

5. Remember that spreads, butterflies, condors, packs and bundles will usually be priced tighter by the market than by implied pricing. In faster moving markets, opportunities can exist in strategies, particularly those that are not subject to implied pricing (e.g. Euronext.liffe butterflies, condors, packs and bundles).

6. Use the spread matrix and butterflies as alternative ways to enter or exit trades.

7. Be aware of the effects of incentive schemes and rebates on total commissions.

8. Try to find a trading niche in the markets which balances the trader's propensity for risk against their expectations of profit.

9. Maintain a healthy scepticism toward technical analysis and systems. Technical studies invariably look better in hindsight, due to their laggard nature and predictors can often give the same signal for considerable periods of time. The simpler analyses, such as support and resistance, seem to be the most widely used and traders should be aware of their levels.

10. If the markets are tough to trade, just sit them out. Likewise with extremely volatile markets. Opportunities will always come around again.

Appendices

The appendices contain the following data:

- A list of **STIR futures contracts** listed around the world

- **Contract specifications** for Eurodollar, Euribor, Short Sterling and Euroswiss STIR futures

- A directory of major **futures exchanges** listing STIR futures

- A directory of the major **Clearing Members**

- A directory of **independent software vendors** (ISV)

- A directory of **trading arcades**

- A list of **economic calendars**

- Tabular data of key **interest rate changes** (GBP, SWF, EUR, USD)

Note: Updated data for the above can be found at: www.stirfutures.co.uk.

STIR Futures Contracts

A list of futures on short-term interest rates.

Table A.1: Futures on short term interest rates

Contract	Exchange	Country	Currency	Notional value	Notes
Eurodollar	CME, LIFFE, SGX	US	US Dollar	1,000,000	
1 Month LIBOR	CME	US	US Dollar	3,000,000	12 sequential months
Euribor	LIFFE EUREX	Europe	Euro	1,000,000	
Short Sterling	LIFFE	UK	Pounds	500,000	
Euroswiss	LIFFE	Switzerland	Swiss Franc	1,000,000	
Euroyen	TFE, LIFFE, SGX, CME	Japan	Yen	100,000,000	
BAX	Montreal exchange	Canada	Canadian Dollar	1,000,000	3 month Canadian Bankers Acceptance futures
30 Day Interbank Cash	SFE	Australia	Australian Dollar	3,000,000	Out to 12 months only
90 Day Bank bills	SFE	Australia	Australian Dollar	1,000,000	Out to five years
3 month BUBOR	Budapest Stock exchange	Hungary	Forint	10,000,000	
91 day notional T Bills	NSE	India	Rupee	200,000	
KLIBOR	BURSA MALAYSIA	Malaysia	Ringgit	1,000,000	
NZ 90 day bank bills	SFE	New Zealand		1,000,000	
JIBAR	SAFEX	South Africa	Rand	1,000,000	
SEK STIBOR	OMX	Sweden	SEK	1,000,000	
Long ID	BM&F	Brazil	Real		Underlying asset is the 1 Day Interbank Deposit future expiring 6 mths after expiry of this contract
1 Day Interbank Deposit	BM&F	Brazil	Real	100,000 (discounted)	Priced as an interest rate

BM&F – Brazilian Mercantile & Futures; CME – Chicago Mercantile exchange; EUREX – Deutsche Borse; LIFFE – Euronext.liffe; NSE- National Stock exchange – India; SGX - Singapore exchange; SAFAX – South African Futures exchange; SFE – Sydney Futures exchange; TFE - Tokyo Financial exchange.

Contract Specifications For Eurodollar, Euribor, Short Sterling and Euroswiss

Table A.2: Contract specifications

Contract	Eurodollar	Euribor	Short Sterling	Euroswiss
Exchange	CME	Euronext.liffe	Euronext.liffe	Euronext.liffe
Notional Value/Unit of trading	$1,000,000	€1,000,000	£500,000	SFr 1,000,000
Delivery months	March, June, Sept, Dec + 4 serial, making a total of 40 delivery months	March, June, Sept, Dec + 4 serial months to a total of 24 delivery months	March, June, Sept, Dec + 2 serial months to a total of 22 delivery months	March, June, Sept, Dec, to a total of 8 quarterly delivery months
Price quotation	100.00 minus rate of interest	100.00 minus rate of interest	100.00 minus rate of interest	100.00 minus rate of interest
Minimum price movement	0.005	0.005	0.01	0.01
Tick value	$25	€25	£12.50	SFr25
Last trading day	Second business day preceding the third Wednesday of the contract month	10.00 - Two business days prior to the third Wednesday of the delivery month	11:00 - Third Wednesday of the delivery month	11:00 - Two business days prior to the third Wednesday of the delivery month
Delivery day	Two business days after the last trading day	First business day after the Last Trading Day	First business day after the Last Trading Day	First business day after the Last Trading Day

Exchanges

Euronext LIFFE

Cannon Bridge House
1 Cousin Lane
London EC4R 3XX
Tel. 44 20 7623 0444
Web: www.euronext.com

STIR futures: Euribor, Short Sterling, Euroswiss, Eurodollar

Other interest rate futures: €Swapnote, $Swapnote

Chicago Mercantile Exchange (CME)

20 South Wacker Drive
Chicago, Illinois 60606
USA
Tel: (312 9301000
Web: www.cme.com

UK Office-
Pinnacle House 23-26 St. Dunstan's Hill
London EC3R 8HN
Tel: 020 7623-2550

STIR futures: Eurodollar

Other interest rate futures: $ Swap futures.

Eurex

Deutsche Börse AG
UK Representative Office
One Canada Square, Floor 42, Canary Wharf
London E14 5DR, United Kingdom
Tel: 020 78627222
Web: www.eurexchange.com

Interest rate futures: Schatz, Bobl, Bund

Chicago Board of Trade (CBOT)

141 W. Jackson Blvd
Chicago, IL 60604
Tel: 312 3413439
Web: www.cbot.com

UK Office -
St. Michael's House
1 George Yard
London EC3V 9DH
Tel: 020 7929 0021

Other interest rate futures: 2-Year Treasury note, 5-Year Treasury note, 10-Year Treasury note, $ 5-year swaps

Clearing Members

London

ADM Investor Services International Ltd

10th Floor, Temple Court
London EC4N 4TJ
Tel: 020 77168000
Web: www.admisi.com

Fortis Bank Global Clearing

Camomile Court
23 Camomile St
London EC3A 7PP
Tel:020 7444 8800
Web: www.informationbanking.fortisbank.com

GH Financials Ltd

Vintners Place
68 Upper Thames St
London EC4V 3BJ
Tel: 020 7653 6400
Web: www.ghf.co.uk

Goldenberg Hehmeyer & Co.

50 Bank Street – 3rd Floor
Canary Wharf
London, E14 5NS
Tel: 020 7390 3301
Web: www.ghco.com

Man Financial & GNItouch

Sugar Quay
Lower Thames St
London EC3R 6DU
Tel: 020 7144 5500
Web: www.mandirect.com

Marex Financial

Trinity Tower
9 Thomas More St
London E1W 1YH
Tel: 020 7488 3232
Web: www.marexfinancial.com

The Kyte Group Ltd

Business Design Centre
52 Upper St
London N1 OQH
Tel: 020 7390 7777
Web: www.kytegroup.com

TRX futures

3 Finsbury Square
London EC2A 1AE
Tel: 020 7880 6050
Web: www.trxfutures.com

Chicago

ADM Investor Services

Suite 1600A
Chicago Board of Trade
141 W Jackson
Chicago 60604
Tel: 312 242 7000
Web: www.admis.com

Fortis Clearing Chicago LLC

Chicago Board of Trade
Suite 1800
141 W Jackson
Chicago 60604
Tel: 312 612 1610
Web: www.fortisclearingus.com

Goldenberg Hehmeyer & Co

Customer Trading
Chicago Board of Trade
141 W. Jackson Boulevard
Suite 1701-A
Chicago, IL 60604
Tel: 312 356 6040
Web: www.ghco.com

Rosenthal Collins Group, LLC

216 W. Jackson Blvd.
Suite 400
Chicago, Illinois 60606 - 6918
Tel: 312 460-9200
Web: www.rcgdirect.com

Independent Software Vendors (ISV)

Easyscreen PLC

78 Cannon St
London
EC4N 6HH
Tel: 020 7645 4600
Web: www.easyscreen.com

Chicago office:

101 North Wacker Drive
Suite 602
Chicago IL 60606
Tel: 312 939 9185

EccoWare Ltd

40 Bank Street,
London
E14 5DW
Tel: 020 7894 8910
Web: www.eccoware.com

Chicago office:

222 West Adams
Suite 1900,
Chicago, IL 60606
Tel 312 469 7500

Ffastfill PLC

1-3 Norton Folgate
London E1 6DB
Tel: 020 7665 8900
Web: www.ffastfill.com

Chicago office:

30 South Wacker Drive
Suite 1716
Chicago, IL 60606
Tel: 312 637 7090

GL Trade Ltd

47/53 Cannon Street
EC4M 5SH
London
Tel: 020 7665 6200
Web: www.gltrade.com

Chicago office:

440, South Lasalle Street
Suite 2202
Chicago, IL 60605
Tel: 312 386 2400

Patsystems PLC

Cottons Centre
Hays Lane
London
SE1 2QP
Tel: 020 7940 0490
Web: www.patsystems.com

Chicago office:
141 W. Jackson Blvd
Suite 3100
Chicago, IL 60604
Tel: 312 922 7600

RTS Realtime Systems Ltd

Cannon Centre
78 Cannon St
London EC4N 6HH
Tel: 020 7861 0700
Web: www.rtsgroup.net

Chicago office:

29 South La Salle St
Suite 1205
Chicago IL 60603
Tel: 312 242 3600

Trading Technologies UK Ltd

Capital House
85 King William Street, 7th Floor
London, EC4N 7BL
Tel:020 7929 6161
Web: www.tradingtechnologies.com

Chicago office:

222 South Riverside Plaza
Suite 1100
Chicago, IL 60606
Tel: 312 476 1000

Trading Arcades

These are two of the largest trading arcades out of approximately 30. Mention here does not confer an endorsement. For more trading arcades see:

www.euronext.com >for our clients>liffe connect>market access>trading bureaux

www.trade2win.com/traderpedia/Trading_Arcade_Index

Marex Trading Ltd

155 Bishopsgate
London EC2M 3XA
Tel 020 7377 2456
Web: www.marextrading.com

(Clearing through: Marex Financial Ltd.)

Schneider Trading Associates Ltd

One Whittington Avenue
London EC3V 1LE
Tel: 020 7664 4200
Web: www.schneidertrading.com

(Clearing through: Man Financial)

Economic Calendars

- http://research.cibcwm.com/res/Eco/ArEcoEUR.html

- http://www.dailyfx.com

- http://www.fxstreet.com/fundamental/economic-calendar/

Key Interest Rate Changes (GBP, SWF, EUR, USD)

GBP

Table A.3: Bank of England (BOE) key interest rate changes since 2000

Date	Direction	Rate (%)
Jan 13, 2000	---	5.75
Feb 10, 2000	↑	6.00
Feb 8, 2001	↓	5.75
Apr 5, 2001	↓	5.50
May 10, 2001	↓	5.25
Aug 2, 2001	↓	5.00
Sep 18, 2001	↓	4.75
Oct 4, 2001	↓	4.50
Nov 8, 2001	↓	4.00
Feb 6, 2003	↓	3.75
Jul 10, 2003	↓	3.50
Nov 6, 2003	↑	3.75
Feb 5, 2004	↑	4.00
May 6, 2004	↑	4.25
Jun 10, 2004	↑	4.50
Aug 5, 2004	↑	4.75
Aug 4, 2005	↓	4.50
Aug 3, 2006	↑	4.75

Source: BOE

SWF

Table A.4: Swiss National Bank (SNB) interest rate changes since 2000

Date	Direction	Range (%)
Feb 3, 2000	---	1.75 - 2.75
Mar 23, 2000	↑	2.50 - 3.50
Jun 15, 2000	↑	3.00 - 4.00
Mar 22, 2001	↓	2.75 - 3.75
Sep 17, 2001	↓	2.25 - 3.25
Sep 24, 2001	↓	1.75 – 2.75
Dec 7, 2001	↓	1.25 - 2.25
May 2, 2002	↓	0.75 - 1.75
Jul 26, 2002	↓	0.25 - 1.25
Mar 6, 2003	↓	0.00 - 0.75
Jun 17, 2004	↑	0.00 - 1.00
Sep 16, 2004	↑	0.25 – 1.25
Dec 15, 2005	↑	0.50 – 1.50
Mar 16, 2006	↑	0.75 – 1.75
Jun 15, 2006	↑	1.00 – 2.00
Sep 14, 2006	↑	1.25 – 2.25

Source: Reuters

Note: The SNB switched to a target band system in 2000 which aims for the mid point of a three-month Swiss franc LIBOR range.

EUR

Table A.5: European Central Bank (ECB) Eurozone interest rate changes (Main Refinancing Rate) since 1999

Date	Direction	Rate (%)
Jan 1, 1999	---	3.00
Apr 8, 1999	↓	2.50
Nov 4, 1999	↑	3.00
Feb 3, 2000	↑	3.25
Mar 16, 2000	↑	3.50
Apr 27, 2000	↑	3.75
Jun 8, 2000	↑	4.25
Aug 31, 2000	↑	4.50
Oct 5, 2000	↑	4.75
May 10, 2001	↓	4.50
Aug 30, 2001	↓	4.25
Sep 17, 2001	↓	3.75
Nov 8, 2001	↓	3.25
Dec 5, 2002	↓	2.75
Mar 6, 2003	↓	2.50
Jun 5, 2003	↓	2.00
Dec 1, 2005	↑	2.25
Mar 2, 2006	↑	2.50
Jun 8, 2006	↑	2.75
Aug 3, 2006	↑	3.00
Oct 5, 2006	↑	3.25

Source: Reuters

USD

Table A.6: Federal Reserve (FED) US interest rate changes (Federal funds rate) since 2000

Date	Direction	Rate (%)
Feb 2, 2000	---	5.75
Mar 21, 2000	↑	6.00
May 16, 2000	↑	6.50
Jan 3, 2001	↓	6.00
Jan 31, 2001	↓	5.50
Mar 20, 2001	↓	5.00
Apr 18, 2001	↓	4.50
May 15, 2001	↓	4.00
Jun 27, 2001	↓	3.75
Aug 21, 2001	↓	3.50
Sep 17, 2001	↓	3.00
Oct 2, 2001	↓	2.50
Nov 6, 2001	↓	2.00
Dec 12, 2001	↓	1.75
Nov 6, 2002	↓	1.25
Jun 25, 2003	↓	1.00
Jun 30, 2004	↑	1.25
Aug 10, 2004	↑	1.50
Sep 21, 2004	↑	1.75
Nov 10, 2004	↑	2.00
Dec 14, 2004	↑	2.25
Feb 2, 2005	↑	2.50
Mar 22, 2005	↑	2.75
May 3, 2005	↑	3.00
Jun 30, 2005	↑	3.25
Aug 9, 2005	↑	3.50
Sep 20, 2005	↑	3.75
Nov 1, 2005	↑	4.00
Dec 13, 2005	↑	4.25
Jan 31, 2006	↑	4.50
Mar 28, 2006	↑	4.75
May 10, 2006	↑	5.00

Source: Reuters

Bibliography

Options, Futures and Other Derivatives

John C Hull, Prentice Hall

Academic textbook giving an excellent fundamental overview of derivatives markets.

The Eurodollar Futures and Options Handbook

Galen Burghardt, McGraw Hill

Excellent but technical book, specifically aimed at the US markets. Seminal text for term spreads.

The Treasury Bond Basis

Galen Burghardt, Irwin

Seminal text for bond basis trading. Good sections on bond futures but aimed solely at US market.

The Futures Bond Basis

Moorad Choudhry, Yieldcurve Publishing

Good bond basis book geared towards UK market

Mastering Financial Calculations

Robert Steiner, FT Pitman

Easy to understand and nicely presented equations

No Bull

Michael Steinhardt, Wiley

A lighter read, about the trading times of top hedge fund manager Michael Steinhardt.

Market Wizards

Jack Schwager, HarperCollins

Entertaining collection of interviews with top traders – see also *New Market Wizards* by same author

Free online introductory material

http://www.cme.com/edu/course/intro/index.html

http://liffe.npsl.co.uk/liffe/site/login_new.acds?lang=en

Index

F

G

Z